The Companion
to
Italian Cinema

Geoffrey Nowell-Smith
with James Hay and Gianni Volpi

CASSELL

BFI PUBLISHING

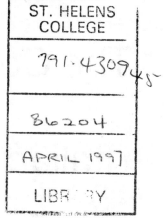
First published in 1996 by
Cassell
Wellington House
125 Strand
London WC2R 0BB
and the
British Film Institute
21 Stephen Street
London W1P 2LN

The British Film Institute exists to promote appreciation, enjoyment, protection and
development of moving image culture in and throughout the whole of the United
Kingdom. Its activities include the National Film and Television Archive; the National
Film Theatre; the Museum of the Moving Image; the London Film Festival; the
production and distribution of film and video; funding and support for regional
activities; Library and Information Services; Stills, Posters and Designs; Research,
Publishing and Education; and the monthly *Sight and Sound* magazine.

British Library Cataloguing-in-Publication Data
A catalogue record for this book is available from the British Library.

ISBN 0 304 34197 5

Cover design by Jamie Tanner
Cover: Sophia Loren, courtesy of The Kobal Collection

Typesetting by Fakenham Photosetting Ltd
Fakenham, Norfolk

Printed and bound in Great Britain by Redwood Books, Trowbridge,
Wiltshire

CONTENTS

ACKNOWLEDGMENTS

The Companion to Italian Cinema regroups and updates all the Italian material written for the Cassell/BFI *Encyclopedia of European Cinema* (1995). Our gratitude therefore goes in the first place to all those who made the *Encyclopedia* possible. We are also grateful to the writers who contributed to the entries on European issues included in the 'Italian Cinema in Europe' section: Chris Darke, Richard Dyer, Joseph Garncarz and Simon Horrocks. The following people should be thanked for their painstaking editing and checking work: Simon Horrocks, Guy Jowett, Markku Salmi, Gian-Luca Sergi and David Wilson. We are grateful to Gianna Cappello for her translations. We also owe special thanks to the staff of the BFI Library, and especially David Sharp and Gillian Hartnoll, and to Sue Bobbermein, Ed Buscombe and Roma Gibson in BFI Publishing.

A work such as this inevitably relies on other sources: trade publications, data provided by embassies and film commissions, journals, filmographies, catalogues, dictionaries, monographs, etc. It is impossible to cite them all, though many appear in the bibliographical notes at the end of some entries and in the final bibliography, as well as with the statistics. May they all be thanked collectively here, including the BFI Library, as well as Annette Kuhn for permission to reproduce in altered form one entry from the *Women's Companion to International Film* (Virago, 1990).

Stills were provided by BFI Stills, Posters and Designs.

Geoffrey Nowell-Smith, James Hay and Gianni Volpi
Ginette Vincendeau, series editor and editor of
The Encyclopedia of European Cinema
London, February 1996

Geoffrey Nowell-Smith is Director of the Media Programme's Joint European Filmography (JEF) and General Editor of the *Oxford History of World Cinema*; **James Hay** is Professor of Cinema Studies at the University of Illinois; **Gianni Volpi** is a freelance writer on Italian cinema.

INTRODUCTION
Geoffrey Nowell-Smith

The Italian cinema is one of the most important in Europe. Cinema has played a significant role in Italian national culture, particularly in the period 1930–80, and it has enjoyed international esteem and success – first in the years immediately preceding the First World War when Italian 'spectaculars' such as *Cabiria* (Giovanni Pastrone, 1914) took the world by storm, and then again after 1945 with neo-realism and in the 1960s and 1970s with Italian contributions to the international art film and with the Italian (or 'spaghetti') Western. But unlike France, cinema in Italy has been marked by severe discontinuity and the glorious years have been interspersed with periods in which both the quantity and the quality of production have slumped to very low levels.

At the present time Italian cinema is going through one of its fallow periods. The share of the Italian box-office taken by home-produced films has sunk to little more than 15% and few Italian films make it on to the international market. Gianni Amelio's masterly *Lamerica* (1994) has yet to be seen in Britain. Italy's most famous contemporary film-maker, Bernardo Bertolucci, has made most of his recent films abroad. But it would be premature to say that Italian cinema will not recover from the doldrums. Movies remain an important part of Italian cultural life, even if most of what people now watch is American films, and on television.

The importance of cinema for audiences of all classes and cultural backgrounds has had a great effect on the sort of cinema Italy has produced. This has ranged from bargain-basement popular genres to the pinnacles of art cinema. Significantly, however, all of cinema has been seen as one. Popular comedians (like Totò) or singers (Domenico Modugno) have appeared in films by 'art cinema' directors such as Pasolini, while top writers (like Ennio Flaiano) and directors (Bertolucci) have not hesitated to dirty their fingers with genres such as the spaghetti Western. Films by Fellini (*La dolce vita*) and Visconti (*Rocco e i suoi fratelli/Rocco and his Brothers*) have been smash-hit box-office successes, while popular melodramas such as those by Raffaello Matarazzo and horror films by Mario Bava or Dario Argento have been the object of cult admiration by intellectuals. And in between the high and the low branches of film there has always been a middle cinema, wide in its appeal and offering vehicles for performances by star actors and actresses, some of whom (Marcello Mastroianni, Sophia Loren) are well known abroad but others of whom (Silvana Pampanini, Nino Manfredi, Ugo Tognazzi and more recently Roberto Benigni) have remained relatively unknown outside their home country.

It is above all the middle cinema that is at the heart of this

Companion to Italian Cinema. Ever since the 1930s and despite severe censorship (first under Fascism and then under postwar Christian Democracy), the cinema has been a faithful mirror of Italian life, reflecting its realities, dreams and nightmares. It has traced changes in sexual mores, and documented political corruption. It has provoked tears, laughter and, where necessary, anger. Out of the fertile ground of this rich cinematic culture – far richer than any provided by literature or television – there have then arisen those works which do more than just hold up a mirror to life, the masterpieces for which Italian cinema will always be remembered. To name but a few: Roberto Rossellini's *Paisà* (1946) and *Viaggio in Italia* (1954); Vittorio De Sica and Cesare Zavattini's *Bicycle Thieves* (1948); Luchino Visconti's *La terra trema* (1948) and *The Leopard* (1963); Michelangelo Antonioni's *L'avventurra* (1960) and *Beyond the Clouds* (1995); Federico Fellini's $8\frac{1}{2}$ (1963) and *Amarcord* (1973); Francesco Rosi's *Salvatore Giuliano* (1962) and *Christ Stopped at Eboli* (1979); Pier Paolo Pasolini's *Medea* (1970); Bernardo Bertolucci's *The Conformist* (1970); Sergio Leone's *C'era una volta in America/Once upon a Time in America* (1983). Not many cinemas can boast such a list. Nor can they boast such a wealth of more ordinary films which have given pleasure to audiences and equally deserve their place in the history books.

Contents

The Companion to Italian Cinema contains the following:

1. An historical overview of Italian cinema. Readers unfamiliar with this national cinema are encouraged to read this first, before 'browsing' or looking up entries.
2. The core of the book is made of over 150, alphabetically arranged entries, on personnel (directors, actors, critics, musicians, producers, set designers), critical concepts (e.g. Neo-realism) and institutions (e.g. Cinecittà). Entries were written by the following writers, signalled by their initials at the end of each entry:
CJ – Carol Jenks; GB – Giuliana Bruno; GC – Gianni Canova; GF – Goffredo Fofi; GLS – Gian-Luca Sergi; GM – Gaetana Marrone; GNS – Geoffrey Nowell-Smith; GV – Ginette Vincendeau; GVo – Gianni Volpi; JHa – James Hay; MMa – Millicent Marcus; MMo – Morando Morandini; PDA – Paolo D'Agostini; PM – Paolo Mereghetti; PV – Paolo Vecchi; RD – Richard Dyer; SH – Simon Horrocks.
3. A section entitled 'Italian cinema in Europe', which draws on material from *The Encyclopedia of European Cinema* and includes entries on pan-European issues (for instance European art cinema, Lesbian and gay cinema in Europe).
4. Two appendices:
– Appendix I: production and audience statistics in Europe.
– Appendix II: select bibliography on European and Italian cinema.

Conventions

Personnel entries are classified under their surname or most common name. This is followed by their date and place of birth and, as the case may be, death, as well as their real name. The country of birth/death is only mentioned if it *not* Italy. As a rule, biographical details such as marriage and children are indicated only if considered relevant to the work or achievement of this person.

Film titles and dates, and filmographies. For space reasons, filmographies are not necessarily exhaustive. Three cases apply:
• all films, or all important films, are mentioned in the text, in which case no filmography follows;
• all other films made by the person (and not mentioned in the text) are added at the end. This is indicated by 'Other films', followed by the films in chronological order. If a complete filmography is provided, it is indicated as 'Films';
• a selection of other major films made by the person (and not mentioned in the text) are added at the end. This is indicated by 'Other films include', followed by the films in chronological order.

Whenever possible, the date indicated is that of the release of the film in Italy.

Bibliography. Some entries are followed by a single short bibliographical reference (under 'Bib') in an abbreviated form, to direct the reader to further reading. There is also a bibliography on European cinema, as well as Italian cinema in appendix II.

Cross-referencing. Throughout the text, persons, institutions and concepts which have their own entry in the rest of the book are signalled by an asterisk placed after the name. Alternatively, an arrow can point to related material. Between entries, other terminologies or related persons may be signalled.

THE COMPANION
TO
ITALIAN CINEMA

ITALY: AN HISTORICAL OVERVIEW

For convenience the history of Italian cinema can divided into three overlapping formations. The first of these occurs between 1900 and 1930, when film production was widely dispersed and 'Italian cinema' had no clear, stable identity. The second lasts from 1928 to 1980, when production became relatively centralised in Rome, film attendance generally increased or remained stable, and Italian cinema acquired both a domestic and a global identity. The third formation began to emerge around 1968 and is marked by increasing co-production with television, by a decline in the importance of Rome as the centre of Italian film-making, and by widespread laments that 'Italian cinema' was either passing away or becoming increasingly difficult to dissociate from television.

1900–1931

The first Italian fiction film – Filoteo Alberini's *La presa di Roma – 20 settembre 1870/The capture of Rome, 20 September 1870* – was not produced until 1905. But the years prior to 1905 nevertheless saw the emergence of a flourishing pattern of exhibition of (mainly French) films. Until 1915 dedicated movie theatres were mainly confined to the centres of a few large cities. Elsewhere, films were shown in existing cabarets and theatres, or as part of travelling carnivals.

Italian film production between 1905 and 1931 can hardly be described as an *industry*. The 500 or so production companies, mainly located in Rome, Milan, Turin and Naples, lacked a centralised structure and the localised nature of film-making contributed to stylistic variances among the films. Weather and lighting in the often cloudy northern cities, for instance, encouraged indoor shooting in glass-covered studios with artificial lighting, which film-makers in Rome or Naples were less quick to adopt. On the production side, the period before 1931 falls into two halves – rapid expansion before World War I, followed by decline and eventual collapse of the production system. The period of expansion was itself marked by contradictory and somewhat opposing impulses. Much of the early expansion, for example, was driven by motives other than profit. Film-making responded in many cases to local needs – a phenomenon particularly evident in Naples. It was often associated with traditional systems of artistic patronage (numerous Italian aristocrats subsidised early films) and with a traditional aesthetic culture, evident in the collaboration of famous Italian literary authors such as Gabriele D'Annunzio, Di Giacomo, Luigi Capuana and Giovanni Verga. There were, however, cases where the expansion of film production before 1915 was driven by a profit motive on a grand scale. The most famous and successful production company organised along those lines was Cines*; its principal backer, Adolfo

Pouchain, secured investment capital from his industrialist relatives and the Banco di Roma, turning Cines into the most successful international distributor of Italian films before World War I.

By 1914, over fifty Italian production companies were distributing their films to movie theatres across Italy, but just as importantly Italy had become the most successful national distributor in an international market. Turin had developed a variety of production facilities, which attracted the most famous film-makers of the era and would only be rivalled (and eventually replaced) by those in Hollywood. Italian films were readily exportable because they worked within genres – primarily the drawing-room melodrama and the historical spectacular – already popularised in the West through theatre and literature. Consequently, the image of Italy in its early, internationally successful films had less to do with the public culture or the everyday landscape and life of contemporary Italy than with a mythic past and the private settings of bourgeois melodrama. The geographic and financial dispersal of film production, however, and the disorganised distribution practices made it difficult for Italian producers to overcome the difficulties generated by World War I. When the war ended, they also had to compete with the rapidly growing popularity of Hollywood films both in Italy and abroad. After 1921, Hollywood films dominated Italian film theatres, comprising nearly 80 per cent of films exhibited through the late 1920s. And by the late 1920s virtually every major Hollywood studio had distribution (and, in some cases, postproduction) offices in Italy.

One of the strategies for maintaining competitiveness involved the creation in 1919 of the Unione Cinematografica Italiana, a trust made up of eleven of the largest production companies in Italy. Although this consortium helped increase film production between 1919 and 1921, its monopolistic structure also reduced competition, and by 1923 the consortium collapsed, exacerbating the instability of Italian production. By the late 1920s domestic film production amounted to less than ten films a year, and some of the most successful silent directors and actors went to work abroad [> EMIGRATION AND EUROPEAN CINEMA]. Throughout the 1920s, production companies attempted to compete with the increasingly successful Hollywood films by futilely relying upon prewar narrative formulas. Significantly, however, one genre – the peplum* – successfully reworked the conventions of the early historical spectacular. Whole series of remakes and retakes involving the escapades of muscular, Olympian-named heroes such as Maciste*, Ajax and Saetta achieved substantial popularity both in Italy and in parts of Europe.

1928–1980

Two major factors contributed to the centralisation of Italian film production and to the formation of a film culture with a national and nationalistic scope. One was the success of entrepreneur Stefano Pittaluga*. The other was the transformation of national, public, economic and cultural policy accompanying the rise to power of Fascism after 1922.

The Fascist government was instrumental in centralising film production in Rome through the setting up of the Istituto Nazionale LUCE* in 1926 and its subsequent support for the construction of the Centro Sperimentale* and Cinecittà*, adjacent to LUCE, in the mid-1930s. The government also supported a national film industry through (albeit feeble) protectionist policies limiting the import and exhibition of Hollywood (and, later, non-Axis) cinema. While this did little to curb the widespread distribution of Hollywood films in Italy or to diminish their appeal, it did help organise film distribution. Contemporaneously the government was involved in 'popular cultural' initiatives such as the mobile cinema caravans that exhibited movies across rural Italy. In the late 1930s, it also encouraged the export of Italian films. But despite its interest in centralising and protecting film production, in producing documentaries and newsreels for national and international distribution, and in nationalising cinema as part of a broad economic policy and cultural initiative, the Fascist government exercised little direct control over domestic feature-length films during the 1920s and 1930s. But censorship was severe, and the government's insistence on having all foreign films dubbed in Italian studios (as a way of controlling what was on the soundtrack) caused dubbing to become a generalised practice in Italian film-making, even for Italian films.

The government was also able to build on the foundations created by Pittaluga in the 1920s. Starting as an exhibitor, Pittaluga had moved into distribution and then production, where he was responsible for the revival of Cines and the making of Italy's first sound films, including Alessandro Blasetti's* *Sole/Sun* (1929) and Mario Camerini's* *Rotaie/Rails* (1929). After Pittaluga's death in 1931, Cines was taken over by the industrialist Lodovico Toeplitz, who appointed Emilio Cecchi* as director of production. Under Cecchi's leadership, Cines embarked on an ambitious production programme which included innovative documentaries as well as comedies and melodramas. Even more important than the international prestige gained by films such as Walther Ruttmann's *Acciaio/Arbeit macht Frei/Steel* (1934) was the steadily improving performance of Italian films at the domestic box office, making Italy less dependent on imports and able to plan further expansion.

When the Cines studio burned down in 1935, it was replaced by the Cinecittà facilities, which became the primary locus for Italian film production up to the 1970s. Cinecittà rapidly became identified with the genres characteristic of Italian cinema of the period, ranging from 'white telephone' (bourgeois) comedies to the historical costume dramas which became the most conspicuous affirmation of Fascism's epic vision of the nation. But by the time of Italy's entry into World War II in 1940 other tendencies were at work which were to change the face of Italian cinema. In the field of the historical film, a small

3

group of scriptwriters and directors known as the 'calligraphers' (Alberto Lattuada*, Renato Castellani*, Mario Soldati* and Luigi Chiarini*) withdrew from nationalistic bombast and, with their elegant adaptations of late nineteenth and early twentieth-century naturalistic fiction, began to offer an alternative picture of Italian culture, one less oriented towards heroic hyperbole. Meanwhile a resurgence of small-scale production led to a more modest type of popular comedy, often using street locations – particularly evident in the work of Ferdinando Maria Poggioli (*Le sorelle Materassi/The Materassi Sisters*, 1943).

More importantly, major cultural changes were afoot, which came to fruition with the fall of Fascism in 1943 and the liberation in 1945. With *Ossessione* (1942, starring Massimo Girotti*), Luchino Visconti* drew on his prewar experience as an assistant to Jean Renoir and on an unlikely literary source (James Cain's crime novel *The Postman Always Rings Twice*) to produce an unvarnished picture of Italian rural life which shocked the censors and proved a forerunner of neo-realism*. In 1945, with Fascism discredited and the economy in ruins, a group of film-makers including Visconti, Lattuada, Vittorio De Sica* and Roberto Rossellini* set out to produce a new type of cinema, with a different relation to popular and national life. Unable or unwilling to use Cinecittà as a production site, they shot their films on location, often with non-professional actors, bringing their material back for editing and sound dubbing in such studio facilities as remained operational. Characteristically their subject matter was the current state of the nation and the recent past of German occupation and local resistance, epitomised by Rossellini's *Roma città aperta/Rome Open City* (1945).

The style pioneered in the immediate postwar years, and generically referred to as neo-realism*, was a product partly of material and economic conditions and partly of a cultural-political imperative to interrogate social conditions and look forward to the future. As such as it was part of a general climate of cultural regeneration which sought to sweep away the residues of Fascism and reaffirm alternative cultural traditions such as that of turn-of-the century realism, or *verismo*. In the turn towards realism the cinema was seen as having a privileged role to play, and the ideas put forward by film theorists such as Umberto Barbaro* and Luigi Chiarini* in the magazines *Cinema* and *Bianco e Nero* found wide acceptance, not only in film circles but in the culture at large. These ideas had been germinating in the last years of Fascism and came to fruition dramatically in the immediate postwar period.

By 1950, however, conditions had changed. American films had reappeared on the market, to the delight of the public. Cinecittà re-opened and the domestic industry was beginning to revive. Production rose from twenty-five films in 1945 to 104 in 1950 and 201 in 1954, steadily increasing its box-office share. The Christian Democrat government elected in 1948 was hostile both to the makeshift production methods and to the leftist ideology of most neo-realist film-makers and favoured the rebuilding of an industry based on studio production. Neo-realism as a movement began to break up. Its stylistic features and socio-political ambitions, however, continued to influence Italian cinema, setting a notional standard against which subsequent Italian films were compared. Meanwhile, the former neo-realists were increasingly drawn to 'art cinema', while a bizarre legacy remained in the popular cinema in the form of 'rose-tinted' neo-realism (*neorealismo rosa*). This treated the pleasures and miseries of everyday life in a generally optimistic, populist vein and was to become the basis of the *commedia all'italiana** ('comedy Italian-style') of the late 1950s and the 1960s. While neo-realism had stressed poverty and the hope for social change in the uncertain conditions of the 1940s, the 1950s were the years of economic boom, but also of political stagnation. *Commedia all'italiana* reflected these changing conditions, satirising both the survival of the 'old' Italy (its primitive sexual morality, for example) and the emerging 'new' Italy of vulgarity and consumerism.

Commedia all'italiana was but one of many genres that flourished in the 1950s revival. Historical, adventure and costume films continued to be popular, often displaying production values that belied their extremely low budgets. At the lower end of the market, the historical film spawned a distinctive variant, popularly known as the peplum*, based on the exploits of muscular heroes in mythical antiquity. In the mid-1960s, the popularity of the peplum began to wane, and it was replaced by the Italian or 'Spaghetti' Western*, which lasted until the mid-1970s. Higher up the scale, a curious co-existence emerged between Italian cinema and Hollywood. Unable to repatriate the profits made by its films in Italy, in 1949 MGM began using Italian studios as a site for its own productions; by 1950 it had begun production of *Quo Vadis*, the first of many 'super-spectacles' produced or co-produced in Italy by Hollywood companies over the 1950s, garnering for Cinecittà the dubious label of 'Hollywood on the Tiber' [> EUROPEAN CINEMA AND HOLLYWOOD]. Meanwhile Italian producers such as Dino De Laurentiis* and Carlo Ponti* attempted, with some success, to set themselves up in Hollywood. These exchanges affected art films as well as popular genres. As early as 1949, RKO had bankrolled Rossellini's *Stromboli, terra di dio/Stromboli*, while later Carlo Ponti contracted Michelangelo Antonioni* to make three English-language films, *Blowup* (1967, UK), *Zabriskie Point* (1969, US) and *Professione: Reporter/The Passenger* (1975).

1960 was the annus mirabilis for Italian cinema. The share of domestic box-office for Italian films reached 50 per cent for the first time since the war, and two of the films most responsible for this unprecedented development, Federico Fellini's* *La dolce vita* and Visconti's *Rocco e i suoi fratelli/Rocco and His Brothers*, achieved critical acclaim and further box-office revenues internationally as well. The success of those two films (and that of Antonioni's artistically ground-breaking if less commercial *L'avventura*) marked the definitive arrival of Italy's contribution to the European art cinema* of the 1960s. Stars such as

5

Marcello Mastroianni*, Giulietta Masina* and Monica Vitti* became household names, joining those of Sophia Loren*, Gina Lollobrigida*, Anna Magnani*, Alberto Sordi*, Totò* and Vittorio Gassman* among others. New directors came on the scene, including Pier Paolo Pasolini* (*Accattone*, 1961), Bernardo Bertolucci* (*Prima della rivoluzione/Before the Revolution*, 1964), Marco Bellocchio* (*I pugni in tasca/Fists in the Pocket*, 1965) and Paolo and Vittorio Taviani* (*I sovversivi*, 1967). Italian cinema affirmed itself not only in the national culture but as Italy's major contribution to the general cultural ferment of the decade. Other successes in the early 1970s, notably Liliana Cavani's* *Il portiere di notte/The Night Porter* (1974) and Ettore Scola's* *C'eravamo tanto amati/We All Loved Each Other So Much* (1974), seemed a further confirmation of this upward trend.

1968–1995

As the 1970s wore on, however, it became clear that major changes were taking place in Italian cinema. Dependence on the international market was leading to a dissolution of its identity as more and more films took on foreign stars to boost their appeal and more and more directors were tempted into international co-productions. American and other actors had been used in Italian films of the 1950s – Anthony Quinn in Fellini's *La strada* (1954) being a conspicuous example. But in the 1970s the trend accelerated. A landmark in this respect was Bertolucci's *Ultimo tango a Parigi/Last Tango in Paris* (1972), set (as the title indicates) in Paris, and starring Marlon Brando, Maria Schneider, Jean-Pierre Léaud* and – as solitary Italian representative – the ageing Massimo Girotti. Continuation of this international trend can be found in Liliana Cavani's* *Il portiere di notte* (1974, starring Dirk Bogarde and Charlotte Rampling), in Bertolucci's *Novecento/1900* (1976, with Burt Lancaster, Donald Sutherland, Robert De Niro and Gérard Depardieu), and in the further use of Bogarde, Lancaster, Helmut Berger, Anna Karina and others in Visconti's films from the late 1960s onwards.

While the 'art' film became increasingly international (and popular genre cinema increasingly inclined to recycle foreign models, developing the Italian horror film* and the Italian Western*), a distinctively Italian character was maintained throughout the 1970s in two areas. One was the contemporary political film [> ITALIAN POLITICAL CINEMA], usually about the threat to the social order represented by the Mafia on the one hand and terrorism on the other. The other was the revisionary historical film that looked back at the recent past and in particular the legacy of Fascism, a conspicuous absence in Italian film culture before the 1970s. The treatment of Fascism in films as diverse as Bertolucci's *Il conformista/The Conformist* (1970) and Fellini's *Amarcord* (1973) became a way of framing a discourse about nationhood and nationalism, of re-evaluating popular taste, memory and consciousness, and of underscoring the political mission of cinema in national culture and everyday life. Related to this cinematic dialogue with the national past were the growing number of films about the legacy of cinema itself. These include Fellini's *E la nave va/And the Ship Sails On* (1983) and *Ginger e Fred/Ginger and Fred* (1985), the Tavianis' *Good Morning, Babilonia/Good Morning, Babylon* (1987), Giuseppe Tornatore's* *Nuovo Cinema Paradiso/Cinema Paradiso* (1988), Scola's *C'eravamo tanto amati, Le bal* (1983) and *Splendor* (1988), and Maurizio Nichetti's *Ladri di saponette/Icicle Thief* (1989). Some of these acknowledge cinema's role in shaping a national consciousness and popular memory, and some (particularly *Ginger e Fred* and *Ladri di saponette*) involve nostalgic protagonists unable to cope with the ubiquity of television in contemporary Italy.

That cinema attendance and production dropped to dramatically low levels by the late 1970s cannot be attributed wholly to the increased centrality of television in everyday Italian life or entirely, for that matter, to conditions within Italy. Nevertheless, the rapid emergence of private Italian television networks after 1980 contributed to the way movies were produced and consumed and to the transformation of Italian culture. No longer was the Rome-based state-run RAI* the centre of broadcasting and made-for-television co-productions, as it had been in the 1970s; nor could it maintain its role, since the 1950s, of state-sanctioned arbiter of national culture and public taste. The private television networks, the most successful of which were formed by entrepreneur (and later Prime Minister) Silvio Berlusconi, were based in Milan, and they initially competed with the RAI networks by importing/recycling foreign (particularly American) films and television programmes. The proliferation of television channels brought an unprecedented number of movies to the television screens, which, combined with theatrically distributed films and the growing number of those released on video, kept film consumption in the 1980s high. The private networks relied largely upon relatively inexpensive ('B-production') older films – Italian or foreign (largely Hollywood). By the 1990s, however, Berlusconi's Milan-based Fininvest* company began to invest in film productions for domestic and international distribution.

While Italian film production had always been entrepreneurial, not since its earliest years had it been so decentralised. In this environment, even entrepreneurial film-making begat new trends. A number of young film-makers of the 1980s – most notably Roberto Benigni*, Carlo Verdone, and Maurizio Nichetti – made films involving personas they had already developed as performers in other media. Equally significant in this regard is Nanni Moretti*, whose films have adopted a highly confessional style; his *Caro diario/Dear Diary* (1994) is constructed as a nomadic narrative through Rome's neighbourhoods and backstreets and across parts of southern Italy. This 'nomadic' style is also evident in several recent Italian 'road movies' involving characters' alienation and unrequited searchings – again, not a new theme in Italian cinema, but one acquiring a different significance in relation to the decentralisation of national film production and the increased marginalisation of film as a cultural form in Italy. The ironic detach-ment/involvement of characters – and of film-makers as social 'actors' – from/with their material social, and symbolic environments (es-pecially in the quasi-confessional and nomadic films) belies a deep un-certainty in Italian cinema about its mission and, above all, its *place* in contemporary Italian life. After decades of struggling to secure a 'national cinema', however, these practices also attest to the possibility of not envisioning the nation as Utopia, or as a unified space of cul-tural production. JHa/GNS

ITALIAN CINEMA: PERSONNEL, INSTITUTIONS, KEY CRITICAL CONCEPTS

AGE, Agenore Incrocci
ALDO, G. R.
ALESSANDRINI, Goffredo
AMBROSIO, Arturo
AMELIO, Gianni
AMIDEI, Sergio
ANTONIONI, Michelangelo
ARGENTO, Dario
AVATI, Pupi
BARBARO, Umberto
BAVA, Mario
BECCE, Giuseppe
BELLOCCHIO, Marco
BENE, Carmelo
BENIGNI, Roberto
BERTOLUCCI, Bernardo
BLASETTI, Alessandro
BOSÉ, Lucia
BRAZZI, Rossano
CAMERINI, Mario
CARDINALE, Claudia
CASTELLANI, Renato
CAVANI, Liliana
CECCHI D'AMICO, Suso
CECCHI, Emilio
CECCHI GORI, Mario
CENTRO SPERIMENTALE
CERVI, Gino
CHIARI, Walter
CHIARINI, Luigi
CINECITTÀ
CINES
COMENCINI, Luigi
'COMMEDIA
   ALL'ITALIANIA'
COTTAFAVI, Vittorio
CRETINETTI
CRISTALDI, Franco
DE FILIPPO, Eduardo, Peppino
   and Titina
DE LAURENTIIS, Dino
DEL POGGIO, Carla
DE SANTIS, Giuseppe

DE SICA, Vittorio
DI VENANZO, Gianni
DIVISMO
DONAGGIO, Giuseppe
EMMER, Luciano
FABRIZI, Aldo
FELLINI, Federico
FERRERI, Marco
FININVEST
FLAIANO, Ennio
FRANCHI, Franco
FREDA, Riccardo
FREDDI, Luigi
FUSCO, Giovanni
FUTURISM
GALLONE, Carmine
GASSMAN, Vittorio
GENINA, Augusto
GERMI, Pietro
GHIONE, Emilio
GIROTTI, Massimo
GUERRA, Tonino
INGRASSIA, Ciccio
ITALIAN HORROR FILM
ITALIAN POLITICAL
   CINEMA
ITALIAN ('SPAGHETTI')
   WESTERNS
LATTUADA, Alberto
LEONE, Sergio
LIZZANI, Carlo
LOLLOBRIGIDA, Gina
LOREN, Sophia
LUCE
LUX
MACARIO, Erminio
MACISTE
MAGNANI, Anna
MANGANO, Silvana
MARCHESI, Marcello
MASELLI, Francesco
MASINA, Giulietta
MASTROIANNI, Marcello

MATARAZZO, Raffaello
MATTOLI, Mario
METZ, Vittorio
MINGOZZI, Gianfranco
MIRANDA, Isa
MONICELLI, Mario
MORETTI, Nanni
MORRICONE, Ennio
NAZZARI, Amedeo
NEO-REALISM
NEW ITALIAN COMICS
NORIS, Assia
NOTARI, Elvira
OLMI, Ermanno
PAMPANINI, Silvana
PASOLINI, Pier Paolo
PASTRONE, Giovanni
PEPLUM
PETRI, Elio
PIETRANGELI, Antonio
PIRRO, Ugo
PITTALUGA, Stefano
PONTECORVO, Gillo
PONTI, Carlo
RAI
RISI, Dino
RISI, Marco
RIZZOLI, Angelo
ROSI, Francesco

ROSSELLINI, Roberto
ROTA, Nino
ROTUNNO, Giuseppe
SANDRELLI, Stefania
SCARPELLI, Furio
SCOLA, Ettore
SERATO, Massimo
SOLDATI, Mario
SOLINAS, Franco
SONEGO, Rodolfo
SORDI, Alberto
STEELE, Barbara
STENO
STORARO, Vittorio
TAVIANI, Paolo and Vittorio
TITANUS
TOGNAZZI, Ugo
TORNATORE, Giuseppe
TOTÒ
TROISI, Massimo
VALLI, Alida
VENICE
VISCONTI, Luchino
VITTI, Monica
VOLONTÉ, Gian Maria
WERTMÜLLER, Lina
ZAMPA, Luigi
ZAVATTINI, Cesare
ZURLINI, Valerio

A

AGE, Agenore Incrocci   Brescia 1919
and
SCARPELLI, Furio   Rome 1919

Italian scriptwriters. The scriptwriting duo of Age and Scarpelli came
together in the late 1940s, scoring a notable hit with their script for the
comedy *Totò cerca casa/Totò Wants a Home* (1949) and other Totò*
vehicles. They developed a more distinctive style of their own with the
emergence of *Commedia all'italiana*＊ in the late 1950s, writing scripts
for Mario Monicelli* (*I soliti ignoti/Persons Unknown*, 1958; *La
grande guerra/The Great War*, 1959) and other directors. Adept at mixing light comedy, social satire and occasional tragedy, they went on to
write vehicles for the comic actor Alberto Sordi*, for the more theatrical Vittorio Gassman*, and for Marcello Mastroianni* (*I compag-
ni/The Strikers*, 1963). Their biggest success came with Luigi
Comencini's* epic tragi-comedy about the 1943 armistice *Tutti a casa/
Everybody Go Home!* (1960), but they are probably most famous for
their collaboration with director Ettore Scola*, beginning with
Dramma della gelosia/The Pizza Triangle (1970), including *C'eravamo
tanto amati/We All Loved Each Other So Much* (1974), and culminating with *La terrazza/The Terrace* (1979). *La terrazza* was their last important film together but Scarpelli returned to work with Scola on *Il
viaggio del capitan Fracassa* (1990) and *Il Postino* (1994). PDA

ALDO, G. R.   Aldo Rossano Graziati; Scorzè 1905 –
                                         Albara di Pianiga 1953

Italian cinematographer, who emigrated to Paris in 1923 where he became a photographer (from 1937 a set photographer) and acquired experience as a cinematographer, for instance on Marcel L'Herbier's *Les
Derniers jours de Pompei/The Last Days of Pompeii* (1947–50). Back
in Italy he met Luchino Visconti* and was offered the role of director
of photography on *La terra trema* (1947). He also worked with
Augusto Genina* on *Cielo sulla palude/Heaven over the Marshes*
(1949) and *Tre storie proibite/Three Forbidden Stories* (1952), and with
Vittorio De Sica* on *Miracolo a Milano/Miracle in Milan* (1951),
Umberto D. (1952), and *Stazione Termini/Indiscretion of an American
Wife* (1953), during which his concern for the film as a whole rather
than the beauty of Jennifer Jones angered producer David O.
Selznick, who employed Oswald Morris for the close-ups of his wife.
Aldo worked with Orson Welles on part of *Otello/Othello* (1951), and
with directors such as Mario Soldati* (*La provinciale/The Wayward*

Wife, 1953). Profoundly influenced by his stay in France, but at the same time loyal to a mythic vision of Caravaggio's and Venetian painting, Aldò – as he was called by everyone, with the stress on the last syllable – was both a traditionalist and a forerunner of self-conscious modern cinematography. His most immediate successor is Giuseppe Rotunno*, his colleague and friend from 1947. Aldo died in a car accident during the shooting of Visconti's *Senso* (1954), which Rotunno and Robert Krasker went on to complete. MMo

ALESSANDRINI, Goffredo   Cairo, Egypt 1904–78

Italian director. A prolific director of some of the most popular Italian films of the 1930s and early 1940s, Alessandrini worked in a variety of genres, including romantic comedy, melodrama and the biopic, but his fame was (and is) mostly tied to his war epics, which mythologised fascist colonialist initiatives. Many of his films were set in North Africa, the site of Italian occupation in the early twentieth century and the place where the director was reared and to which he frequently returned.

After working as a scriptwriter and assistant director for Alessandro Blasetti* at Cines*, Alessandrini directed his first feature-length film for Cines, *La segretaria privata/The Private Secretary* (1931), an Italian remake of a popular German film. After a stint working for MGM on Italian versions of Hollywood films, he returned to Italy to make *Seconda B* (1934), a quaint and nostalgic melodrama set in 1911 at a girls' school, which he co-scripted with Umberto Barbaro*. Alessandrini then directed *Don Bosco* (1935), a biopic commemorating the founder of the Salesian Catholic order in Italy. The film was funded by the Salesians and (unusually for the period) used mainly non-professional actors. Alessandrini's subsequent epics follow on from *Don Bosco* in the quasi-religious tone they give to the exploits of modern Italian crusaders. *Cavalleria* (1936) charted the rite of passage of a cavalryman played by the young Amedeo Nazzari*, who forgoes his horse for an aeroplane at the outbreak of World War I. In Alessandrini's next film, *Luciano Serra pilota/The Pilot Luciano Serra* (1938), the central character, also played by Nazzari, is a successful World War I pilot whose disillusionment with his country can only be assuaged through his return to the battlefields of North Africa, where he re-emerges as a protector of a 'new' Italy and the future of his soldier son. The quasi-sacred quests of the central characters in these two films are consonant with the more literally religious mission of Cardinal Messias to North Africa in Alessandrini's following film, *Abuna Messias* (1939), which attempts to demonstrate the cultural basis for ties between Ethiopia and Catholic Italy.

The popularity of the colonial war genre in Italy during the late 1930s led to Alessandrini being contracted in 1942 to direct another war epic, *Giarabub* (1942), again set in North Africa. *Giarabub*, made partly in the war zone (drawing Italian soldiers from the battlefront to play the opposing armies) and partly at Cinecittà*, is an ironic allegory of the relation between the cultural politics of film-making and the state politics of war. Alessandrini's other successful epics during the early 1940s include the biography of Caravaggio (*Caravaggio, il pittore maledetto/Caravaggio, The Cursed Painter*, 1941) and *Noi vivi – Addio, Kira!/We The Living* (1942), a long (in some versions, two-part) romantic melodrama set during the Russian revolution, based on a novel by Ayn Rand and starring Alida Valli* and Rossano Brazzi*. Alessandrini's career as a director was significantly limited after the war amid the emerging neo-realist* aesthetic. JHa

AMBROSIO, Arturo   Turin 1869–1960

Italian producer. Ambrosio, the owner of a photographic equipment shop with technical and commercial connections with Pathé, produced *La prima corsa automobilistica Susa-Moncenisio/The First Susa-Moncenisio Car Race* with Roberto Omegna in 1904, followed by a series of short (*c.* five-minute) documentaries. From these modest beginnings Ambrosio rose to worldwide recognition as the founding father of Italian cinema, with Turin as its capital. In 1907 he founded l'Anonima Ambrosio, a well-capitalised and rigorously organised company, with new large studios, new 'cinematographic' actors (Mary Tarlarini, Gigetta Morano, Alberto Collo), cameramen (G. Vitrotti) and scriptwriters (Arrigo Frusta), which produced popular adventure melodramas and comedies, as well as more ambitious films. Of particular interest are Luigi Maggi's *Spergiura!* (1909) with its real settings, Omegna's *Caccia al leopardo/The Leopard Hunt*, entirely shot in Africa; the early epic, *Gli ultimi giorni di Pompei/The Last Days of Pompeii* (1908) and Omegna's documentary *La vita delle farfalle/The Life of Butterflies* (1911), made in collaboration with the poet Guido Gozzano. In 1911–12, Ambrosio produced six dramas written by the poet Gabriele D'Annunzio. Contributing to the worldwide triumph of Italian historical cinema, he produced spectaculars such as Mario Caserini's unforgettable version of *Gli ultimi giorni di Pompei* (1913) and *I promessi sposi* (1913, dir. Ernesto Maria Pasquali). The company also had its regular comedian in 'Robinet' (Marcel Fabre). In 1916, Ambrosio produced the only film performance of stage *diva* Eleonora Duse [> DIVISMO], in Febo Mari's *Cenere*. Ambrosio's company entered a period of crisis after the war. He joined UCI (Unione Cinematografica Italiana, a trust created to fight off international competition), for whom he produced three films, including Gabriellino (the son of Gabriele) D'Annunzio's *La nave/The Ship* (1920). When UCI in turn went bust, he retired to his farm in the country, and returned to cinema only to manage Scalera Film from 1939 to 1943. GVo

AMELIO, Gianni

Italian director. Graduating from assistant on low-budget films, Amelio quickly learnt to apply a personal touch to all sorts of genres, formats and commissions before reaching international recognition in the late 1980s. His talent first emerged in his television work at RAI*, beginning with *La fine del gioco/The End of the Game* (1970), and followed by the philosophical *La città del sole/City of the Sun* (1973, based on Tommaso Campanella's eponymous utopian treatise) and his free adapatations of Aldous Huxley (*Il piccolo Archimede/ Young Archimedes*, 1979) and Anna Banfi (*I velieri/The Sailing Ships*, 1982). Often focusing on the world of the media and the ambiguity of his own role within it, he revealed an acute moral sense of social relations, mingling public and private themes, allied to an alert consciousness of film language. Notable are *Colpire al cuore/Straight to the Heart* (1982), the story of a father–son relationship caught in the poisonous climate of terrorism; *I ragazzi di via Panisperna/The Panisperna Street Boys* (1988), about the complex relationship between a teacher and his pupil; *Porte aperte/Open Doors* (1990), original both in its treatment of Leonardo Sciascia's novel and in Gian Maria Volonté's* central performance; and *Il ladro di bambini/Stolen Children* (1992), a journey from North to South by a policeman and two children, which is also a journey into the depths of Italy, open to many different readings. Most recently *Lamerica* (1994), the encounter of a 'son' without an identity and a 'father' without a present, against the background of the almost biblical exodus of the Albanians into Italy, confirms Amelio's status as one of the most important Italian directors of the present generation. GVo

Other Films Include: *La morte al lavoro/Death at Work* (1978, video); *Effetti speciali/Special Effects* (1978, video).

AMIDEI, Sergio

Italian scriptwriter. Initially a jack of all trades at the FERT studio in Turin, Amidei started to write scripts in 1938 with Pietro Micca. As an anti-fascist in a cinema ruled by dictatorship, he focused on technical proficiency by devising a sort of 'language for cinema'. He worked on genre films, such as the so-called 'Hungarian' comedies, and historical reconstructions for Mario Bonnard, Nunzio Malasomma, Carmine Gallone* and Carlo Ludovico Bragaglia, participating at all levels of production. Only in his work with Ferdinando Maria Poggioli did he manage to work more creatively. His talent achieved full expression in the postwar period. He was Roberto Rossellini's* regular scriptwriter from *Roma città aperta/Rome, Open City* (1945) to *Stromboli, terra di Dio/Stromboli* (1949). His name appears on the credits of films by

Vittorio De Sica* (*Sciuscià/Shoeshine*, 1946), Luigi Zampa* (*Anni difficili/Difficult Years*, 1948; *Anni facili/Easy Years*, 1953), Renato Castellani* (*Sotto il sole di Roma*, 1948), Luciano Emmer (*Una domenica d'agosto/Sunday in August*, 1950), and Carlo Lizzani* (*Cronache di poveri amanti/Stories of Poor Lovers*, 1954). He was thus one of the protagonists (some critics claim an originator) of neo-realism* in all its forms, including *commedia all'italiana** – a genre for which, rightly or wrongly, the scriptwriters rather than the directors have tended to receive the credit. A versatile and pragmatic craftsman, he excelled in a kind of 'everyday epic poetry' inhabited by a wide variety of popular characters, his work ranging from moral reflection on society to criticism of manners. His position on society was, however, shot through with paradox – which, he maintained, 'captures reality more than documentation can' – and with irony which 'releases more truth than anger'. He continued collaborating with Rossellini (for instance, on *La paura/Fear*, 1954, and *Viva l'Italia*, 1961), and worked in comedy, contributing to a number of masterpieces of the genre such as *Un borghese piccolo piccolo/An Average Man* (1977, dir. Mario Monicelli*), and creating many other roles for Alberto Sordi*. *Il mondo nuovo/The New World* (1982), which came out after his death and which is dedicated to him, was the last of more than 150 films written by Amidei. GVo

ANTONIONI, Michelangelo   Ferrara 1912

Italian director. Italy's foremost modernist *auteur*, Antonioni made a successful transition from postwar realism to an abstract, formalist style which embodied his characters' increasingly alienated and dehumanised world view.

Antonioni graduated from the University of Bologna with a degree in economics and business before becoming a film critic for the newspaper *Corriere Padano*. In l939 he moved to Rome, joined the editorial staff of the journal *Cinema*, and studied film-making at the Centro Sperimentale* for three months. After collaborating on the screenplay of Roberto Rossellini's* *Un pilota ritorna* (1942), he travelled to Paris to assist Marcel Carné on *Les Visiteurs du soir* (1942). Upon his return, the agency LUCE* commissioned a documentary on the Po valley (*Gente del Po*, begun in 1943 but not completed until 1947 because of Fascist censorship and wartime interruptions). Antonioni's immediate postwar activities included critical writing, collaboration on screenplays (Giuseppe De Santis'* *Caccia tragica/Tragic Hunt*, 1947, Federico Fellini's* *Lo sceicco bianco/The White Sheik*, 1952) and the shooting of documentaries (*N.U./Nettezza urbana*, 1948, and *L'amorosa menzogna*, 1949). His first feature, *Cronaca di un amore/Story of a Love Affair* (1950), was a conventional story of adultery and intended murder, distinguished by Antonioni's attention to formal values. His next work, a film in three episodes entitled *I*

15

vinti/The Vanquished (1952), incurred the wrath of government censors for its unflinching treatment of drug and crime problems among postwar youth in France, Italy and Britain. In *La signora senza camelie/The Lady Without Camelias* (1953) Antonioni criticised the Italian film industry for its exploitation of women, while Turin high society became his target in *Le amiche/The Girlfriends* (1955, based on Cesare Pavese). *Il grido/The Cry* (1957), his only film with working-class characters, followed its protagonist's desperate odyssey through the film-maker's native Po valley landscape.

Antonioni's *L'avventura*, along with Fellini's *La dolce vita* (both 1960), marked the birth of a new, anti-conventional film language and disjointed narrative structure homologous to the radically altered conditions of Italian life. *L'avventura* inaugurated Antonioni's exploration of the moral and emotional bankruptcy of the bourgeois condition, the difficulty (if not impossibility) of personal intimacy and the individual's increasing alienation from social and natural contexts. It was followed by *La notte/The Night* (1961), *L'eclisse/The Eclipse* (1962) and *Deserto rosso/The Red Desert* (1964). Through Monica Vitti's* intelligent performances in these films, Antonioni focused on the crisis of women in the midst of failed love relationships and non-sustaining social environments. Antonioni's use of *rosso* (red) in the title of *Deserto rosso,* his first colour film, called attention to his aggressive, non-naturalistic colour technique in representing industrialised Ravenna.

Blowup (1966, UK/It.) marked the beginning of Antonioni's international phase. From 1967 to 1982 he filmed outside Italy and his concerns became increasingly abstract and universal. Set in the fashionable London of the mid-1960s, *Blowup* reflected on the knowability and representability of 'the real'. *Zabriskie Point* (1969, US), shot in California, was his attempt to fathom American counter-culture and find a revolutionary film language to represent it. *Professione: Reporter/The Passenger* (1975), the story of a journalist (Jack Nicholson) who impulsively takes on someone else's identity only to learn that his new 'self' was a gun-runner caught in a death trap, raised questions of identity, destiny and the relationship of the mass media to lived experience. Returning to his roots as a documentarist in 1972, Antonioni shot *Chung-Kuo Cina*, a RAI*-sponsored film on China, critically acclaimed in the West but reviled by the Chinese authorities as subversive of official photographic etiquette. Experiments with visual effects and colour culminated in *Il mistero di Oberwald/The Oberwald Mystery* (1980), an adaptation of a Cocteau play starring Vitti and featuring the latest video and laser technology. Antonioni's next feature was *Identificazione di una donna/Identification of a Woman* (1982), a reworking of earlier concerns with bourgeois crisis and the impossible quest for intimacy. Plagued by ill-health, Antonioni was not able to complete several projects, but his career has received widespread recognition, including lifetime achievement awards at film festivals in Taormina (1981), Cannes (1982) and Venice (1983), and most recently an Oscar (1995). In 1995 he recovered sufficiently from the effects of a serious stroke to make (with help from his wife and from the German director Wim Wenders) *Par-delà les nuages/Beyond the Clouds/Al di la delle nuvole*, an episode film based on some of his short stories. MMa

Bib: Sam Rohdie, *Antonioni* (1990).

Other Films: **Documentaries**: *Superstizione, Sette canne, un vestito* (1949); *La funivia del Faloria, La villa dei mostri* (1950); *Kumbha Mela* (1989); *Roma* (1990). **Features**: *Amore in città/Love in the City* (1953, ep., *Tentato suicidio*); *I tre volti/Three Times* (1965, ep. *Il provino*).

ARGENTO, Dario   Rome 1940

Italian director, son of producer Salvatore Argento and Brazilian photographer Elda Luxardo. After an abortive start as a film critic for the Roman daily *Paese Sera*, Argento started working as a scriptwriter, collaborating with Bernardo Bertolucci* and director Sergio Leone* on the writing of *C'era una volta il West/Once Upon a Time in the West* (1968). His directorial debut came in 1970 with *L'uccello dalle piume di cristallo/The Gallery Murders*, a tense and realistic thriller which achieved unexpected public success. The subsequent *Il gatto a nove code/The Cat o' Nine Tails* (1971), *Quattro mosche di velluto grigio/ Four Flies on Grey Velvet* (1971), *Le cinque giornate/Five Days* (1973) and *Profondo rosso/Deep Red* (1975) confirmed Argento's visionary talent and contributed to a revival of the Italian horror* B-movie tradition, marked by excess and violence. A turning point came with *Suspiria* (1977) in which the gradual eruption of horror and breakdown of narrative logic prepared the ground for the baroque fantasies and lurid neo-gothic delirium of *Inferno/Hell* (1979), *Tenebre/Unsane* (1982), *Phenomena/Creepers* (1985) and *Opera* (1987). Argento also worked as a producer for young Italian directors in the horror genre inspired by his example (Lamberto Bava, Michele Soavi) and helped his American friend George A. Romero, maker of *Zombi* (1978), with whom he directed *Due occhi diabolici/Two Diabolical Eyes* (1990), a two-part film based on tales by Edgar Allan Poe (Argento's part was called *Il gatto nero/The Black Cat*). With *Trauma* (1993), shot in the US with his daughter Asia in a starring role, he returned to the thriller atmosphere of his early films. The outcome, however, was largely disappointing and confirmed that bloodthirsty and irrational horror is indeed the only genre which really suits him. He made *La sindrome di Stendhal/The Stendhal Syndrome* in 1995. GC

AVATI, Pupi

Giuseppe Avati; Bologna 1938

Italian director. After spending his youth as an amateur jazz player, making a living in various jobs (including as knitwear salesman), Avati, at the age of thirty, finally discovered his ideal medium of self-expression: cinema. He made his debut with *Balsamus, l'uomo di Satana/Blood Relations* (1968), where he freely expressed his naive and provocative taste for the esoteric, the supernatural and black magic – a tendency he pursued throughout his career, especially in his films of the 1970s. A penchant for horror and impressive effects characterised *La casa dalle finestre che ridono/The House with the Laughing Windows* (1976), *Tutti defunti ... tranne i morti* (1977), the horror-style remake of *Zeder/Revenge of the Dead* (1983), and *Magnificat* (1993), a film imbued with ambiguous millenarian pessimism. The eclectic Avati moved between genres, stepping easily from farce and comedy (*La mazurka del barone, della santa e del fico fiorone*, 1974) into the musical (*Aiutami a sognare/Help Me Dream*, 1980; *Jazz Band*, 1978 [TV]; *Dancing Paradise*, 1981) and historical drama (*Noi tre/The Three of Us*, 1984, about Mozart's journey to Bologna). His most personal vein can be found in the nostalgic evocations of past provincial life (in particular his native Emilia Romagna) which occasionally slide into mawkishness. In all these films, however, Avati displayed a remarkable talent for choosing and directing young actors. *Una gita scolastica* (1983) and *Storia di ragazzi e ragazze* (1989) skilfully recreate the 1930s and 1940s with their old-fashioned prudery but also moral values which seem now to have disappeared. More ambiguous are the films shot in contemporary settings (*Impiegati*, 1985; *Festa di Laurea*, 1985; *Regalo di Natale*, 1986; *Fratelli e sorelle*, 1992), which, despite a certain introspective finesse, fail to probe sufficiently their petit-bourgeois milieux. PM

Other Films Include: *Thomas ... gli indemoniati/Thomas ... The Possessed* (1969); *Bordella* (1975); *Le strelle nel fosso* (1979); *Ultimo minuto* (1987); *Sposi* (1988); *Bix* (1990); *L'amico di infanzia* (1994); *Dichiarazioni d'amore* (1994).

B

BARBARO, Umberto

Acireale 1902 – Rome 1959

Italian theoretician and scriptwriter. The erudite, self-taught Barbaro placed cinema at the centre of a multiplicity of interests and experi-

Rossano Brazzi, Alida Valli and Fosco Giachetti in Goffredo Alessandrini's anti-Communist epic *Noi vivi (We the Living,* 1942), based on the novel by Alyn Rand.

Gianni Amelio's *Lamerica* (1994).

Maria Schneider and Jack Nicholson in Antonioni's
The Passenger (*Professione: Reporter,* 1975).

Michael Brandon in Dario Argento's *Quattro mosche di velluto grigio*
(*Four Flies on Grey Velvet,* 1971).

Mario Bava's *Terrore nello spazio* (*Planet of the Vampires*, 1965).

Lou Castel and Paola Pitagora in Marco Bellocchio's
Fists in the Pocket (1965).

Bernardo Bertolucci

Alessandro Blasetti's Risorgimento epic *1860* (1934).

Assia Noris and Vittorio De Sica in Mario Camerini's
Il Signor Max (1937).

Claudia Cardinale

Dirk Bogarde and
Charlotte Rampling
in Liliana Cavani's
The Night Porter
(1973).

Marcello Mastroianni with Daniela Rocca in Pietro Germi's
Divorce Italian Style (1961).

The comedian André Deed, known in Italy as Cretinetti, in
Cretinetti e le donne (1908).

Vittorio De Sica shooting *Umberto D* (1952).

Francesca Bertini

The influence of Futurism on Italian film: Anton Giulio
Bragaglia's *Thais* (1917).

ences. Also a novelist (*Luce fredda, L'isola del sole*), he founded a late futurist movement ('Immaginismo') [> FUTURISM], edited literary reviews, wrote comic plays and translated theoretical writings on film by Rudolf Arnheim, Béla Balázs and Vsevolod Pudovkin among others. In the early 1930s, at the height of the Fascist dictatorship, he acquainted himself with the works of Freud and Marx. Together with art historian Roberto Longhi he made the documentaries *Carpaccio* (1947) and *Caravaggio* (1948). He worked for Cecchi Gori's* Cines*, for which he directed a Walther Ruttmann-style social documentary (*I cantieri dell'Adriatico*, 1933) and scripted Goffredo Alessandrini's* melodrama *Seconda B* (1934). Although an anti-Fascist, he was offered a teaching position at the new Centro Sperimentale* in 1935. A leading light of the Italian cultural changes of the late 1930s, he developed a notion of neo-realism* as synthesis of the 'national tradition' and elaborated a materialist aesthetic as well as an anti-idealist notion of 'collective creativity'. After the fall of Fascism, he worked at the Centro Sperimentale (1944–47) as special commissioner, and taught at the Polish film school in Łódź. He combined all this with scriptwriting (for instance for Giuseppe De Santis'* *Caccia tragica/Tragic Hunt*, 1947) and directing (the unsuccessful *L'ultima nemica/The Last Enemy*, 1938). A journalist for *L'Unità* and *Vie Nuove*, his communist stance became increasingly rigid and his 'poetics of realism' turned into absolute, normative criteria. Some of his writings were collected posthumously by his students in *Il film e il risarcimento marxista dell'arte* (1960) and *Servitú e grandezza del cinema* (1962), which document thirty years of research on film, from the 1932 preface to Pudovkin's writings to an unfinished treatise on general aesthetics. GVo

BAVA, Mario   San Remo 1914 – Rome 1980

Italian director and cinematographer. A highly inventive photographer, Bava started his career as an assistant cameraman, graduating to cinematographer in the late 1930s and working for directors as diverse as Roberto Rossellini*, Steno, Mario Monicelli*, Dino Risi*, G. W. Pabst and Federico Fellini*. Moving into direction, he became a master of ultra-low-budget special effects in the studio. His first full direction credit was on *La maschera del demonio/Mask of the Demon/Black Sunday* (1960), which launched the career of British-born actress Barbara Steele* as unquestioned star of the Italian horror film*. Though he ventured into other genres, such as the peplum* (*Ercole al centro della terra/Hercules in the Haunted World*, 1961), it was in the mainstream Italian horror film – for instance *La frusta e il corpo/Night is the Phantom* (1963) and *I tre volti della paura/Black Sabbath* (1963) – that his visual imagination and skill with lighting and decor were put to best effect. GF

BECCE, Giuseppe Lonigo, Italy 1877 – Berlin 1973

Italian composer who worked in Germany, adapting existing musical compositions for Messter-Film and other companies in 1913 (for instance *Richard Wagner* in which he starred as the composer), while simultaneously writing original accompanying music which he called '*Autorenillustrationen*' (author's illustrations). Becce decisively shaped the musical dramaturgy of German silent cinema and his *Kinothek*, an alternative to foreign music compilations, appeared in print from 1919. In the 1920s Becce became head of Ufa's music division. His most notable compositions were incidental music for F. W. Murnau's *Tartüff* (1926, use of leitmotif and quotations) and *Der letzte Mann/The Last Laugh* (1924, rhythm). He remained one of Germany's most productive film composers of the sound era. Famous from the later period are his soundtracks for Luis Trenker's Berge in *Flammen/The Doomed Battalion* (1931) and *Der Berg ruft/The Challenge* (1938), and Leni Riefenstahl's *Das blaue Licht/The Blue Light* (1932). SG

BELLOCCHIO, Marco Piacenza 1939

Italian director. Born to a well-off middle-class provincial family and educated at religious schools, Bellocchio enrolled at the Centro Sperimentale* in Rome, graduating in 1962 with a 55-minute film, *Ginepro fatto uomo*. In 1965, he made a sensational debut with *I pugni in tasca/Fists in the Pocket*. Autobiographical acrimony and expressive violence mingled in the young protagonist's abstract rages against family values, bigoted provincialism and normality, in a manner so radical and so remote from the humanism of neo-realism* that public and critics were violently split over it. In his later films Bellocchio coherently pursued a critique of institutions such as the family, the middle classes and reformist parties, Catholicism, the press, the army and psychiatric institutions: *La Cina è vicina/China is Near* (1967), *Nel nome del padre/In the Name of the Father* (1971), *Sbatti il mostro in prima pagina* (1972), *Marcia trionfale/Victory March* (1976), the pitiless *Salto nel vuoto/Leap into the Void* (1979) and the gentler *Gli occhi, la bocca/The Eyes, The Mouth* (1982). *Nessuno o tutti/Matti da slegare* (1974) was an outstanding investigative documentary on mental hospitals in two versions, shot with Silvano Agosti, Stefano Rulli and Sandro Petraglia, who were also co-directors of the five-part television programme *La macchina cinema* (1978). After two interesting literary adaptations – Chekhov's *Il gabbiano/The Seagull* (1977) and Pirandello's *Enrico IV/Henry IV* (1984) – Bellocchio's work entered a new and controversial phase in which he drew more explicitly on psychoanalysis (influenced by his own psychoanalyst, the unorthodox Massimo Fagioli): *Diavolo in corpo/Devil in the Flesh* (1986), which remains the best film on post-terrorism Italy, *La visione del Sabba* (1987) and *La condanna* (1991). He directed *Il sogno della farfalla* in 1994. MMo

BENE, Carmelo
Campi Salentina 1937

Italian actor and director. A restless personality, intolerant of any form of academicism, Bene made a name for himself as a leading exponent of theatrical reform. Plays staged by him include *Salomè, Faust* and *Hamlet*, based on reworked extracts taken from classics. In the cinema, he had a small part in Franco Indovina's *Lo scatenato* (1967), after which he was an excellent Creon in Pier Paolo Pasolini's* *Edipo re/Oedipus Rex* (1967). As a film director, he began by adapting his own novel *Nostra Signora dei Turchi/Our Lady of the Turks* (1968). This film, a dazzling baroque phantasmagoria about the landing of the Turks in Otranto, was awarded a special jury prize at the Venice festival. Bene's later films, *Capricci* (1969), *Don Giovanni* (1970) and *Salomè* (1972), confirmed his iconoclastic fury and experimental provocativeness with their gaudy colour schemes and abrupt changes in rhythm. With *Un Amleto di meno* (1973) Bene went further in experimentation, attempting to dissolve the image just as his plays had sought to dissolve words. He subsequently moved away from the cinema, concentrating on theatre and literature. Particularly well known in this context are his experiments with verse and sound during public readings of cantos from Dante's *Divine Comedy*. GC

BENIGNI, Roberto
Misericordia 1952

Italian actor and director, one of Italy's most popular comic actors of the 1980s and 1990s. Benigni's fourth film as director and actor, *Johnny Stecchino* (1991), a hilarious light-hearted comedy about the Mafia, broke all box-office records in Italy for either Italian or American films. He had already achieved similar, if less spectacular, success in 1984 with the boisterous *Non ci resta che piangere* (co-written, co-directed and co-acted with Massimo Troisi*) and in 1988 with *Il piccolo diavolo/The Little Devil*, the story of the catastrophic apprenticeship of a mischievous imp. Benigni's first experience as a director was with *Tu mi turbi* (1983), an unusual film composed of four monologues, first conceived as comic sketches; but he had already made a name for himself in 1975 with *Cioni Mario fu Gaspare di Giulia*, a monologue written with Giuseppe Bertolucci, Bernardo's brother, which toured experimental theatres throughout Italy and was eventually used as a source for *Berlinguer, ti voglio bene* (1977). With his transgressive and boorish sense of comedy, his mixture of rustic intelligence and surrealist whims, it was not long before Benigni started to make his mark in television with such programmes as *Onda libera* ('Free Wave', from *Televacca* – 'Cow TV' – a local network pretending to broadcast from a cowshed) and *L'altra domenica* ('The Other Sunday') where he created the figure of a bizarre but ultimately acute film critic. Benigni once defined himself as 'the product of a dispute between God and the PCI' (the former Italian communist party), which in fact continue to be two important sources of inspiration for his humour. He has also been described as 'a dung-heap Woody Allen'. In reality, he is an oddly aggressive and surrealistic genius, an 'innocently' malign spirit who subjugates the audience with the frenetic use of his body and voice. He has essentially remained faithful to these characteristics in his film performances, from 'low' comedies to dramatic films by *auteurs* such as Luigi Zampa* and Antonio Pietrangeli*, Bertolucci (*La luna*, 1979), Marco Ferreri* (*Chiedo asilo*, 1979) and Federico Fellini* (*La voce della luna/The Voice of the Moon*, 1990), as well as, in the US, Jim Jarmusch (*Down by Law*, 1985) and Blake Edwards (*The Son of the Pink Panther*, 1993). *Tuttobenigni* (1985), directed by Giuseppe Bertolucci, is an account of one of Benigni's theatre tours. He directed and acted in *Il mostro* in 1994. MMo

BERTOLUCCI, Bernardo   Parma 1941

Italian director. The son of the renowned poet Attilio Bertolucci, Bernardo Bertolucci was himself awarded the Viareggio Prize for a first poetry work in 1962.

Bertolucci began his career in the cinema as assistant director on Pier Paolo Pasolini's* *Accattone* (1961); his own first film, *La commare secca/The Grim Reaper* (1962), was heavily indebted to his mentor's style. His next film, *Prima della rivoluzione/Before the Revolution* (1964), contained all the ideological and aesthetic tensions that would play themselves out during the course of his career. Set in his native Parma, this semi-autobiographical work is a coming-of-age story about a young man, Fabrizio, who is radicalised sexually by his aunt, and ideologically by his Marxist teacher, but who ultimately abandons the ideal of the revolution to accept his bourgeois birthright. Like Fabrizio, Bertolucci has struggled throughout his career to negotiate the rival claims of his high-cultural, materially privileged patrimony and the ideological imperatives of the left. The arena for this struggle has frequently been the cinema's built-in tendency towards spectacle, which Bertolucci has sometimes resisted but more often embraced with varying degrees of ambivalence. The cerebral, Godard-inspired *Partner* (1968), for example, forgoes the pleasures of cinematic spectacle, whereas his brilliant version of Moravia's novel, *Il conformista/ The Conformist* (1970), brings back those pleasures, albeit in the service of a politically responsible message (the denunciation of Fascism). The made-for-television film *Strategia del ragno/The Spider's Stratagem* (1970), an adaptation of José Luis Borges' short story 'The Theme of the Traitor and the Hero', foregrounds the relationship between political identity and spectacle by having the anti-Fascist hero-turned-traitor decide to transform his execution into public martyrdom during a performance of the opera *Rigoletto*.

In 1972, Bertolucci abandoned politically committed film-making for eroticism. *Ultimo tango a Parigi/Last Tango in Paris*, the story of two strangers (Marlon Brando and Maria Schneider) whose sexual encounters in a Parisian apartment serve as a metaphor for the psychodynamics of human relations, was a clamorous *succès de scandale*, banned in Italy until 1987 and accorded an 'X' rating in the US. Its box-office earnings made possible the ambitious *Novecento/1900* (1976), a panoramic vision of Italian political, social and cultural history from the beginning of the century to the present, filtered through the parallel and intersecting lives of a peasant (Gérard Depardieu) and a land-owner (Robert De Niro). In this extravaganza (311 min., reduced to 245 min. for commercial distribution, and re-released in 1991 in its full-length version) Bertolucci indulges his love of spectacle, while trying, at the same time, to balance it with his ideological concerns. Political spectacle is the theme of the Academy-award-winning *The Last Emperor* (1987), the story of China's twentieth-century evolution, ending with Mao's cultural revolution of the late 1960s. At the centre of this grand epic resides the supreme paradox of an absolute ruler who is powerless, the ostensible maker of history who becomes the dupe of historical processes.

Bertolucci returned to literary adaptation in *The Sheltering Sky* (1990, UK/It.), based on the existentialist novel by Paul Bowles. The story of a couple seeking 'authenticity' on a journey to the remote reaches of the Sahara desert, the film finds its own authenticity in its nearly wordless, visually dazzling second half, as the young wife, newly widowed, assimilates into desert existence. With *Little Buddha* (1993, Fr./UK, starring Keanu Reeves) a new tranquillity has entered Bertolucci's work, unexpected in an author whose characters have generally been driven by a violent restlessness. MMo

Bib: Donald Ranvaud and Enzo Ungari, *Bertolucci by Bertolucci* (1987).

Other Films Include: *Amore e rabbia* (1969, ep. *L'agonia*); *I poveri muoiono prima* (1971, documentary); *La tragedia di un uomo ridicolo/ Tragedy of a Ridiculous Man* (1981); *Sleeping Beauty* (1996).

BLASETTI, Alessandro   Rome 1900

Italian director and scriptwriter. Blasetti began as a film critic and theorist and as a spokesperson for the revitalisation of the flagging Italian film industry during the 1920s. In 1925 he became a film critic for the newspaper *L'Impero*, and in 1927 editor of the magazines *Cinematografo* and *Lo spettacolo d'Italia*. In 1928, Blasetti and journalist friends formed the production company Augustus, with the aim of putting into practice their critical ideals of a cinema that would be 'organically Italian' and at one with current cultural politics. The first product of this company was *Sole/Sun* (1929), for which Blasetti received directing credit, though it was very much a collective effort and Blasetti's formal training as director consisted of a brief excursion to the Ufa studios in Germany. *Sole* was seen by critics as heralding a new type of consciously 'Italian' film – an ideal most evident in Blasetti's use of non-professional actors in the role of the 'people'. Unfortunately the film had very limited distribution (no complete copy of it seems to have survived) and Augustus ran into financial difficulties. Blasetti went on to work for Cines*, the company owned by Stefano Pittaluga*, whom Blasetti had previously attacked as an enemy of his ideals. For Cines he made *Resurrectio* (1931), an urban melodrama involving the struggle of a disillusioned orchestra conductor to return to the stage, and *Nerone* (1930), a film organised around parodic sketches by the Italian stage comedian Ettore Petrolini. More central to his concerns was a third film made later the same year – *Terra madre/Mother Earth*, the story of a son who inherits a rural estate and rediscovers the power and fertility of the land (a metaphor for the nation). Subsequent films made for Cines by Blasetti include *Palio* (1932, set around the historic horse race in Siena), *1860* (1933, a historical film about the Italian Risorgimento, set in Sicily), and *Assisi* (a documentary on the medieval Umbrian town). Like *Terra madre*, these films involve returns to provincial settings where 'popular' causes (a working-class hero's ride to victory in *Palio*; the struggle of inhabitants of rural Sicily to expel foreign mercenaries in *1860*) form the basis of myths of national political awakening.

In 1934, after the demise of Cines, Blasetti made *Vecchia guardia/ Old Guard*, a film that reworks many of his Cines motifs, but through the story of a group of Fascists attempting to restore order in a small town destabilised by striking workers. This was followed by *Aldebaran* (1935), on the call to duty of a young submarine officer. Despite the fact that the film's hero is a Fascist soldier, *Aldebaran* was picked up for distribution by MGM. By the late 1930s, Blasetti had come to be Italy's most famous stylist of epic costume films (such as *La corona di ferro/The Iron Crown*, 1941), many loosely based on nineteenth- and early twentieth-century historical novels and melodramas, but from the early 1940s he adapted to changing circumstances with a group of pre- or quasi-neo-realist* films, including *Quattro passi fra le nuvole/ Four Steps in the Clouds* (1942, about the efforts of a petit-bourgeois patriarch to defend the honour of a husbandless pregnant woman), *Nessuno torna indietro/Nobody Goes Back* (1943, on the love affairs of young women sharing a boarding house in Rome), and *Un giorno nella vita/A Day in the Life* (1946, about a group of partisans who take refuge in a remote convent while pursued by German soldiers). After the war Blasetti continued to make historical costume films such as *Fabiola* (1948), *La fiammata* (1952) and *Altri tempi/Infidelity* (1952,

24

the first of many episodic films made in Italy). In the 1950s, Blasetti also made fairly successful films in the style of the *commedia all'italiana**, including *Peccato che sia una canaglia/Too Bad She's Bad* (1954) and *La fortuna di essere donna/Lucky to Be a Woman* (1956), films that launched Sophia Loren*.

Besides feature films, Blasetti directed documentaries, plays and television programmes. He also appears (playing himself) in Luchino Visconti's* *Bellissima* (1951). While he enjoyed more success after World War II than any other Italian director from the 1930s, he (like Mario Camerini*) could never quite overcome his association with the Fascist period. JHa

Other Films Include: *La tavola dei poveri* (1932); *Ettore Fieramosca* (1938); *Un'avventura di Salvator Rosa* (1939); *La cena delle beffe* (1941); *Prima comunione* (1950); *Tempi nostri/A Slice of Life* (1953); *Amore e chiacchiere* (1957); *Io amo, tu ami ...* (1960); *Liolà/A Very Handy Man* (1964); *Io, io, io ... e gli altri* (1966); *La ragazza del bersagliere* (1967); *Simon Bolivar* (1969).

BOSÉ, Lucia   Milan 1931

Italian actress, who won the title of Miss Italy in 1947, competing against such outstanding finalists as Gina Lollobrigida*, Gianna Maria Canale and Eleonora Rossi Drago. After appearing in *1848* (1948), a short film by Dino Risi*, she was given a leading part in *Non c'è pace tra gli ulivi* (1950), directed by Giuseppe De Santis*, who then cast her in a longer and more dramatic role in *Roma, ore 11* (1952). But it was in the early films of Michelangelo Antonioni*, *Cronaca di un amore/Story of a Love Affair* (1950) and *La signora senza camelie/The Lady Without Camelias* (1953), that her stylish brunette elegance was most dramatically revealed. Working with Luciano Emmer*, she showed a quality of self-confident freshness in *Parigi è sempre Parigi* (1951) and again in *Le ragazze di Piazza di Spagna* (1952). With Walter Chiari*, her fiancé at the time, she played in a number of mediocre romantic comedies. In 1955 Bosé married the famous bullfighter Luis Dominguin, giving birth to two daughters and a son, Miguel Bosé, who has become a moderately successful singer and an actor in films by Pedro Almodóvar among others. In Spain she starred in Juan Antonio Bardem's *Muerte de un ciclista/Death of a Cyclist* (1955), where she reverted to her Antonioni character of the 'thoroughbred' middle-class woman, immersed in existentialist sadness. This was further reflected in Francesco Maselli's* *Gli sbandati* (1955), Luis Buñuel's *Cela s'appelle l'aurore* (1955, Fr./It.), and Jean Cocteau's *Le Testament d'Orphée* (1960, Fr.). After a ten-year break, she returned to the cinema in 1968 to make three Spanish films and in 1969 she went back to Italy, appearing in the Taviani* brothers' *Sotto il segno dello Scorpione/Under the Sign of Scorpio* (1969) and Federico Fellini's*

Fellini Satyricon (both 1969). A number of other films followed, including Mauro Bolognini's *Metello* (1970) and *Per le antiche scale/ Down the Ancient Stairs* (1975); in France, Marguerite Duras' *Nathalie Granger* (1972) and Jeanne Moreau's *Lumière* (1976); and in Switzerland, Daniel Schmid's *Violanta* (1977), in which she displayed a new, strong dramatic presence, as she had already done in Liliana Cavani's* *L'ospite/The Guest* (1971). After another ten-year absence, she made further appearances in television dramas and in the film version of a successful novel, *Volevo i pantaloni* (1990). MMo

BRAZZI, Rossano   Bologna 1916 – Rome 1994

Italian actor and director. Considering his active participation in the anti-Fascist movement, it is ironic that Rossano Brazzi found his early film roles in classic examples of Mussolini's Fascist cinema such as *La forza bruta* (1941). An international star in the 1950s, the dashingly handsome Brazzi was initially signed up by David O. Selznick, but his talent was hardly extended as the distinctly unromantic German professor in the 1948 version of *Little Women*. It was 1954 before Brazzi was given a chance to prove his potential as a Hollywood leading man, when he had his first stock part as a 'Latin lover' opposite Jean Peters in *Three Coins in the Fountain*. Despite newspaper speculation about his relationships with a succession of female co-stars, Brazzi was much more than a handsome foil. Katharine Hepburn was so impressed with his acting that she suggested Brazzi's name should accompany hers above the titles of *Summertime/Summer Madness* (1955, US/UK). Apparently his singing voice was not quite as attractive; the musical parts of Brazzi's role in *South Pacific* (1958) were dubbed by Giorgio Tozzi. Falling out of favour with Hollywood in the 1960s, Brazzi returned to Italy, also turning his hand to directing (sometimes under the pseudonym of Edward Ross). Perhaps revelling in his cameo as the criminal mastermind of *The Italian Job* (1969, UK), Brazzi was notoriously arrested in 1984 for his alleged involvement in an arms-smuggling conspiracy. He ended his long career with television appearances, notably in the British productions *The Far Pavilions* (1984) and an episode of the *Ruth Rendell Mysteries* (1990). SH

Films as Director: *The Christmas That Almost Wasn't/Il natale che quasi non fu* (1966, US/It.); *Sette uomini e un cervello* (1968); *Salvare la faccia/Psychout for Murder* (1969, Argentina/It.); *Cappucetto rosso, Cenerentola ... e voi ci credete* (1972).

C

CAMERINI, Mario   Rome 1895 – Gardone Riviera 1981

Italian director. Alongside Alessandro Blasetti*, Camerini was one of
the most successful, influential, innovative and popular film-makers in
1930s Italy. He began his film career after World War I as a
scriptwriter, assistant director and director at Cines*, where he often
worked for his cousin Augusto Genina*. His early collaboration with
Genina included *Marito, moglie, e ...* (1922, co-dir.), *Cyrano de
Bergerac* (1923, co-dir. and co-scriptwriter), *Jolly, clown da circo*
(1924), a film Camerini claims to have directed, though only Genina's
name appears as director, and *Kiff Tebbi* (1927), a silent film Genina
is reputed to have begun but left to Camerini. In the 1920s Camerini
also directed two films involving the popular film 'superheroes'
Maciste* and Saetta. Significantly, *Maciste contro lo sceicco* (1925) and
Kiff Tebbi take place in Africa, a setting that had as much to do with
Italian colonialism as with the popularity of Rudolph Valentino's *The
Sheik*. After *Kiff Tebbi*, Camerini worked briefly as an editor and sub-
titler before going on to direct *Rotaie/Rails*, shot in 1929 as a silent film
with a musical score and released in 1931 with a soundtrack. Along
with Blasetti's *Sole/Sun* (1929), *Rotaie* was widely heralded as sig-
nalling the revival of the Italian film industry. Throughout the 1930s
Camerini worked in various genres, but he is perhaps best known for
his 'populist' light comedies that always verged (as in the German
Kammerspielfilm) on 'dark' realist melodrama. For this reason, films
such as *Rotaie, Gli uomini, che mascalzoni ...* (1932), *T'amerò sempre*
(1933), *Il signor Max/Mr Max* (1937), *Grandi magazzini* (1939) and
Batticuore (1938) have led film historians to compare Camerini with
such diverse directors from that period as René Clair, Ernst Lubitsch,
Frank Capra and F. W. Murnau. All these films concerned petit-
bourgeois protagonists who struggled amid the artifice of a decadent
upper class, a society given to consumerism, and the modern urban
landscape of Italy. Many of them also launched two new matinee idols,
Vittorio De Sica* and Assia Noris*, Camerini's wife. Despite his success and popularity during the Fascist years, only one of Camerini's
films, *Il grande appello/The Last Roll-call* (1936), overtly depicts a project of the Fascist state, namely the military activities of the Italians in
North Africa, a return to a setting Camerini had mythologised in his
1920s films.

Although neither Camerini nor his films were directly attacked after
1945, his style was dismissed as 'escapist' and denigrated as contrary to
the aesthetics of neo-realism* (though his 1945 film *Due lettere anon-
ime* has much in common with 'neo-realist' films). Like Blasetti, he
was never quite able to overcome being associated with the Fascist
period, particularly by younger critics. JHa

Other Films Include: *Voglio tradire mio marito, Saetta principe per un giorno* (1925); *Figaro e la sua gran giornata, L'ultima avventura* (1931); *Giallo* (1933); *Il cappello a tre punte/The Three-Cornered Hat, Come le foglie* (1934); *Ma non è una cosa seria/But It's Nothing Serious* (1936); *Il documento* (1939); *Centomila dollari, Una romantica avventura* (1940); *I promessi sposi/The Spirit and the Flesh* (1941); *Una storia d'amore* (1942); *L'angelo e il diavolo/The Angel and the Devil* (1946); *La figlia del capitano/The Captain's Daughter* (1947); *Molti sogni per la strada/The Street Has Many Dreams* (1948); *Il brigante Musolino* (1950); *Moglie per una notte* (1952); *Gli eroi della domenica* (1953); *Ulisse/Ulysses* (1954); *Suor Letizia* (1956); *Primo amore/First Love* (1959); *Via Margutta/Run with the Devil, Crimen/Killing at Monte Carlo* (1960); *I briganti italiani/Seduction of the South* (1961); *Kali Yug la dea della vendetta* (1963); *Il mistero del tempio indiano* (1964); *Delitto quasi perfetto/Imperfect Murder* (1966); *Don Camillo e i giovani d'oggi* (1972).

CARDINALE, Claudia   Tunis, Tunisia 1939

Italian actress. At the age of seventeen Cardinale won a contest for the most beautiful girl of Italian origin in Tunis. Rewarded with a trip to the Venice festival, she later moved to Italy to prepare for a career as a film actress. Although initially chosen for her physical charms rather than her acting prowess, she soon developed into an intelligent and versatile actress, equally at home in serious and comedy roles. Her early career was fostered by producer Franco Cristaldi*, whom she married. Cristaldi gave her roles in films he produced, beginning with Mario Monicelli's* *I soliti ignoti/Persons Unknown* (1958), but also looked after her career in general. She gave fine performances for a number of major directors, notably Luchino Visconti* (*Rocco e i suoi fratelli/Rocco and His Brothers*, 1960; *Il gattopardo/The Leopard*, 1963; *Vaghe stelle dell'orsa/Sandra*, 1964), but also for, among others, Valerio Zurlini*, Francesco Maselli* (*Gli indifferenti/Time of Indifference*, 1963), Luigi Comencini* (*La ragazza di Bube/Bebo's Girl*, 1963), and Federico Fellini* ($8\frac{1}{2}$, 1963). After her divorce from Cristaldi her career went into decline and she mostly made undistinguished films until the early 1980s, when she re-emerged in a number of international productions, including Werner Herzog's *Fitzcarraldo* (1982, Ger.) and Diane Kurys' *Un Homme amoureux/A Man in Love* (1987, Fr./It.). She went on to give proof of a new maturity as an actress with superbly modulated performances in Marco Bellocchio's Pirandello adaptation *Enrico IV* (*Henry IV*, 1984) and in Luigi Comencini's* *La storia/The Story* [or *History*], 1986). She also gave a moving performance as the mother in Henri Verneuil's autobiographical films *Mayrig* (1991, Fr.) and *588, rue Paradis* (1992, Fr.) GNS

CASTELLANI, Renato
Finale Ligure 1913 –
Rome 1985

Italian director. After studying architecture in Milan, Castellani entered cinema first as a journalist and then as a scriptwriter for films by Augusto Genina*, Mario Camerini*, Mario Soldati* and in particular Alessandro Blasetti* (*La corona di ferro/The Iron Crown*, 1941). At the time of his directorial debut with *Un colpo di pistola* (1941) and *Zazà* (1942), both written by Alberto Moravia but not signed by him because of racial laws, Castellani was one of the leading exponents of the 'calligraphy' movement, whose narrative formalism was trying to counter Fascist rhetoric. His postwar trilogy about the poor – *Sotto il sole di Roma/Under the Sun of Rome* (1948), *È primavera/It's Forever Springtime* (1949) and *Due soldi di speranza/Two Cents Worth of Hope* (1951) – added to the *commedia romanesca* ('Roman-style comedy') elements of realism such as actors taken from the street. This lively, vibrant and optimistic vision of popular life led to the so-called 'rose-tinted' neo-realism*, as opposed to the pessimism of a film like Vittorio De Sica's* *Umberto D.* (1952). An intelligent craftsman and sharp observer of social reality, Castellani has also often been charged with formalism. Such controversial qualities can be seen in films like *Giulietta e Romeo/Romeo and Juliet* (1954), the bitter *I sogni nel cassetto* (1957), and the prison film *Nella città l'inferno/And the Wild, Wild Women* (1958), starring Anna Magnani* and Giulietta Masina*. An affected but sincere account of land occupation in Calabria, *Il brigante* (1961) can be seen as a late tribute to a neo-realism which Castellani had been accused of trying to bury. His cinema career ended in the 1960s with a number of mediocre films. He then worked for television, making popular and historically accurate serials such as *Leonardo da Vinci* (1971) and *Verdi* (1982). GVo

Other Films Include: *La donna della montagna* (1943); *Mio figlio professore/Professor, My Son* (1946); *Mare matto* (1963); *Controsesso* [ep. *Una donna d'affari*], *Tre notti d'amore/Three Nights of Love* [ep. *La vedova*] (1964); *Questi fantasmi* (1967); *Una breve stagione* (1969).

CAVANI, Liliana
Capri 1937

Italian director. Cavani's work, in both documentary and fiction, represents a significant response to the revolutionary social and political changes in Italy since the 1960s. Her dramatisation of socio-historical concepts has led her to create cinematic character who are 'rebels', 'visionaries' or 'madmen', experiencing in acute form the conflict between historical and spiritual reality, past and present.

After studying at the Centro Sperimentale* in Rome, Cavani became a freelance television director for RAI*. Her first major assignments were documentaries on the Third Reich (1962), Stalin (1962) and women in the Resistance (1965), followed by the 1965 Venice prize-winner, *Philippe Pétain, Processo a Vichy/Philippe Pétain, Vichy on Trial*. Her first feature, *Francesco d'Assisi* (1966), starring Lou Castel (the schizophrenic hero of Marco Bellocchio's* *I pugni in tasca/Fists in the Pocket*), was based on the meticulous observation of everyday reality mastered during her apprenticeship as a documentarist, and became an emblem of emerging Catholic dissent. Her commitment to a visionary expression of social issues continued with *Galileo* (1968), *I cannibali/The Cannibals* (1969) and *L'ospite/The Guest* (1971), which all focus on repressive mechanisms and challenge traditional assumptions about authority. The turning point in her career came with *Il portiere di notte/The Night Porter* (1974), starring Dirk Bogarde and Charlotte Rampling, whose huge box-office success made her reputation as one of the most provocative (not least within feminist circles) film-makers of the 1970s. Her choice of controversial themes, graphic use of sexuality and forceful apolitical stance underline a complex vision of the contemporary world. Her German trilogy continued with *Al di là del bene e del male/Beyond Good and Evil* (1977) and *Interno berlinese/Berlin Interior* (1978), in which games of erotic enslavement and domination reflect a complex historical situation (Nazism). Her most recent films – *Francesco* (1989, with Mickey Rourke in the role of Saint Francis) and *Dove siete? Io sono qui/Where Are You? I Am Here* (1993) – continue to place individuals in extreme situations. In 1979 Cavani added opera to her repertoire, directing Berg's *Wozzeck* for the Maggio Musicale Fiorentino. Since then she has worked for the Paris opera and for La Scala, Milan. GM

Other Films Include: *Milarepa* (1974); *La pelle/Skin* (1981); *Oltre la porta/Beyond the Door* (1982).

CECCHI, Emilio   Florence 1884 – Rome 1966

Italian producer, scriptwriter, critic and director. Although Cecchi worked in various capacities in the Italian film industry from the 1930s to the 1950s, he is mostly remembered for his early 1930s work. Cecchi was hired by Cines*, first as artistic director in March 1931, and then as director of production in April 1932, a position he held only until November 1933; his tenure occurred, however, at the height of the revival of Italian cinema (depleted since the 1920s) and at a time when Cines was responsible for most Italian film production. Before working at Cines, Cecchi had little direct experience of film production. He had been a successful writer, had published film criticism (1930–31), and spent some time in Hollywood while lecturing in California. As director of production, he came to embody the multiple aims and contradictions surrounding an Italian cinema attempting to produce 'art for the people'. He is credited with having encouraged a cosmopolitan film style congruent with the European avant-garde [> AVANT-GARDE CINEMA IN EUROPE] by attracting directors such as Walther Ruttmann and Carlo Bragaglia and writers such as Luigi Pirandello; a modernist formalism is also evident in many of the documentaries he produced. On the other hand, the 'Cecchi era' brought Italian film production closer to a 'popular' style that, as never before, emphasised Italian locations and everyday life. Significantly, Cecchi's vision of film as a popular art was bound up with his admiration for Hollywood films, whose virtues he had extolled in his first film reviews.

In the early 1940s, Cecchi worked as scriptwriter on such films as *Piccolo mondo antico/Old-Fashioned World* (1941), *Sissignora* (1941) and *Giacomo l'idealista* (1943). He revised the scripts of *I promessi sposi/The Spirit and the Flesh* (1941) and *Vespro siciliano* (1949). He wrote commentaries for documentaries and directed short features such as *Vita e morte degli etruschi* (1947) and *Anatomia del colore* (1948). In 1949 he returned to the reorganised Cines as 'artistic consultant' and in 1952 as part of its administrative council. Throughout the 1950s and 1960s he was mostly engaged in writing literary criticism and history. JHa

CECCHI D'AMICO, Suso   Rome 1914

Italian scriptwriter. The daughter of Emilio Cecchi and wife of music critic Fedele D'Amico, Suso Cecchi D'Amico must count as Italy's most distinguished scriptwriter. Starting as a script translator, she made her first original contribution as co-scriptwriter (with her father) on Renato Castellani's* *Mio figlio professore/Professor, My Son* in 1946. Her contribution to Luigi Zampa's* *Vivere in pace/To Live in Peace* (1946) won her a Silver Ribbon (Italy's equivalent of an Oscar). She worked with Cesare Zavattini* and Ennio Flaiano* on the scripts of *Ladri di biciclette/Bicycle Thieves* (1948) and *Roma città libera* (1946) respectively. She soon emerged as a writer with a style of her own, first on neo-realist* subjects and then social and moral satire. She was scriptwriter on many important films by distinguished directors, including Vittorio De Sica's* *Miracolo a Milano/Miracle in Milan* (1951), Alessandro Blasetti's* *Altri tempi/Infidelity* (1952), Michelangelo Antonioni's* *Le amiche/The Girlfriends* (1955), Francesco Rosi's* *Salvatore Giuliano* (1962), Franco Zeffirelli's* *The Taming of the Shrew* (1967, US/It.), Luigi Comencini's* *La storia/The Story* [or *History*] (1986), and most recently Nikita Mikhalkov's *Oci ciornie/Ochi chërnye/Dark Eyes* (1987). Many of her collaborations were long-standing, the most celebrated with Luchino Visconti*, for whom she was the major scriptwriter on almost all his films from *Bellissima* (1951) to *L'innocente/The Innocent* (1976). Particularly when working with Visconti, the depth of her culture, her sense of realism and attention to the text enabled her to play a major creative role. MMo

CECCHI GORI, Mario   Brescia 1920 – Rome 1993

Italian producer. Throughout his long career, in association with Dino De Laurentiis* from 1948 and with his son Vittorio from the 1970s, Cecchi Gori produced some 170 films. After the creation of his own production house in 1957, he opened an important phase for Italian cinema by 'inventing' *commedia all'italiana**, the genre which exploded during the years of the 'economic boom'. He demonstrated a remarkable commercial intuition, typical of a 'salesman' according to his detractors but in fact the result of the skills of a great artisan. He produced Luigi Zampa's* popular comedies, as well as those of Ettore Scola* and many others, including especially many directed by Dino Risi*: *Il mattatore/Love and Larceny* (1960), *Il sorpasso/The Easy Life* (1962), *La marcia su Roma/The March to Rome* (1962), *I mostri/The Monsters* (1963), *Il gaucho* (1964), *Il tigre/The Tiger and the Pussycat* (1967), all starring Vittorio Gassman*. Gassman embodied the company's image in over twenty films, being eventually replaced in this role by Ugo Tognazzi*, Nino Manfredi, and the singer Adriano Celentano (the latter starring in 'lighter' productions). In the 1970s and 1980s Cecchi Gori's name was linked to the 'new Italian comics'*, particularly Paolo Villaggio. He addressed his films to a middle-brow audience, although he also produced a series of ambiguous political/judiciary movies (such as Damiano Damiani's *L'istruttoria è chiusa: dimentichi*, 1971). His presence within Italian cinema grew even larger with the creation in 1989 of Penta, a joint venture with Silvio Berlusconi [> FININVEST], which produced many run-of-the-mill films as well as more prestigious ones such as those of Carlo Verdone (*Borotalco*, 1982; *Perdiamoci di vista*, 1994), Roberto Benigni* (*Il piccolo diavolo/The Little Devil*, 1988; *Johnny Stecchino*, 1991), Gabriele Salvatores (*Mediterraneo*, 1991), Giuseppe Tornatore*, and Marco Risi, and films by *auteurs* such as Ermanno Olmi* (*La leggenda del santo bevitore/The Legend of the Holy Drinker*, 1988), Gianni Amelio* (*Lamerica*, 1994) and Federico Fellini* (*La voce della luna/The Voice of the Moon*, 1990). Penta has recently suffered from the effects of its rapid and excessive growth and from internal dissensions, especially over risky endeavours such as the creation of Pentamerica, an American subsidiary, and participation in the Italian pay-TV channel Telepiú. GVo

CENTRO SPERIMENTALE

Italian institution. The Centro Sperimentale di Cinematografia is Italy's oldest national film school. It was created in 1934 through the re-formation of the much smaller National School of Cinematography, established (in 1932) and headed by director Alessandro Blasetti*. Although its formation was the direct result of initiatives by the Fascist government, it operated quasi-independently from state control and without precise political objectives. While there were earlier models of national film schools outside Italy, such as the Soviet VGIK, the Centro grew out of very specific conditions in 1930s Italy: a shared interest among some film-makers, theorists and the state to centralise, institutionalise and promote cinema as a form of national culture, and to guarantee a future for the Italian film industry, whose production had fallen to just a few films a year during the late 1920s. Throughout the 1930s the Centro Sperimentale was directed by film-maker and critic Luigi Chiarini*. It was situated in a school in Rome until 1939, when it was relocated to its current site in the new cinema complex adjacent to Cinecittà* on the via Tuscolana in the southern suburbs of Rome. Since its inauguration, the Centro has offered professional training in all areas of film production. It has also served as a forum for film theory and criticism, producing a series of books that ranged from translations of S. M. Eisenstein and Béla Balázs to writings by Italian intellectuals. JHa

CERVI, Gino
Bologna 1901 – Castiglione della Pescaia 1974

Italian actor. Cervi was one of the most famous protagonists of Italian action-adventure films during the late 1930s and early 1940s. His prolific career spanned five decades. A stage actor since 1923, he started working in film in the early 1930s, appearing as a supporting character actor in several unsuccessful low-budget films before being given the lead in Alessandro Blasetti's* *Aldebaran* (1935), one of the first military dramas of the period. Between 1935 and 1942 he made five films with Blasetti, including *Ettore Fieramosca* (1938), *Un'avventura di Salvator Rosa* (1939), *La corona di ferro/The Iron Crown* (1941) and *Quattro passi fra le nuvole/Four Steps in the Clouds* (1942). In many respects, Cervi's screen persona became as inextricable from Blasetti's adventure films as Vittorio De Sica's* was from Mario Camerini's* romantic comedies. But whether for Blasetti or Camerini, with whom he also made two films in the early 1940s (*Una romantica avventura* in 1940 and *I promessi sposi/The Spirit and the Flesh* in 1941), Cervi became a familiar presence in Italian historical films. Although he appeared in various film genres and international productions until 1972, he was best known in the postwar years for his role as Peppone, the Communist mayor in the very popular Franco-Italian *Don Camillo* comic series, co-starring Fernandel as Don Camillo (except in the last film made after Fernandel's death): *Le Petit monde de Don Camillo* (1952) and *Le Retour de Don Camillo* (1953), both directed by Julien Duvivier, were followed by four other sequels, two (in 1955 and 1961) directed by Carmine Gallone* and two (in 1965 and 1972) by Luigi Comencini*. JHa

CHIARI, Walter

Walter Annichiarico; Verona 1924–91

Italian actor. The very young Chiari gained wide popularity at the end of the war through variety shows and musical comedies. Throughout the 1950s and 1960s, his persona of the boasting lovable rogue, his ability to improvise and his brilliant talkativeness made him one of the first Italian television stars. As man and artist, Chiari was inclined to dissipation, living 'some hundred real and imaginary lives'; like many other 'kings' of variety shows (Erminio Macario*, Ugo Tognazzi*, among others), he 'wasted' his film acting, confining his roles to parody and character sketches (*Totò al giro d'Italia*, 1948; *Mogli e buoi...*, 1956; *Gli zitelloni*, 1958; *Un dollaro di fifa*, 1960; *Walter e i suoi cugini*, 1961; *I magnifici tre*, 1962), sometimes playing doubles or twins (*I cadetti di Guascogna*, 1950; *I gemelli del Texas*, 1964). From 1947 to 1968 he made eighty-five films. Among his few dramatic roles, some consideration must be given to Giorgio Pastina's *Vanità* (1947), where he plays a 'tough' guy living in early twentieth-century Milan, and to Luchino Visconti's* *Bellissima* (1951), where he is the unforgettable Annovazzi, a mean trickster trying to take advantage of Anna Magnani*. Indeed, there was in Walter Chiari a really dramatic (if clownish) vein, a hidden and perhaps more authentic dimension, hinted at in films such as Mario Monicelli's* *Donatella* (1956), Alessandro Blasetti's* *Io, io, io ... e gli altri* (1966), Nanni Loy's *Made in Italy* (1965), and fully exploited only by Dino Risi's* *Il giovedí* (1962), the story of a clumsy divorced father who spends a gloomy afternoon with his son, and by Damiano Damiani in *La rimpatriata* (1963). Apart from Orson Welles' *Campanadas a medianoche/Chimes at Midnight* (1966), where he plays a hilarious Silence, in the last years of Chiari's life only a few young directors were able to exploit his melancholy histrionics: Peter del Monte in *Tracce di vita amorosa* (1990) and especially Massimo Mazzucco in *Romance* (1986). GVo

CHIARINI, Luigi

Rome 1900–75

Italian critic and director. During the 1930s and 1940s Chiarini, along with Umberto Barbaro*, played an important role in the promotion of Italian cinema. From its foundation in 1934, he directed the Centro Sperimentale* in Rome, contributing to its magazine *Bianco e nero* as well as writing his book *Cinque capitoli sul film* (1941). Influenced by the idealist philosophy of Giovanni Gentile, he insisted on the need to consider cinema in all its complexity, saying that 'film is an art, cinema is an industry'. He called for the expressive specificity and autonomy of cinema, summed up in his formula 'film as an absolute form', a formula he developed in the five films he directed: *Via delle Cinque Lune* (1942), *La bella addormentata/Sleeping Beauty* (1942), *La locandiera* (1943), *Ultimo amore* (1947) and *Patto col diavolo* (1950). These are highly theoretical, erudite, 'literary' movies, sophisticated from a figurative point of view but ultimately academic. During the postwar period Chiarini became a crucial presence in the Italian cultural landscape. He was then influenced by the Marxist Gramsci, although still within a Gentilian perspective, and published his most mature books: *Il film nei problemi dell'arte* (1949), *Il film nella battaglia delle idee* (1954), *Cinema quinto potere* (1954), *Arte e tecnica del film* (1952), all of which were attentive to the problems of the media and culture industries. After leaving the Centro Sperimentale in 1951, Chiarini was the first person in Italy to teach film history, first at the University of Pisa (1961–66) and eventually at the University of Urbino. His ideas may today appear a little outdated, but he remains an important figure for the affirmation of cinema as an art form and a language. From 1964 to 1968 he was director of the Venice* Film Festival, a position from which he was displaced both by the political radicalism of 1968 and changes in the media industries. GVo

CINECITTÀ

Italian studio. This complex of film studios in Rome, opened in 1937, has served as a major centre of Italian film production for decades. After a mysterious fire destroyed Carlo Roncoroni's Cines* studios in 1935, Roncoroni and Luigi Freddi* struck an agreement to construct, with state subsidies, a new production complex on a large site on the outskirts of Rome. The facility, envisioned as a new 'cinema city' ('Cinecittà'), was designed by Freddi and architect Gino Peresutti. Its construction began in January 1936, with Mussolini ceremonially laying the cornerstone, and it was opened, again by Mussolini, in 1937. Government subsidies for its construction were spread over four years (1935–39), during most of which Cinecittà was technically owned and operated by Roncoroni. After his death in September 1938, it was taken over by the government and run by a senator and former industrialist, Giovanni Tofani. By 1939, Cinecittà had become the largest cinema complex in Italy, centralising Italian film production more than it had ever been. Between 1937 and 1939, Cinecittà's ten sound stages became the production sites for almost two-thirds of all films made in Italy. By 1942, the number of sound stages had grown to twelve (with two additional ones at the nearby Centro Sperimentale*), as compared to twelve other sound stages in Rome, four in Turin, and three in Tirrenia.

With the fall of Fascism, Cinecittà came to symbolise for many Italian film-makers a kind of film too closely associated with the regime. In 1945 its facilities were briefly taken over by the Allies for use as a refugee camp. But in the 1950s Cinecittà once again became one of the most important sites for Italian film production, whether by producers of genre films such as the peplum* or *auteur* films such as Federico Felllini's* $8\frac{1}{2}$ (1963). JHa

CINES

Italian production company. The name Cines has, for some fifty years, been linked with a succession of quite different enterprises. The original company was founded in Rome in 1906 by Filoteo Alberini, a pioneer of Italian silent cinema, with support from the Banco di Roma. It started by imitating Pathé, and then specialised in historical and costume films with Mario Caserini and Enrico Guazzoni as its most prominent directors. It was a diversified company with studios in Rome in Via Vejo and a film stock production facility near Padua. In 1919 it joined the UCI consortium put together as a response to the postwar crisis but collapsed in 1924. In 1929 the Via Vejo studio was taken over by Stefano Pittaluga's* company Cines-Pittaluga, which made the first Italian sound film, *La canzone dell'amore* (1930), and produced films by Mario Camerini*, Goffredo Alessandrini* and others. After Pittaluga's death in 1931 control passed to the banker Ludovico Toeplitz, who made Emilio Cecchi* his director of production. This was a period of great success for Cines. But in 1935 Cines was restructured as part of the state-owned holding company IRI; its distribution and exhibition arms came under the state-run ENIC (Ente Nazionale Industrie Cinematografiche) while studios and production were taken over by Carlo Roncoroni under the name Cines-SAISC. A mysterious fire destroyed the Via Vejo studio in 1935 and Cines ceased to exist until 1941, when it was reconstituted in the name of the corporate state by Luigi Freddi* and subsequently produced films by Luigi Chiarini*, Carmine Gallone*, Alessandro Blasetti*, Mario Camerini* and Roberto Rossellini* (*L'uomo dalla croce*, 1942). Transferred briefly to Venice during the German occupation, the new Cines was put into liquidation in 1945. Cines returned, still as a state company, in 1949, and produced a number of films, most of them (with the exception of some by Pietro Germi* and by Luigi Zampa*) undistinguished. Deeply in debt, Cines was definitively liquidated in 1957. GVo

COMENCINI, Luigi   Salò 1916

Italian director. After spending his childhood in France, Comencini returned to Italy and graduated in architecture from Milan, where he became one of the founders of the Italian Film Library. A film critic as well as a scriptwriter for Mario Soldati*, Alberto Lattuada*, Pietro Germi* and Dino Risi*, he made several noteworthy short films before his first feature, *Proibito rubare* (1948), a sort of *Boys Town* with a Neapolitan setting and an interest in childhood, a dominant theme in his subsequent films. Important landmarks of Comencini's career are the excellent *La finestra sul Luna Park* (1957) in which, in a post-neo-realism* scenario, he subtly alludes to the drama of emigration and affirms the supremacy of affection over blood ties, as well as *Incompreso* (1967); he also made a philosophical 'Casanova' for children: *Infanzia, vocazione e prime esperienze di Giacomo Casanova veneziano* (1969), and a utopian 'Pinocchio' for adults: *Le avventure di Pinocchio* (1971). A highly versatile artist and a great storyteller, Comencini moved easily from populism to 'rose-tinted' neo-realism (*neorealismo rosa*), and from social drama to thriller and to opera and episode film. It was, however, with two early examples of what was to become *commedia all'italiana** – *Pane, amore e fantasia/Bread, Love and Dreams* (1953) and *Pane, amore e gelosia/Bread, Love and Jealousy/Frisky* (1954), starring Gina Lollobrigida* and Vittorio De Sica* – that he first left an important and identifiable mark. This propensity was refined during the 1950s in light comedy works and reached its peak in *Tutti a casa/Everybody Go Home!* (1960), which, alongside Mario Monicelli's* almost contemporary *La grande guerra/ The Great War* (1959), introduced history to the comic film and vice versa. PV

Other Films Include: *L'imperatore di Capri* (1949); *Persiane chiuse/ Behind Closed Shutters* (1950); *La bella di Roma* (1955); *Le sorprese dell'amore* (1959); *A cavallo della tigre/Jail Break* (1961); *La ragazza di Bube/Bebo's Girl* (1963); *Lo scopone scientifico* (1972); *Delitto d'amore, Mio Dio, come sono caduta in basso!/Till Marriage Do Us Part* (1974); *La donna della domenica/The Sunday Woman* (1976); *L'ingorgo/Bottleneck* (1979); *Voltati Eugenio* (1980), *La storia/The Story* [or *History*] (1986); *La Bohème* (1987); *Un ragazzo di Calabria* (1987); *Buon Natale, Buon Anno* (1989); *Marcellino, pane e vino* (1992).

'COMMEDIA ALL'ITALIANIA'

Italian genre. *Commedia all'italiana*, or 'Comedy – Italian style', a satirical form spiced with elements of social and moral criticism and originally a mixture of comedy and drama, emerged in the late 1950s. Its distant origins lay in the popular cinema of the Fascist period (notably the work of Mario Camerini*), and an element of continuity can be found in the career of Vittorio De Sica*, both as an actor for Camerini in the 1930s and as a director (and again actor) in the 1940s and 1950s. But a more important source was the 'rosy' or 'rose-tinted' neo-realism* (*neo-realismo rosa*) which appeared in the late 1940s and early 1950s when films like Luigi Zampa's* *L'onorevole Angelina* (1947), Luciano Emmer's* *Domenica d'agosto/Sunday in August* (1950), Renato Castellani's* *Due soldi di speranza/Two Pennyworth of Hope* (1951) and indeed De Sica's *L'oro di Napoli/The Gold of Naples* (1954) signalled the first symptoms of a move towards a more indulgent notion of neo-realism, inclined to dwell on the minor misfortunes of daily life, materially poor but rich in optimism and hope.

Also important were the films of Totò*, and the contributions made to them by writers like Age* and Scarpelli and directors Steno* (Stefano Vanzina) and Mario Monicelli*, future stalwarts of the fully developed *commedia all'italiana*.

A watershed in the development of the genre came with *Pane, amore e fantasia/Bread, Love and Dreams* (1953), directed by Luigi Comencini* and starring Vittorio De Sica* and Gina Lollobrigida*, and Dino Risi's* *Poveri ma belli/Poor but Beautiful* (1956). The rustic style of *Pane, amore e fantasia* (and its sequel) was complemented, and eventually replaced, by a more incisive type of urban humour, typified by actor Alberto Sordi's* versatile characterisations of the 'average Italian' in the changing society of the 1950s economic boom: *Il seduttore/The Seducer* (1954), *Il moralista/The Moralist* (1959), *Mafioso* (1962). A shift to a more complex and mature form was achieved with Monicelli's *I soliti ignoti/Persons Unknown* (1958), starring Vittorio Gassman* with a full supporting cast including Totò. This marked the beginning of the golden age of the genre. Some of the films combined comic characters, actors and language with a reinterpretation of Italian history (Monicelli's *La grande guerra/The Great War*, 1959) and Comencini's *Tutti a casa/Everybody Go Home!*, 1960). In others, such as Risi's *Il sorpasso/The Easy Life* (1962), changes in social customs and the new status symbols favoured by the emerging classes were put under the microscope: the 'modernity' of sexual liberation, the enthusiasm for the motor car, mass travel, tourism, beach life, popular music and the consumer goods foisted on the public by television advertising were relentlessly mocked. Central to the genre were actors Sordi, Gassman, Ugo Tognazzi* and (later) Nino Manfredi, with roles also played by emerging stars Marcello Mastroianni* and Monica Vitti*. Writers including Rodolfo Sonego*, Leo Benvenuti, Piero De Bernardi and Ruggero Maccari contributed to the genre, as did Ettore Scola*. Among the directors who entered its orbit were Nanni Loy, Antonio Pietrangeli*, Lina Wertmüller* and Pasquale Festa Campanile. Important titles include Monicelli's *L'armata Brancaleone* (1966), Pietro Germi's* *Signore e signori/Ladies and Gentlemen* (1966), Loy's *Il padre di famiglia/The Head of the Family* (1967), Risi's *Straziami ma di baci saziami/Hurt Me, but Cover Me With Your Kisses* (1968), Manfredi's *Per grazia ricevuta/For Grace Received* (1971), Wertmüller's *Mimí metallurgico ferito nell'onore/The Seduction of Mimi* (1972), and Franco Brusati's *Pane e cioccolata/ Bread* and *Chocolate* (1974).

By this time, however, the capacity of the genre to keep up with social change, particularly the new youth movements, was blunted. The army of comedians from the 'boom' years was ageing and began to disperse. The last great exponent of the *commedia all'italiana* was Scola, with *C'eravamo tanti amati/We All Loved Each Other So Much* (1974) and *La terrazza/The Terrace* (1980), which combine a wealth of familiar motifs with a rare narrative skill. Meanwhile the genre was falling apart. Although the intervening generation supplied important comedians, such as Giancarlo Giannini and Mariangela Melato, there is really no continuity between the classic *commedia all'italiana* and the 'New Italian comics'* who emerged in the 1980s. PDA

Bib: Enrico Giacovelli, *La commedia all'italiana* (1990).

COTTAFAVI, Vittorio   Modena 1914

Italian director. Although he worked in many genres, Cottafavi is celebrated as the *auteur* of the peplum*. With relatively large budgets, films like *La vendetta di Ercole/The Vengeance of Hercules* (1960) and *Ercole alla conquista di Atlantide/Hercules Conquers Atlantis/Hercules and the Captive Women* (1961) forge coherent worlds out of disparate classical and fantasy elements, rendered with a kitsch finesse, filling the wide screen with brilliant colour effects. Some of Cottafavi's films, such as *Messalina, Venere imperatrice/Messalina, Imperial Venus* (1960), have a tragic tone, but his Hercules is an amiable hero, reluctantly drawn into conflict and amused at the world about him. RD

Bib: 'Vittorio', *Présence du Cinéma* (special issue, 1961).

CRETINETTI (André DEED)   André [de?] Chapuis,
Le Havre 1884 – Paris 1938 [some sources: 1879–1931]

French actor with a prominent career in Italy. Deed was one of the major comic stars of early world cinema. Like many comics, Deed came from the music hall, where he had been a singer and an acrobat. At Pathé, he starred in a popular comic series as the character Boireau (1906–09). His fame greatly increased when he was lured to Giovanni Pastrone's* Itala studios in Turin in 1909, where under the pseudonym of Cretinetti he starred in more than a hundred films, some directed by himself (in Spain he was Torribo or Sanchez, in English-speaking countries Foolshead or Jim). Typical of early farce and chase films, his humour was physical and violent, based on a character who gets into trouble and makes things worse in his struggle to escape the consequences. He is described by Richard Abel as 'a grotesquely bewildered clown and a skilful practitioner of physical gags'. As the popularity of the early comic genres waned, so did Deed's and he died in neglect and poverty. GV

Bib: Richard Abel, *The Ciné Goes to Town: French Cinema 1896–1914* (1994).

CRISTALDI, Franco

Turin 1924 – Monte Carlo, Monaco 1992

Italian producer. The son of a lawyer and partisan, Cristaldi founded his own production company, Vides, in Turin in 1947, initially concentrating on documentaries and newsreels. He later moved into fiction with an unusual film on the Risorgimento, *La pattuglia sperduta* (1954) by Piero Nelli. He moved to Rome but maintained links with the northern industrial capitals, imposing a new style of work on the Italian cinema of the 1960s. For him cinema should be dominated by the director, but also by the highly professional producer. His view was that 'we don't have to produce films which sell, but we do have to sell the films that we produce'. He considered plots more important than stars and he chose films for their ability to capture the 'mood of a particular period'. He produced works by, among others, Luchino Visconti* (*Le notti bianche/White Nights*, 1957; *Vaghe stelle dell'Orsa/ Sandra*, 1965); Pietro Germi* (the Oscar winner *Divorzio all'italiana/ Divorce – Italian Style*, 1961; *Sedotta e abbandonata/Seduced and Abandoned*, 1964); Mario Monicelli* (*I soliti ignoti/Persons Unknown, 1958; I compagni/The Strikers*, 1963); and Luigi Comencini* (*La ragazza di Bube/Bebo's Girl*, 1963). He produced all Francesco Rosi's* films from *I magliari* (1959) to *Cristo si è fermato a Eboli/ Christ Stopped at Eboli* (1979), including *Salvatore Giuliano* (1962), which he pushed through to completion in spite of ostracism by the authorities and the banks. He was particularly dedicated to the discovery of such talents, which he regarded as part of his duty. He thus promoted the early careers of Gillo Pontecorvo*, Francesco Maselli*, Elio Petri*, Ugo Gregoretti (*Omicron*, 1964), Nanni Loy (*Un giorno da leoni*, 1961) and Marco Bellocchio*. He was a 'padre padrone' (despotic father) figure, as seen in the case of Giuseppe Tornatore* and his *Nuovo Cinema Paradiso/Cinema Paradiso* (1988), which was cut, reassembled and brought out several times before achieving worldwide success and winning many prizes, including an Oscar. His – contradictory – respect for *auteurs*' wishes and for meeting estimated budgets earned him a love-hate attitude from many directors, including Federico Fellini*, for whom he produced *Amarcord* (1973, another Oscar) and *E la nave va/And the Ship Sails On* (1983). Winner of a record number of awards, Cristaldi was forced to compromise increasingly during the 1980s as a result of the overpowering influence of television. He nevertheless continued to produce international successes, including Jean-Jacques Annaud's *Der Name der Rose/The Name of the Rose* (1986). GVo

D

DE FILIPPO, Eduardo Naples 1900 – Rome 1984
DE FILIPPO Peppino Naples 1903 – Rome 1980
DE FILIPPO, Titina Annunziata De Filippo;
Naples 1898 – Rome 1963

Italian film and theatre family. (Eduardo: playwright-director-actor; Peppino: actor-playwright; Titina: actress). Eduardo De Filippo was unquestionably, alongside Luigi Pirandello, the greatest Italian playwright of the twentieth century, raising the Neapolitan tradition to the level of European high culture. Son of actor-playwright Eduardo Scarpetta, Eduardo made his stage debut with his father's company at the age of four. Having started in variety, in the late 1920s he founded, with his brother and sister, the 'Teatro umoristico', and shortly afterwards the family moved hesitantly into film. Eduardo and Peppino began their film career in Mario Bonnard's *Tre uomini in frac*. They were then invited by Mario Camerini* to star in his delightful adaptation of the Spanish story *Il cappello a tre punte/The Three-Cornered Hat* (1934), which Mussolini personally censored. Other films followed, including Raffaello Matarazzo's* *Sono stato io/I Did It* (1937), which marked Titina's film debut, but their films remained secondary to their theatrical work throughout the period.

In 1944 Peppino flamboyantly left the company, a breach that was never healed. An author of lightweight comedy and farce, he was perhaps the better actor, with an extraordinary comic presence. He flourished in minor films, starring opposite Totò* in a series of films with titles like *Totò, Peppino e la malafemmina/Totò, Peppino and the Wicked Woman* (1956) and also opposite Aldo Fabrizi*. He created the hugely popular television character Pappagone and was marvellously used by Federico Fellini*, for instance in *Luci del varietà/Variety Lights* (1950). Eduardo was never a spectacular film actor, but his achievements were more varied. Declaring that his ambition was 'not to turn the man in the street into an actor, but the actor into a man in the street', he created an original style in parallel with that of neorealism*, aided by the talents of his sister Titina and of Totò. He directed and acted in a number of films, including adaptations of his theatrical masterpieces of the late 1940s, most notably *Napoli milionaria* (film: 1950; English title: *Side Street Story*). Other film acting credits include Vittorio De Sica's* *L'oro di Napoli/The Gold of Naples* (1954) and Luigi Comencini's* *Tutti a casa/Everybody Go Home!* (1960). For her part Titina continued to act in her brother's plays and films, creating the title role in *Filumena Marturano* (play: 1946; film: 1950), and in films by other directors (for instance in Luchino Visconti's* *Bellissima*, 1951), until forced by illness to give up the stage. GVo

DE LAURENTIIS, Dino

Torre Annunziata 1919

Italian producer. After acting classes at the Centro Sperimentale* in Rome and appearing in Mario Camerini's* *Batticuore* (1938), De Laurentiis became a producer. He set up Real Cine in Turin in 1941 and then became production manager for Riccardo Gualino's Lux*. Among the films he produced there were Alberto Lattuada's* *Il bandito* (1946), and Giuseppe De Santis'* *Riso amaro/Bitter Rice* (1949), which launched the career of Silvana Mangano* (who soon became his wife). Owner of the Farnesina studios in Rome with Carlo Ponti*, De Laurentiis founded Ponti-De Laurentiis in 1950, which produced films by Lattuada as well as by Roberto Rossellini*, Vittorio De Sica*, Luigi Zampa* and Federico Fellini*, and historical epics such as Camerini's *Ulisse/Ulysses* (1954) and King Vidor's *War and Peace* (1956, US). But it was the more lowbrow productions, particularly films starring Totò*, which achieved spectacular box-office success. Totò and De Laurentiis in fact set up a company, DDL, to exploit their success. In 1957 Ponti and De Laurentiis went their separate ways, the latter to pursue his own dream of becoming a great international producer. He set up a large production unit called Dinocittà on the outskirts of Rome, where films such as Richard Fleischer's *Barabba* (1961) and John Huston's *La Bibbia/The Bible In the Beginning ...* (1966) were shot, together with Mario Monicelli's* *La grande guerra/The Great War* (1959), Alberto Sordi's* films and others. A man with a genuine passion for the cinema and for taking risks, he was forced to sell Dinocittà in 1971 for financial reasons. He moved to the US, where he worked as executive producer on *Serpico* (1973), *Death Wish* (1974) and *Three Days of the Condor* (1975). He set up his own company, De Laurentiis Entertainment, and worked once again with super-productions like *King Kong* (1976), *Hurricane* (1979), *Flash Gordon* (1980) and *Dune* (1984), the last-named directed by David Lynch and on which the executive producer was De Laurentiis' own daughter Raffaella. But he also remained committed to prestige *auteur* cinema, producing films directed by Robert Altman, Ingmar Bergman, Miloš Forman and Michael Cimino among others. In the early 1980s he invested part of his capital in a chain of Italian fast food restaurants. In the early 1990s, in a changed Hollywood climate, he had more failures than successes but remained determined not to abandon the field. MMo

DEL POGGIO, Carla

Maria Luisa Attanasio; Naples 1925

Italian actress. Carla Del Poggio was discovered at the Centro Sperimentale* in Rome by Vittorio De Sica*, who cast her as the whimsical heroines of *Maddalena ... zero in condotta* (1940) and *Un garibaldino al convento* (1942). After these lighter roles, she became a

42

dramatic actress, epitomising the 'tragic young woman' in the films of Alberto Lattuada*, whom she married in 1945: as sister and prostitute in *Il bandito* (1946); as the cursed lover of a black soldier in *Senza pietà/Without Pity* (1948); as frustrated bride in *Il mulino del Po/The Mill on the Po* (1949); and as the aspiring artiste in *Luci del varietà/Light of Variety/Variety Lights* (1950, co-dir. Federico Fellini*). Her parts in Giuseppe De Santis'* *Caccia tragica/Tragic Hunt* (1947) and *Roma ore 11* (1952) were no less troubled. More unusual but less successful were her digressions into the imaginary (in Mario Camerini's* *L'angelo e il diavolo/The Angel and the Devil*, 1946) and melodrama (Pietro Germi's* *Gioventù perduta/Lost Youth*, 1947). After a number of minor roles, particularly in France, and a disappointing *Cose da pazzi/Das Bekenntnis der Ina Kahr* (1954), directed by a weary G. W. Pabst, Carla Del Poggio's career came to an end alongside Peter Ustinov in Hugo Fregonese's *I girovaghi/The Wanderers* (1956), a 'chaotic and absurd' film belonging to the 'Hollywood on the Tiber' period of Italian cinema. GVo

DE SANTIS, Giuseppe   Fondi 1917

Italian director. After studying philosophy, De Santis made a name for himself as a short story writer, then as a critic for the magazine *Cinema*. He was assistant director to Luchino Visconti* (*Ossessione*, 1942), Aldo Vergano and Roberto Rossellini* and wrote a number of scripts. In 1945 he assisted Mario Serandrei on a documentary on the Resistance, *Giorni di gloria/Days of Glory*. Starting with *Caccia tragica/Tragic Hunt* (1947) and *Riso amaro/Bitter Rice* (1949; his best-known film, starring Silvana Mangano*), De Santis set out to create a new form of neo-realism*. His films were popular-populist, baroque melodramas influenced both by classical American cinema and by Soviet Socialist Realism, and making suggestive use of landscapes as well as eroticism. From the farmers' co-operatives of the lower Po to the rice fields of Vercelli and the sheepfolds of his native Latium countryside in the hieratic *Non c'è pace tra gli ulivi* (1950), he offered an epic cross-section of rural Italy, embracing its confused post-Resistance aspirations. De Santis then turned his attention to urban environments with two admirable films, *Roma ore 11* (1952), based on a dramatic news event (the collapse of a staircase on which hundreds of young women were queuing for a job interview), and *Un marito per Anna Zaccheo* (1953), a strikingly modern portrait of a woman (Silvana Pampanini*) seeking an impossible balance between her desires and societal constraints. Later works, such as the Fordian *Cesta duga godinu dana/La strada lunga un anno/The Road a Year Long* (1958), an Italian-Yugoslav co-production filmed in Yugoslavia, the bourgeois drama *La Garçonnière* (1960) and the unusual war film *Italiani brava gente/Attack and Retreat* (1964), are not without interest, but De Santis remains a director tied to the immediate postwar period of Italian film history. PV

Other Films Include: *Giorni d'amore* (1954); *Uomini e lupi/Men and Wolves* (1956); *Un apprezzato professionista di sicuro avvenire* (1972).

DE SICA, Vittorio   Sora 1901 – Neuilly-sur-Seine, France 1974

Italian actor and director. De Sica's career exemplifies the heights as well as the banalities of four decades of Italian film-making, progressing from the so-called 'white telephones' of the 1930s, to neo-realism* and later 'rose-tinted' comedies [> 'COMMEDIA ALL'ITALIANA'], and to the romantic realism of the 1970s. De Sica's film career began in 1918 when he appeared as young Clémenceau in Bencivenga's *Il processo Clémenceau*. He continued working in the theatre, including with his own acclaimed company, ZaBum. Although by 1932 he had appeared in two more films (*La compagnia dei matti*, 1928, and *La vecchia signora*, 1931), he was still mainly known as a stage actor. However, *Gli uomini, che mascalzoni* ... (1932), his first film for director Mario Camerini*, turned him into the most popular male star in 1930s Italian cinema. He appeared in four more Camerini films during that period: *Darò un milione* (1935), *Ma non è una cosa seria/But It's Nothing Serious* (1936), *Il signor Max/Mr Max* (1937) and *Grandi magazzini* (1939), romantic comedies which firmly established his screen persona as the petit-bourgeois hero and (as one critic put it) the 'bravo ragazzo' (the nice guy).

The 1940 romantic comedy *Due dozzine di rose scarlatte/Two Dozen Red Roses* launched a brief series of films, including *Maddalena ... zero in condotta* (1940) and *Teresa Venerdì/Doctor Beware* (1941), for which De Sica is credited as both actor and director. The last two films, as well as *Un garibaldino al convento* (1942), all concern the 'coming of age' of a young female character who becomes romantically attracted to an older man, played by De Sica in two of the films. The films, however, evolved gradually away from the conventions of 1930s romantic comedy. In *Teresa Venerdì and Un garibaldino al convento*, the female protagonists are caught in oppressive youth institutions (orphanage, boarding school), themes that form a bridge to De Sica's later neo-realist films. *Sciuscià/Shoeshine* (1946), *Ladri di biciclette/Bicycle Thieves* (1948), *Miracolo a Milano/Miracle in Milan* (1951) and *Umberto D.* (1952), all scripted by Cesare Zavattini*, placed De Sica at the forefront of the neo-realist movement, along with Roberto Rossellini* and Luchino Visconti*. While each film is constructed around a specific postwar social problem (respectively: juvenile crime, unemployment, homelessness, and the plight of the aged), De Sica's lyricism departs from the purely didactic by inviting a powerful emotional engagement. With *Umberto D.*, neo-realism reached a state of 'terminal purity' in its rigorous adherence to Zavattini's 'poetics of immediacy', and the film's box-office failure ushered in a period of commercial compromise for the financially strapped director. His next project, *Stazione Termini/Indiscretion of an American Wife* (1953), indeed involved concessions to David O. Selznick, who financed the production provided it showcased his wife, Jennifer Jones. De Sica resumed his acting career, appearing in France in Max Ophuls' *Madame de .../The Earrings of Madame de ...* (1953) with Danielle Darrieux and Charles Boyer, and in Italy with Gina Lollobrigida* in Luigi Comencini's* immensely popular *Pane, amore e fantasia/Bread, Love and Dreams* (1953) and *Pane, amore e gelosia/ Bread, Love and Jealousy/Frisky* (1954); he also delivered a brilliant performance as the lead in Rossellini's *Il generale Della Rovere* (1959). After a five-year hiatus, De Sica returned to directing with *La ciociara/Two Women* (1960), a well-crafted adaptation of the Moravia novel set in a ravaged World War II Italy and starring Sophia Loren*. De Sica launched the lucrative team of Loren and Marcello Mastroianni* in several 'rose-tinted' hits, including *Ieri, oggi, domani/Yesterday, Today and Tomorrow* (1963) and *Matrimonio all'italiana/Marriage – Italian Style* (1964), followed by undistinguished commercial ventures such as *Sette volte donna/Woman Times Seven* (1967) and *Amanti/A Place for Lovers* (1968), starring Shirley MacLaine and Faye Dunaway respectively. With *Il giardino dei Finzi-Contini/The Garden of the Finzi-Continis* (1970), De Sica made a conscious return to committed film-making, incorporating the lessons of commercial cinema into an unflinching account of Jewish persecution under the Fascist regime and the Nazi occupation of Ferrara. 'I am happy that I made it,' he said, 'because it brought me back to my old noble intentions.' JHa/MMa

Other Films as Director: *I bambini ci guardano* (1943); *La porta del cielo* (1944); *L'oro di Napoli/The Gold of Naples* (1954); *Il tetto/The Roof* (1956); *Il giudizio universale/The Last Judgment* (1961); *Boccaccio '70* (ep. *La riffa*), *I sequestrati di Altona/The Condemned of Altona* (1962); *Il boom* (1963); *Un mondo nuovo/A Young World* (1965); *Caccia alla volpe/After the Fox* (1966); *Le streghe* (1967, ep. *Una sera come le altre*); *I girasoli/Sunflower* (1969); *Le coppie* (1970, ep. *Il leone*); *Lo chiameremo Andrea* (1972); *Una breve vacanza/A Brief Vacation* (1973); *Il viaggio/The Journey* (1974).

DI VENANZO, Gianni   Teramo 1920 – Rome 1966

Italian cinematographer. Di Venanzo started young as a camera assistant on some of the most important neo-realist* films, including Luchino Visconti's* *Ossessione* (1942), and films directed by Roberto Rossellini* and Vittorio De Sica*. He was director of photography for the first time on Carlo Lizzani's* *Achtung! Banditi!* (1951) and *Cronache di poveri amanti/Stories of Poor Lovers* (1954) and went on to work with directors such as Francesco Maselli*, Mario Monicelli*, Lina Wertmüller* and Luigi Comencini*. His fame, however, is mostly due to his work with Michelangelo Antonioni* on such films as *Le amiche/The Girlfriends* (1955), *Il grido/The Cry* (1957), *La notte/The Night* (1961), *L'eclisse/The Eclipse* (1962), and with Francesco Rosi* on *La sfida* (1958), *Salvatore Giuliano* (1961), *Le mani sulla città/Hands Over the City* (1963). Di Venanzo significantly influenced lighting techniques: he challenged classical schemes and revolutionised black-and-white cinematography by eliminating 'theatre light' (*luce teatro*) in favour of 'light everywhere' (*luce dovunque*). He pionereed the use of soft lights known as 'photo-flood' and 'photo-spot' (although Antonioni claimed that Enzo Serafin was the first to use them on his early feature *Cronaca di un amore/Story of a Love Affair* in 1950). All of this contributed to a distinctive style '*à la* Di Venanzo', which at the same time was flexible enough to adapt to the directors' own styles: Rosi's dramatic realism, Antonioni's 'visual ambiguity', Fellini's avant-gardist '*mise-en-scène* of light' in $8\frac{1}{2}$ (1963) and orchestration of visions and ghosts in *Giulietta degli spiriti/Juliet of the Spirits* (1965), one of Di Venanzo's rare ventures into colour. GVo

DIVISMO

Italian star phenomenon. *Diva* in Italian means goddess and by extension other objects of worship such as (female) film stars. *Divismo* describes the phenomenon of star worship (and star power), with particular reference to the silent period. It acquired currency in terms of the role of operatic prima donnas and lead actresses of theatre companies in Italy in the early years of the century. In these companies not only was the *diva* the star attraction around which the performance of the rest of the company revolved, but often she was also formally or informally the head of the company and able to determine the repertoire. Actresses like Eleonora Duse and Emma Gramatica enjoyed great power as well as great reputation, and the practice soon spread to the cinema. Lyda Borelli and Francesca Bertini emerged as film stars first and foremost around 1914, to be joined by Pina Menichelli and Leda Gys. In a meteoric film career lasting only five years, Borelli's intense appearance, striking poses and sinuous movements provide the central focus of all her films, notably *Ma l'amor mio non muore/But My Love does not Die* (1914), *Fior di male/Flower of Evil* (1915) and *Malombra* (1917), and the whole *mise en scène* and the performances of the rest of the cast are little more than supporting elements as she goes through her routines of joy and (more often) suffering. Bertini was a more accomplished actress, able to interpret a variety of roles, and she had a longer career. She performed alongside Leda Gys as a pantomime character in *Histoire d'un pierrot* (1914), becoming a star with *Assunta Spina* in 1915. The post-1918 crisis in the Italian cinema brought an abrupt end to the *diva* genre. Bertini and Borelli both married aristocrats and were able to retire, although Bertini returned sporadically to the screen as late as the 1950s. Her career (and that of other *dive*) is commemorated in a documentary by Gianfranco Mingozzi*, *L'ultima diva; Francesca Bertini/The Last Diva; Francesca Bertini* (1982). GNS

DONAGGIO, Giuseppe [Pino] Bruano 1941

Italian composer. Donaggio's prolific career has been marked by a high number of international productions, second only in this respect to Ennio Morricone*. In particular, his professional partnership with American director Brian De Palma covers over twenty years and includes, among others, popular films such as *Carrie* (1976), *Dressed to Kill* (1980) and *Body Double* (1984). Although his scores were mostly composed for horror films and thrillers (apart from the De Palma films, there was Joe Dante's *Piranha*, 1978, and *The Howling*, 1981), Donaggio has also worked on more 'intimate' scores for films ranging from the family melodrama of Liliana Cavani's* *Oltre la porta/Beyond the Door* (1982) to the political cinema of Giuseppe Ferrara's *Il caso Moro/The Moro Affair* (1986). GLS

E

EMMER, Luciano Milan 1918

Italian director. Emmer started his film career in the 1940s, first in collaboration with Enrico Gras and then on his own, as a maker of innovative short landscape films and documentaries about art and artists. He branched out into feature film-making in the 1950s, beginning with the appealing *Una domenica d'agosto/Sunday in August* (1950), based on a story by Sergio Amidei* (who also produced). But he continued to make films about artists, notably *Leonardo da Vinci* (1952) and the very striking *Picasso* (1954). Finding fewer opportunities to make cinema films, either documentary or feature, since the 1960s he has worked mainly for television. GNS

F

FABRIZI, Aldo
Rome 1905–90

Italian actor and director. A man of modest background, Fabrizi started his career in 1931 in variety theatres, bringing in the warm and 'human' vein of Roman dialect comedy. In his many film parts he was tolerant and gently ironic but also imbued with petit-bourgeois moralism, for example as the tram driver in *Avanti c'è posto* (1942) and the fishmonger in *Campo de' Fiori/The Peddler and the Lady* (1943), both directed by Mario Bonnard. Roberto Rossellini* discovered his dramatic talent, casting him as Don Pietro in *Roma città aperta/Rome Open City* (1945), a symbol of the new Italy. With his down-to-earth common sense and a touch of sentimentality, Fabrizi bridged the period of reconstruction and neo-realism*, embodying a peasant under the Occupation in Luigi Zampa's* *Vivere in pace/To Live in Peace* (1946), a grumpy but sympathetic police inspector in Mario Monicelli's* *Guardie e ladri/Cops and Robbers* (1951) and a janitor in Renato Castellani's* *Mio figlio professore/Professor, My Son* (1946). However, his greatest successes are perhaps those in which he played more grotesque roles, such as the tyrant Nicolao in Rossellini's *Francesco giullare di Dio/The Flowers of St Francis/Francis, God's Jester* (1950), or when he demonstrated pathos, as in Alberto Lattuada's* *Il delitto di Giovanni Episcopo/Flesh Will Surrender* (1947). During these early years he also directed a number of films which exploited his previous screen characters. Notable are *Emigrantes/Gli emigranti* (1949), made in Argentina, and the episode *Marsina stretta* (from a Pirandello short story) in *Questa è la vita/Of Life and Love* (1954). His good-humoured characters occasionally gave way to a somewhat unsympathetic cynicism. This was fully exploited by Ettore Scola* in *C'eravamo tanto amati/We All Loved Each Other So Much* (1974), Fabrizi's last performance of some quality, given that throughout the 1960s he had turned to more indulgent comedies, such as *I tartassati* (1959), *Totò, Fabrizi e i giovani d'oggi* (1961), *I quattro monaci* (1963) and *Frà Manisco cerca guai* (1964). GVo

Other Films as Director Include: *Benvenuto, reverendo!* (1950); *La famiglia Passaguai* (1951); *La famiglia Passaguai fa fortuna* (1952); *Papà diventa mamma* (1952); *Una di quelle* (1953); *Hanno rubato un tram* (1954); *Il maestro* (1958).

48

FELLINI, Federico Rimini 1920 – Rome 1994

Italian director and scriptwriter. Fellini's extravagant inventiveness and carnivalesque style, and his authorship of ground-breaking films such as *La strada* (1954), *La dolce vita* (1960) and *Amarcord* (1973), have made him synonymous in the popular imagination with Italian cinema itself.

Fellini was born and raised in Rimini, the setting of *I vitelloni/The Spivs* (1953) and *Amarcord*. He moved to Florence in 1938 and to Rome in 1939, where he joined the editorial staff of the humorous magazine *Marc'Aurelio*. After the war, he worked in The Funny-Face Shop, drawing caricatures of American G.I.s. He also wrote gags and scripts for film and radio, including the show *Cico e Pallina* about a young married couple, whose co-star Giulietta Masina* became his wife in 1943. Through a friend, the actor Aldo Fabrizi*, Fellini met Roberto Rossellini* and contributed to the screenplay of *Roma città aperta/Rome Open City* (1945). In addition to four other collaborations with Rossellini, *Paisà* (1946), *Il miracolo/The Miracle* (1948), *Francesco giullare di Dio/The Flowers of St Francis/Francis, God's Jester* (1950) and *Europa '51* (1952), Fellini wrote scripts for such directors as Alberto Lattuada*, Pietro Germi*, Luigi Comencini* and Eduardo De Filippo*. Lattuada gave the aspiring film-maker his start as co-director of *Luci del varietà/Lights of Variety/Variety Lights* (1950), a film which anticipates Fellini's lifelong fascination with the tackiness and glitz of the vaudeville stage. But it was *Lo sceicco bianco/The White Sheik* (1952), his first solo effort, which established important elements of his *auteur-ism*: the collaboration with playwright Tullio Pinelli and scriptwriter Ennio Flaiano* until 1965, and with the composer Nino Rota* until Rota's death in 1979; the thinly veiled autobiography (the provincial newly-weds' arrival in Rome as a replay of his own recent past), and a fondness for popular culture (here photoromance). The paradigm was repeated in *I vitelloni*, an even more transparently autobiographical film about Fellini's hometown peer group whose fantasies kept them in a state of permanent adolescence. The Giulietta Masina trilogy – *La strada* (1954), *Le notti di Cabiria/Cabiria/Nights of Cabiria* (1957), and *Giulietta degli spiriti/Juliet of the Spirits* (1965) – explored her characters' drive to transcend the constraints of everyday life. Gelsomina (in *La strada*), a simpleton sold into slavery to a sideshow strongman, Zampanò, has 'breakthrough' experiences of a preternatural order; Cabiria, a spunky prostitute, seeks redemption through religion and romantic love; Giulietta, a middle-class housewife abandoned by her husband, discovers her own spiritual resources.

Though highly original, Fellini's 1950s films were still bound to realist codes. *La dolce vita* (1960) signalled a quest for a radical new film language reflecting the breakdown of traditional values in the Italy of the postwar 'boom'. *$8\frac{1}{2}$* (1963), with its mixture of lived experience, dream, memory and fantasy, went even further. Both films added important chapters to Fellini's cinematic autobiography; Marcello Mastroianni* played the alter ego figure of the artist newly arrived from the provinces and attempting to adjust to metropolitan life in *La dolce vita*, and was the director in the throes of a mid-life crisis in $8\frac{1}{2}$. Two decades later, Mastroianni resumed this role in Fellini's encounter with feminism, *La città delle donne/City of Women* (1980) and in *Ginger e Fred/Ginger and Fred* (1985), a nostalgic look at a lifetime of performance in the context of televised vulgarity. Other transparently autobiographical films include *Roma/Fellini's Roma* (1972), a pastiche of personal impressions of the Eternal City, and *Amarcord* (1973), a poetic return to the film-maker's adolescence in Rimini during the Fascist era. Two highly self-referential films merge personal reminiscences with reflections on the cinematic apparatus: *I clowns* (1970), a documentary about the director's quest for the world's great clowns, and *Intervista* (1987), a celebration of Cinecittà's* fiftieth anniversary in the form of an extended interview for Japanese television.

Though opposed in principle to literary adaptations, Fellini has adapted a series of texts, beginning with Edgar Allan Poe for *Tre passi nel delirio/Histoires extraordinaires/Tales of Mystery* (1968, ep. *Toby Dammit*). Petronius' *Satyricon* attracted him as a series of fragments whose gaps begged to be filled in (*Fellini-Satyricon*, 1969), and the lists of sexual conquests in Casanova's *Memoirs* (which Fellini found as boring as a telephone directory) invited his demystification (*Casanova*, 1976). Finally, Ermanno Cavazzoni's story of a simpleton's odyssey in *Poema dei lunatici* prompted Fellini to survey a postmodern landscape through the astonished eyes of Roberto Benigni* in *La voce della luna/The Voice of the Moon* (1990).

In 1993, Fellini was given an Oscar for Lifetime Achievement, a fitting tribute to his ability to create a filmic mythology both intensely private and universal in its reach. MMo

Bib: Peter Bondanella, *The Cinema of Federico Fellini* (1992).

Other Films as Director: *Amore in città/Love in the City* (1953, ep. *Agenzia matrimoniale*); *Il bidone/The Swindlers* (1955); *Boccaccio '70* (1962, ep. *Le tentazioni del dottor Antonio*); *Block-notes di un regista/ Fellini: A Director's Notebook* (1969); *Prova d'orchestra/Orchestra Rehearsal* (1978); *E la nave va/And the Ship Sails On* (1983).

FERRERI, Marco   Milan 1928

Italian director who also worked in Spain and France. In Italy, Ferreri began working in advertising and film production and then experimented with newsreels. While selling film equipment in Spain, he met the comedy writer Rafael Azcona*, who was to contribute to many of his films. Two of his features became milestones of the Spanish cinema: *El pisito/The Little Flat* (1958) and *El cochecito/The Wheelchair*

(1960). Anticipating the black humour of Luis García Berlanga's films, *El pisito* shows a young couple postponing their wedding until they find a flat. Out of desperation, the young man (José Luis López Vázquez) marries an aged woman, hoping for her early death. Marriage, however, revitalises the old woman and the young couple's plans are frustrated. *El cochecito* covers a similarly grotesque territory.

Ferreri split the rest of his career between Italy and France, producing one of the most original and disturbing bodies of work of the European art cinema* of the 1960s and 1970s, a startling blend of socio-political critique (sex, consumerism, alienation), black humour and misogyny. *Una storia moderna: l'ape regina/The Conjugal Bed* (1963) ends with Ugo Tognazzi* reduced to a wheelchair by women's sexuality. Ferreri reflected on male obsessions in *Break-up* (1965, uncensored version released 1969); in *Dillinger è morto/Dillinger is Dead* (1969), he portrayed a fetishistic and alienated world. His attention focused increasingly on changing sexual roles, culminating in *L'ultima donna/The Last Woman* (1976), where Gérard Depardieu, in a celebrated scene, emasculates himself with an electric knife (as a response to feminism). Undoubtedly, though, Ferreri's 'scandalous' reputation rests principally on *La Grande bouffe/La grande abbuffata* (1973), an allegory of the ravages of consumerism, in which a team of European stars (Marcello Mastroianni*, Tognazzi, Philippe Noiret, Michel Piccoli) literally eat themselves to death. His films of the 1980s reflected the intellectual weariness both of Italy and of the director himself, who seemed to be simply pandering to an audience waiting to be provoked (*La carne*, 1991). However, with *La casa del sorriso* (1992), and above all *Diario di un vizio* (1993), Ferreri seems to have returned to his most scathing vein. PM

Other Films Include: *Los chicos* (1960); *Le italiane e l'amore* (1961, ep.); *La donna scimmia/The Ape Woman* (1963); *Controsesso* (1964, ep.); *Marcia nuziale* (1966); *L'harem* (1967); *L'udienza* (1971); *Liza/La cagna* (1972); *Touche pas la femme blanche* (1975); *Ciao maschio/Bye Bye Monkey, Il seme dell'uomo/The Seed of Man* (1978); *Chiedo asilo* (1979); *Storie di ordinaria follia* (1981); *Storia di Piera* (1983); *Il futuro è donna* (1984); *I Love You* (1986); *Come sono buoni i bianchi* (1987).

FININVEST

Italian production company. Silvio Berlusconi's television networks developed an interest in film production in the mid-1980s, first by acquiring broadcasting rights and then by participating directly in production itself through the production house, Reteitalia. The money invested in this operation was considerable: in 1986, out of a total national investment in film production of 220 billion lire (*c.* £100 million), Berlusconi's company was responsible for some 90 billion, and in 1990, together with the Cecchi Gori* company, 180 billion out of a total 240 million. Initially, the results failed to attract large television and cinema audiences. In 1989, after Fininvest declared a 'loss' of 200 billion lire on its investment in Italian cinema, an agreement with the Cecchi Goris led to the creation of a joint production and distribution venture, Penta. In addition to a large number of 'low/middle-brow' productions and some 'quality' films directed by the likes of Marco Risi* and Bernardo Bertolucci*, Penta came to promote the majority of Italian films by both young and established directors. However, the death of Mario Cecchi Gori* in November 1993, the expiry of Penta's five-year agreement and Berlusconi's election as Prime Minister of Italy in 1994 slowed down Fininvest's activity, although its role within Italian cinema remains significant. GVo

FLAIANO, Ennio   Pescara 1910 – Rome 1972

Italian scriptwriter. A prominent name in Italian journalism and litera-ture, Flaiano started as a film reviewer, first on the weekly *Oggi*, be-ginning immediately before the war, and later on *Il Mondo*. After a few experiments in film writing, he wrote the wittily unorthodox text of *Roma città libera* (1946, dir. Marcello Pagliero) which examines the bewilderment of Romans under the Allied occupation. His talents were diverse: comedy of manners, in Alessandro Blasetti's* films such as *Tempi nostri/A Slice of Life* (1953), in Gianni Franciolini's *Villa Borghese/It Happened in the Park* (1953), and in Mario Monicelli's* much-censored *Totò e Carolina* (1953); caustic humour in films by Luis García Berlanga such as *El verdugo/The Executioner* (1963), where he collaborated with Rafael Azcona; the world of the fantastic, little ex-plored by Italian cinema, with *Camilla* (1954), *Fortunella* (1958) and *Fantasmi a Roma/Phantom Lovers* (1961). However, Flaiano's true comic inspiration as a disillusioned moralist was mostly linked (in col-laboration with the more 'metaphysical' Tullio Pinelli) to the films of Federico Fellini*, beginning with *Luci del varietà/Lights of Variety/Variety Lights* (1950, co-dir. Lattuada*), and continuing through *I vitelloni/The Spivs* (1953), *La strada* (1954), *La dolce vita* (1960), *8½* (1963) and *Giulietta degli spiriti/Juliet of the Spirits* (1965). Flaiano also specialised in 'made-to-measure' subjects, for instance for a particular actor, some of which were collected posthumously. A great source of original subjects and witticisms, he was a great 'squanderer' of ideas, some of which remained unacknowledged; *Roman Holiday* (1953), for example, devised by Ben Hecht for Audrey Hepburn's debut, was written by Flaiano and Suso Cecchi D'Amico*. Flaiano's plans to film his novel *Melampus* came to nothing, though the story eventually be-came the basis of Marco Ferreri's* *Liza/La cagna*, made in 1972, the year of Flaiano's death. GVo

Other Films Include: *Pastor Angelicus* (1942); *La freccia nel fianco* (1943); *Fuga in Francia/Flight into France* (1948); *Guardie e ladri/Cops and Robbers* (1951); *Lo sceicco bianco/The White Sheik* (1952); *Peccato che sia una canaglia/Too Bad She's Bad* (1954); *Il bidone/The Swindlers* (1955); *La donna del fiume/Woman of the River* (1955); *Le notti di Cabiria/Cabiria/Nights of Cabiria* (1957); *La notte* (1961); *La decima vittima/The 10th Victim* (1965); *I protagonisti* (1968).

FRANCHI, Franco

Franco Benenato;
Palermo 1922 – Rome 1992

and
INGRASSIA, Ciccio

Palermo 1923

Italian actors. In the 1960s and the early 1970s, Ciccio and Franco were the only surviving representatives of *commedia all'italiana**. These 'two cine-idiots most cine-watched in the country', as they were once defined, started in open-air theatre in Sicily, working their way through variety shows. They were discovered by the popular singer Domenico Modugno and offered small parts in Mario Mattoli's *Appuntamento a Ischia* (1960) and De Sica's* *Il giudizio universale/The Last Judgment* (1961). They finally starred in *L'onorata società* (1961), directed by the Neapolitan writer and comedian Riccardo Pazzaglia.

Franchi and Ingrassia were a perfect duo. 'Dividing us', they used to say, 'would be like tearing a photograph in two.' Their film roles and plots were rigidly set, endlessly reproducing the patterns of the popular variety shows of the day. Franco, the plebeian with rough working-class appearance, exaggerated gestures and expressions and sardonic/idiotic laugh, embodied basic instinctive needs, while Ciccio, whose physique recalled that of a gaunt decaying aristocrat, displayed a mature dignity, pushed to the limits of hysteria by the surreal foolishness of his companion. Together they made more than a hundred films whose titles point to their symbiotic relationship: *002 agenti segretissimi/00-2 Most Secret Agents* (1964), *I due mafiosi/The Two Mafiosi* (1964), *I due pompieri/The Two Firemen* (1968) and, inevitably, *Don Chisciotte e Sancho Panza* (1968). They revelled in parody, mimicking successful films by means of titles (many, alas, untranslatable) such as *Sedotti e bidonati* (1964), *Le spie vengono dal semi-freddo/Dr Goldfoot and the Girl Bombs* (literally 'The spies who came in from the semi-cold', directed by Mario Bava* in 1966), *Brutti di notte* (1968), *Satiricosissimo* (1970), and two 'low-grade' cult movies, *Ultimo tango a Zagarol/The Last Italian Tango* (1973) and *Farfallon* (1974). Eventually, they made it to art cinema, playing in the puppets episode, *Che cosa sono le nuvole?*, directed by Pasolini* for *Capriccio all'italiana* (1968), in the 'jar' episode of the Tavianis'* *Kaos* (1984) and, as the Cat and the Fox, in Luigi Comencini's* *Le avventure di Pinocchio*

(1972). In 1974, Ciccio on his own wrote, directed and played *Paolo il freddo* and *L'esorciccio/The Exorcist – Italian Style*. He was also the unforgettable Teo, the mad uncle of Fellini's* *Amarcord* (1973). But in spite of these solo ventures and some furious quarrels they stayed together, united 'first by hunger and then by success'. GVo

FREDA, Riccardo
Alexandria, Egypt 1909

Italian director. A master craftsman of popular films in many different genres, Freda began his directing career making 'heroic' epic films such as *Don Cesare di Bazan* (1942), *Aquila nera/The Black Eagle* (1946) and a version of *Les Misérables, I miserabili* (1947). An admirer of classical American cinema, he persevered with various types of historical and costume pictures, from *Beatrice Cenci* (1956) to *Roger-la-Honte* (1966, Fr./It.), including peplum* films such as *I giganti della Tessaglia/The Giants of Thessaly* (1960). In the 1960s he turned his attention to the horror genre with *L'orribile segreto del Dottor Hichcock/The Terror of Doctor Hichcock* (1962) and *Lo spettro/The Spectre* (1963), well-crafted claustrophobic films displaying a dark and sadistic aspect [> ITALIAN HORROR FILM]. With time his perspective became increasingly disenchanted, as he struggled to express his considerable talents and culture in the face of inadequate budgets and shoddy scripts. He co-wrote but did not direct (as planned) the comic 1994 swashbuckler *La Fille de D'Artagnan/D'Artagnan's Daughter*, shot by Bertrand Tavernier. GF

FREDDI, Luigi
Milan 1895 – Sabaudia 1977

Italian producer. The most important political and entrepreneurial figure in the Italian cinema in the 1930s, Freddi was put in charge of the state-sponsored sector of the industry after it was 'corporatised' by the Fascist government in 1934. As General Director of Cinematography, Freddi pursued a rigorously commercial policy, helping to make Italian films competitive with Hollywood imports. He was responsible for centralising the industry, concentrating on efficient studio production, and for the construction of the Cinecittà* studios (1935–37). He fell from favour because of his outspoken opposition to the protectionist proposals in the government's 'Alfieri law' of 1938, which led to the withdrawal of the Hollywood majors from the Italian market, but returned to take over the revived Cines* company in 1941. A dedicated (but non-ideological) Fascist, his close associations with the regime led him to be made a scapegoat in 1945, when he was stripped of his powers and even, for a while, deprived of his pension rights. GNS

FUSCO, Giovanni

Sant'Agata dei Goti 1906 –
Rome 1968

Italian composer. Although his name is not as immediately recognisable as that of more popular Italian composers such as Ennio Morricone* and Nino Rota*, Fusco was a very influential figure whose name appears on the credits of such landmark films as Michelangelo Antonioni's* *L'avventura* (1960) and Alain Resnais' *Hiroshima mon amour* (1959) and *Le Guerre est finie/The War Is Over* (1966). A graduate of the prestigious Accademia di Santa Cecilia, Fusco was notably eclectic, his skills and experience ranging from chamber music to the theatre, and in film from documentaries to fiction. Such an openness to experimentation marked his career and his ability to create new musical 'landscapes' was an invaluable help to the exploration of the relationship between images and sounds in the cinema of *auteurs*. Although Fusco worked with several directors such as Damiano Damiani, Mario Bolognini and the Taviani* brothers, he will be particularly remembered for his collaboration with Antonioni, for whom he wrote most of his scores. GLS

FUTURISM

Italian avant-garde circle, from 1909 through the 1930s, whose most famous spokesperson was F. T. Marinetti. Between 1909 and 1916, the Futurists published numerous manifestos decrying everything traditional about Italian art and culture, celebrating instead signs of modernity: urban landscapes, mechanisation and speed, war and its new technologies. Their wide range of artistic production included painting, theatre, poetry, musical performance, prose texts, sculpture, assemblages, architecture, furniture, ceramics, clothing and culinary preparations. Individual productions often co-opted techniques from different media. While the Futurists' manifestos often valorised cinema for its potential to the movement, their actual output of films and photography was minimal, and none of it is known to exist today.

Between 1909 and 1912, Futurists Bruno Corra and his brother Arnaldo Ginna are reputed to have made a sepia-tone photograph entitled 'Christus' and a series of coloured designs conceived as 'chromatic tunes'. Corra wrote in 1912 of having made a film of these designs, *Musica cromatica*, in which the designs were filmed as sequences – a technique that anticipated other avant-garde theories and practices of montage and animation. Concurrently, Anton Giulio Bragaglia linked Futurism to a new kind of photographic 'synthesis', which he described as 'photodynamism' and which he demonstrated through his own experiments with photographic superimposition, collage and (by the mid-1920s) film. For the most part, though, Futurists saw cinema as a potential trope or toy for their theoretical and rhetorical arsenal.

Giacomo Balla, for instance, venerated cinema for its use of image, while Marinetti saw in cinematic montage the apotheosis of his literary ideal of 'word montage'. In 1916, Marinetti and five other Futurists wrote the first manifesto about cinema, *Cinematografia futurista*. This brief treatise proclaimed that cinema fulfilled their ideal of a Futurist 'synthetic theatre', while being a completely new art. That the Futurists described cinema as 'synthetic theatre' had as much to do with their effort to transform art and culture through provocative syntheses and performance as with their belief that a Futurist film was itself a performance. Significantly, the 1916 manifesto was written the same year as a group of Futurists made what is now believed to be the only Futurist film – *Vita Futurista* (dir. Arnaldo Ginna) – initially shown between other Futurist performances at the Niccolini Theatre in Florence in 1917 and reputed to have involved eight sequences running roughly 1,200 metres.

After World War I, the context of such film productions and of the Futurist project changed significantly. While Futurism re-emerged during the 1920s, increasingly supportive of Italian Fascism, its members saw less potential in the progressively industrialised cinema. Film remained of interest to this generation of Futurists less in itself than in its 'co-penetration', to use Balla's term, with other forms. Significantly, there is evidence of Futurism's impact on mainstream Italian cinema after 1916, particularly in Enrico Prampolini's set designs for Anton Giulio Bragaglia's *Thais* (1916) and *Perfido incanto* (1916), and later in Carlo Ludovico Bragaglia's *O la borsa o la vita* (1933), and Guido Brignone's *La voce lontana* (1933). Several Futurists, including Marinetti, were appointed alongside Fascist political figures to the first national film council in 1926. [> AVANT-GARDE CINEMA IN EUROPE] JHa

G

GALLONE, Carmine   Taggia 1886 – Rome 1972

Italian director. The most consistent feature of Gallone's long career as a director (from the 1910s to the 1960s) is an enduring interest in opera and a distinctively Italian operatic and melodramatic aesthetic. He began directing films for the rapidly expanding Cines* company in 1914. Often starring the *diva* Lyda Borelli [> DIVISMO], and sometimes his wife Soave Gallone, his early films were closely aligned with the tradition of stage melodrama, with a mainly static camera allowing full play to the *diva*'s eye-catching performance.

Along with Augusto Genina*, Gallone was one of the few Italian film-makers to find work in Italy's crumbling film industry in the early and mid-1920s. But after his costly and critically unacclaimed remake of the successful silent epic *Gli ultimi giorni di Pompei/The Last Days of Pompeii* (1926, co-dir. Amleto Palermi), he, like many Italian silent film directors, went to work abroad. After making films in Germany, France and Britain, Gallone returned to Italy to make *Casta diva/ Chaste Goddess* (1935), a lavish historical melodrama about the life and times of the composer Vincenzo Bellini, which was awarded the Mussolini Cup for best Italian film at the Venice film festival. For the Italian film industry under Fascism, Gallone represented both the Italian cinema's heroic legacy and its potential international appeal, and in 1937 he was chosen to be co-writer and director of the epic *Scipione l'Africano/Scipio Africanus*. Operatic in style and harking back to a silent film aesthetic, *Scipione l'Africano* is one of the most vivid examples of the revival of the early historical epic during the 1930s and one most often linked to Fascist ideals; its central character has often been likened to Mussolini. Not all Gallone's films were so backward-looking. Although similar to Hollywood boxing films and family melodramas from the early 1940s, *Harlem* (1943) evinces many traits later valorised by neo-realism*. In the postwar years, however, he confined himself largely to 'film opera' – a flourishing Italian genre of the late 1940s and 1950s of which he was the major exponent. Gallone directed films about the lives of four famous composers – Verdi, Bellini (*Casta Diva*), Mozart (*Melodie eterne*, 1940), and Puccini – as well as *Casa Ricordi/House of Ricordi*, about the famous music publishing house, told through episodes from the lives of Rossini, Donizetti, Bellini, Puccini and Verdi. In the years following World War II, he also directed eight operatic adaptations. Gallone's consistency and adaptability are most vividly exemplified in his 1946 film *Davanti a lui tremava tutta Roma/Tosca* (1946), wherein performers of *Tosca* become embroiled in anti-Fascist activities. JHa

Other Films Include: *La donna nuda/The Nude Woman* (1914); *La falena/The Moth, Malombra* (1916); *Rendenzione/Maria di Magdala/ Redemption/Mary Magdalen* (1918); *Amleto e il suo clown/Hamlet and His Jester* (1920); *Nemesis* (1921); *Marcella* (1922); *I volti dell'amore/ The Faces of Love, Il corsaro/The Corsair* [co-dir.] (1923); *La cavalca-ta ardente/The Fiery Cavalcade* (1925); *Das Land ohne Frauen/Land without Women* (1929, Ger.); *Le Chant du marin* (1930, Fr.); *Un Soir de rafle* (1931, Fr.); *Giuseppe Verdi* (1938); *Il sogno di Butterfly/The Dream of Butterfly* (1939); *Manon Lescaut, Oltre l'amore/Beyond Love, Amami, Alfredo!/Love Me, Alfredo!* (1940); *L'amante segreta/ The Secret Lover, Primo amore/First Love* (1941); *La regina di Navarra/The Queen of Navarre, Le due orfanelle/The Two Orphans, Odessa in fiamme/Odessa in Flames* (1942); *Harlem, Tristi amori/Sad Loves* (1943); *Il canto della vita/The Song of Life* (1945); *Rigoletto* (1946); *La signora dalle camelie/La traviata, Addio Mimì* (1947); *Il Trovatore, La leggenda di Faust/The Legend of Faust* (1949); *La forza* *del destino/The Force of Destiny* (1949); *Messalina* (1951); *Puccini, Cavalleria rusticana, Senza veli/Without Veils* (1953); *Casta diva* [remake], *Madame Butterfly* (1954); *Don Camillo e l'onorevole Peppone* (1955); *Michele Strogoff, Tosca* (1956); *Polikuska* (1958); *Cartagine in fiamme/Carthage Burning* (1959); *Don Camillo monsignore... ma non troppo* (1961); *Carmen di Trastevere, La monaca di Monza/The Nun of Monza* (1962).

GASSMAN, Vittorio   Genoa 1922

Italian actor, who was established as one of Italy's best stage performers before his cinema career took off with his fourth film, Giuseppe De Santis'* *Riso amaro/Bitter Rice* (1949). Gassman has sometimes been criticised for overacting but, as David Thomson more generously puts it, his 'effusion seems quite natural and innocent'. His good looks, combined with a talent for comedy, led to many characterisations as handsome rogues and comic cads.

Never quite a star of international renown, Gassman attracted attention with his wedding to Shelley Winters in 1952. They made one film together, *Mambo* (It./US) in 1954, and divorced later that year. After a handful of films for MGM, including *Sombrero* (1952) and *Rhapsody* (1953), Gassman went back to Italy where he starred in, and co-directed with Francesco Rosi*, a film version of Jean-Paul Sartre's play *Kean* (1957). The theatre continued to play an important part in his professional life; he formed his own company, Teatro Popolare Italiano, in 1960. Mario Monicelli's* *I soliti ignoti/Persons Unknown* (1958) proved to be a watershed in Gassman's film career. Displaying a great talent for comedy, he then concentrated on humorous roles, notably in a brilliant series of films with Dino Risi*, including *Il sorpasso/The Easy Life* (1962) and *I mostri/The Monsters* (1963); he won the Best Actor award at Cannes in 1975 for his part in Risi's *Profumo di donna/Scent of a Woman* (1974). He continued a regular collaboration with Risi, and made two films with Robert Altman in the US, *A Wedding* (1978) and *Quintet* (1979) as well as one with Alain Resnais, *La Vie est un roman/Life is a Bed of Roses* (1982, Fr.). Gassman won the Nastro d'argento (Silver Ribbon, Italy's equivalent of the Oscars) for Best Actor on two occasions, first for *Kean*, then for *Lo zio indegno/The Uncle* (1989). He published a collection of poems, *Vocalizzi*, in 1988. SH

GENINA, Augusto   Rome 1892–1957

Italian director, scriptwriter, and producer. Along with Carmine Gallone*, the prolific Augusto Genina was one of the few Italian directors of silent films to pursue a long career in sound cinema, in his case up to the 1950s. Like Gallone, too, he worked abroad during the 1920s and early 1930s.

Genina entered Italian film-making at the age of 20, peddling ideas to film companies. By 1913 he had sold stories to Celio Films, and soon after worked as writer and director for Cines*. He scripted most of the films he directed over this decade, including his first, *La moglie di sua eccellenza/His Excellency's Wife* (1913), shot in Barcelona and released by Cines as two separate films. After a series of films for Cines in 1914, he worked for a variety of companies throughout Italy. In 1920 he began co-producing many of his films and in 1922 he was appointed head of the new Unione Cinematografica Italiana, a trust that mediated subsidies from Italian banks to the film industry. Genina's films during the 1910s and early 1920s were romantic melodramas, many adapted from popular literature and drama, mostly about eccentric upper-class characters. His first major success, *La signorina Ciclone* (1916), involved the European escapades of a wealthy American heiress. During the middle and late 1920s, Genina increasingly developed contacts outside Italy. His next major success, *Cyrano de Bergerac* (1923, co-dir. Mario Camerini*), was released in France in a three-colour version. Genina's career really flourished between 1929 and 1937, when he worked mostly in Germany and France, his films influenced by the styles of these national cinemas. *Prix de beauté/Miss Europa* (1930) strikingly exemplifies the influence of a European modernist aesthetic, with a story by G. W. Pabst, script by René Clair and Genina, sets by Robert Gys, and Louise Brooks in the lead. Its consonance with the artistic strategies of the avant-garde* cinema of Europe at the time is most evident in its self-reflexive use of sound and image and meta-narrative about cinema, stardom and mass culture; Brooks plays a rising film star whose death occurs during a screening of her first sound film, her gleefully singing on-screen image counterposed to her lifeless form just off-screen. Despite being offered a contract by Paramount in 1935, Genina returned to Italy, where the film industry had begun to revive, and became involved in films which valorised Italian nationalism. On the one hand were colonialist epics such as *Squadrone bianco/White Squadron* (1936), *L'assedio dell'Alcazar/The Siege of Alcazar* (1940) and *Bengasi* (1942). On the other hand, *Naples au baiser de feu* (1937, Fr.) and *Castelli in aria/Ins blaue leben/Castles in the Air* (1939, Ger./It.) offered touristic visions of Italy as an enchanted land.

Genina directed relatively few films after World War II. The most famous was *Cielo sulla palude/Heaven over the Marshes* (1949), based on the life of Maria Goretti (beatified by the Catholic Church in 1947), and using neo-realist* techniques such as non-professional actors to accentuate the bleakness of Goretti's poor, rural community. However, as film critic Guido Aristarco noted in 1949, the characters' acceptance of their condition makes this film quite different ideologically from other neo-realist films. Furthermore, as André Bazin observed, the contradictions inherent in the neo-realist treatment of a

59

saint makes this one of the most curious Italian films of the period. JHa

Other Films Include: *La doppia ferita/The Double Wound, Lulu* (1915); *Il principe dell'impossibile/Prince of the Impossible, Femmina/ Female, Addio giovinezza!/Farewell Youth!* (1918); *Lo scaldino/The Warming-pan* (1919); *I tre sentimentali/Three Sentimentals* (1920); *Marito, moglie, e ...* (1922, co-dir.); *Il corsaro/The Corsair* (1923, co-dir.); *Il focolare spento/The Cold Hearth* (1925); *L'ultimo lord/The Last Lord, Addio giovinezza!/Inconstant Youth* [remake] (1926); *Quartier Latin* (1928, Fr.); *Les Amours de minuit* (1930, Fr.); *Paris-béguin* (1931, Fr.); *La Femme en homme* [remake of *L'ultimo lord*] (1932, Fr.); *Ne sois pas jalouse, Nous ne sommes plus des enfants* (1934, Fr.); *Vergiss mein nicht/Forget Me Not* [Ger.], *Blumen aus Nizza, La gondala delle chimera/Phantom Gondola* (1936, Austr.); *Frauenliebe-Frauenleid* [Ger.]; *Naples au baiser de feu* [Fr.] (1937); **in Italy**: *Castelli in aria/Castles in the Air*, also Ger. version directed by Genina, *Ins blaue Leben* (1939); *L'edera/Devotion* (1950); *Tre storie proibite/Three Forbidden Stories* (1952); *Maddalena* (1953); *Frou-frou* (1955, Fr./It.).

GERMI, Pietro   Genoa 1914 – Rome 1974

Italian director. Federico Fellini* once described Germi as a 'great carpenter' in recognition of his unique mastery of film craft; he was also a very effective actor both in his own films and in those of others. Germi made his debut with *Il testimone/The Witness* (1946), the beginning of the early, 'dramatic' phase of his work which ended with *Un maledetto imbroglio/A Sordid Affair* (1959). Two films about the problems of southern Italy, *In nome della legge/In the Name of the Law* (1949) and *Il cammino della speranza/Road to Hope* (1950), were great box-office successes but caused controversy, many critics objecting to the extravagant, Hollywood-style approach taken by this 'fellow traveller' of neo-realism*. A similar fate awaited *Il ferroviere/Man of Iron* (1956) and *L'uomo di paglia/Man of Straw* (1958), in which Germi created two powerful portraits of men in a state of crisis, corrupted by their own moralism, superficiality and sentimentality. With his surly humanism and rejection of ideology, Germi was something of a nineteenth-century man. His later films – *Divorzio all'italiana/Divorce – Italian Style* (1961), *Sedotta e abbandonata/Seduced and Abandoned* (1963) and *Signore e signori/The Birds, the Bees and the Italians* (1965) – established him as one of the masters of *commedia all'italiana**, helped by first-rate scripts from Age* and Scarpelli*, Ennio De Concini and Luciano Vincenzoni. His satirical comedy of manners of this period is infused with a bitterness which falls just short of invective. His last films were less successful; he died during the preparation of *Amici miei*, a sharply malicious comedy eventually made by Mario Monicelli*. MMo

Other Films Include: *Gioventù perduta/Lost Youth* (1948); *La città si difende/Passport to Hell* (1951); *La presidentessa/The Lady President* (1952); *Il brigante di Tacca del Lupo/The Brigand of Tacca del Lupo* (1952); *Amori di mezzo secolo, Gelosia* (1953); *L'immorale/The Climax* (1966); *Serafino* (1968); *Le castagne sono buone/Pocketful of Chestnuts* (1970); *Alfredo Alfredo* (1972).

GHIONE, Emilio   Fiesole 1879 – Rome 1930

Italian actor, producer and director, who first appeared in films as a double and in walk-on parts for Aquila Films in Turin, where he grew up. He later moved on to Giovanni Pastrone's* Itala Films, and then to Cines* in Rome, where he was given a part in *Il poverello d'Assisi* (1911). Eventually he was hired by Celio, where, with Francesca Bertini and Alberto Collo, he acted in his first three films, including *Histoire d'un Pierrot* (1914) [> DIVISMO]. In 1913, he directed *Idolo infranto*, and, in 1914, *Nelly la Gigolette* (co-starring Bertini), where he created the character of Za la Mort, the romantic and noble-minded 'apache' gangster, to whom his reputation is inextricably linked. The character was, with Za la Vie (played by Kally Sambucini, his real-life companion), the hero of two serials inspired by Louis Feuillade's *Fantômas* (1913–14) and *Judex* (1917): *Il triangolo giallo/The Yellow Triangle* (1917, four episodes) and *I topi grigi/The Grey Mice* (1918, eight episodes), both outstanding successes. Ghione's performance style was unusual in Italian terms: expressionistic rather than naturalistic, dependent on facial expressions and the use of his body. His outdoor scenes were set in squalid, starkly illuminated peripheral areas of the city. Ghione acted in over a hundred films, among which are some of the most popular mystery and adventure films of the Italian silent cinema. In 1920, he founded Ghione Film but his success waned in an industry undergoing a severe crisis. In the mid-1920s, he emigrated like many others to Germany, where he revived Za la Mort in two films with Fern Andra. In 1926 he played in Carmine Gallone's* and Amleto Palermi's remake of *Gli ultimi giorni di Pompei/The Last Days of Pompeii* and directed a rustic drama, *Senza padre*, his last work. After trying to overcome the crisis by founding the short-lived Compagnia delle Maschere e del Colore, he moved in poverty to Paris, where he tried a new career as a writer. He wrote a long article on cinema in Italy, published in *L'Art cinématographique* in 1929. The same year he was repatriated, by then seriously ill with tuberculosis. MMo

GIROTTI, Massimo   Mogliano 1918

Italian actor. Before his first film role in Mario Soldati's* *Dora Nelson* (1939) Girotti was a professional swimmer, and his early casting had more to do with his athletic body than with training as an actor. For

61

the first three years of his film career, his screen persona was shaped through swashbuckler and costume adventure films. His first major role was as the young hero of Alessandro Blasetti's* lavish medieval fantasy, *La corona di ferro/The Iron Crown* (1941). The same year, he starred as the same character (Tremal-Naik) in two adventure films, *Pirati della Malesia* and its sequel *Le due tigri*. Soon, however, Girotti was increasingly cast in contemporary melodramas. He played a wounded Italian pilot in Roberto Rossellini's* *Una pilota ritorna* (1942), and an Italian boxer in New York in Carmine Gallone's* *Harlem* (1943), but was especially notable as the vagrant mechanic of *Ossessione* (1942), Luchino Visconti's* version of *The Postman Always Rings Twice*. The complexity of his eroticised anti-hero in *Ossessione* resulted in part from his being cast both with and against the athletic and romantic persona of the adventure films. After the war, Girotti appeared in adventure films, peplums* and melodramas, and delivered noteworthy performances for such major directors as Giuseppe De Santis* (*Caccia tragica/Tragic Hunt*, 1947), Pietro Germi* (*In nome della legge/In the Name of the Law*, 1949), Michelangelo Antonioni* (*Cronaca di un amore/Story of a Love Affair*, 1950), Visconti (*Senso*, 1954), and Alberto Lattuada* (*Lettere di una novizia*, 1960). Roles in two Pasolini* films brought him renewed prominence in the art cinema of the late 1960s: as the paradigmatic bourgeois father in *Teorema/Theorem* (1968) and as Creon in *Medea* (1970), he played dignified and sacrificial patriarchs.

Girotti has worked extensively in theatre, including in Visconti's very successful production of *The Cherry Orchard* (1965), and in Italian, French and German television. Girotti's longevity as a performer and his association with Italy's major cinematic movements established him as a living relic, and film-makers began to direct him self-consciously. Thus Bertolucci included Girotti in the line-up of older stars of neo-realism* as part of his iconoclastic strategy in *Ultimo tango a Parigi/Last Tango in Paris* (1972), while Ettore Scola* in *Passione d'amore/Passion of Love* (1981) cast him as a colonel whose performance deliberately recalled that of Ussoni in *Senso*. JHa/MMa

GUERRA, Tonino   Santarcangelo di Romagna 1920

Italian scriptwriter. One of the finest Italian dialect poets of the twentieth century, Guerra was also a gifted prose writer who used ironic and concise simplicity in his somewhat grotesque and fairytale-like depictions of reality. His scriptwriting career started with Giuseppe De Santis'* *Uomini e lupi/Men and Wolves* (1956). He made notable contributions to the work of Michelangelo Antonioni* by creating his suspenseful atmospheres and increasingly free forms from *L'avventura* (1960) to *Identificazione di una donna/Identification of a Woman* (1982). He wrote a series of 'fairytales' for Federico Fellini*, which include *Amarcord* (1973), *E la nave va/And the Ship Sails On* (1983) and

Ginger e Fred/Ginger and Fred (1985). He worked for some considerable time with Elio Petri* (*L'assassino/Assassin*, 1961; *Un tranquillo posto in campagna/A Quiet Place in the Country*, 1968), with Francesco Rosi* (for example on *Cadaveri eccellenti/Illustrious Corpses*, 1975, and *Carmen*, 1984) and on many of the Taviani* brothers' finest films, including *La notte di San Lorenzo/The Night of San Lorenzo* (1982) and *Kaos* (1984). Guerra added poetry to the work of 'prose' *auteurs* such as Rosi and the Tavianis, but was not afraid to superimpose his own style on more 'poetic' directors. His versatility is evidenced by his work for such diverse directors as Andrey Tarkovsky (*Nostalghia*, 1983), Thodoros Angelopoulos (*Taxidi sta Kithira/Voyage to Cythera*, 1984; *O melissokomos/The Beekeeper*, 1986; *Topio stin omihli/ Landscape in the Mist*, 1988) and Marco Bellocchio* (*Enrico IV/Henry IV*, 1984). He even produced some outstanding scripts for less popular directors, such as Franco Indovina (*Lo scatenato/Catch as Catch Can*, 1967, and *Tre nel mille*, 1970), and adapted some of his own stories for the four-episode film *La domenica specialmente/Especially on Sunday* (1992). MMo

Other Films Include: *La strada lunga un anno* (1957); *La notte* (1961); *I giorni contati, L'eclisse/The Eclipse* (1962); *Deserto rosso/The Red Desert* (1964); *La decima vittima/The 10th Victim* (1965); *Blowup* (1966); *C'era una volta/More than a Miracle* (1967); *Zabriskie Point* (1969, US); *Uomini contro* (1970); *Il caso Mattei/The Mattei Affair* (1972); *Un papillon sur l'épaule* (1973, Fr.); *Il mistero di Oberwald/The Oberwald Mystery* (1980); *Il frullo del passero/The Sparrow's Flutter* (1988); *Par-delà les nuages/Beyond the clouds* (1995); *To vlemma tou Odissea/Le Regard d'Ulysse/Ulysses' Gaze* (1995).

I

INGRASSIA, Ciccio – see FRANCHI, Franco

ITALIAN HORROR FILM

Considered by some critics as an inferior imitation of American cinema, the Italian horror film is nonetheless remarkably rich and original. Furthermore, the outstanding level of craftsmanship of its practitioners has enabled it to overcome the limitations of its often ridiculously low budgets.

After a hesitant start, during which it was often influenced by other popular Italian genres such as the peplum*, Italian horror emerged as a category of its own. Films such as Riccardo Freda's* *I vampiri/The Lust of the Vampire* (1957) and Mario Bava's* *La maschera del demonio/Mask of the Demon/Black Sunday* (1960) and *I tre volti della paura/Black Sabbath* (1963) succeeded in integrating modern horror with traditional 'Mediterranean' themes, treating sexuality more openly than in more puritanical countries and creating mesmerising female characters, archetypally played by Barbara Steele*. One founding member of the genre is unquestionably Freda, who, as well as being a skilled creator of swashbucklers and adventure films, was an original explorer of the world of nightmares and fear, notably in *L'orribile segreto del Dottor Hichcock/The Terror of Doctor Hichcock* (1962) and *Lo spettro/The Spectre* (1963). The other is Bava; an accomplished cameraman for Freda's *I vampiri*, he directed films which quickly attained cult status: *I tre volti della paura*, and others such as *La frusta e il corpo/Night is the Phantom* (1963) and *Operazione paura/Curse of the Living Dead* (1966). All his films focus on sexual perversions and pathological states of mind, evoked through brilliant special effects and camera movements, creating a disorienting, nightmarish atmosphere. At the end of the 1960s, Pupi Avati* brought a personal approach to the Gothic and traditional horror themes in his directorial debut *Balsamus, l'uomo di Satana/Blood Relations* (1968) and *Thomas ... gli indemoniati/Thomas ... The Possessed* (1969), which he pursued with *La casa dalle finestre che ridono/The House with the Laughing Windows* (1976) and especially *Zeder/Revenge of the Dead* (1983). The theme of the 'returning dead' is dealt with within the framework of the macabre country fable, immersed in blood and grotesque humour. Through the 1970s the most prolific exponent of the genre was Lucio Fulci, whom many consider the inventor of Italian-style 'gore'. Fulci specialised in fantasy horror, beginning with *Non si sevizia un paperino* (1972) and *Sette note in nero/Murder to the Tune of the Seven* (1977). Defined as the 'poet of the macabre' by French critics and extolled by magazines such as the American *Fangoria*, the unusual Fulci favours menace, repulsion and delirious visionary horrors, reworked from American horror films (the living dead, cursed houses, the buried alive, demonic possession). Films such as *Zombi 2/Zombi Flesh Eaters* (1979), *Paura nella città dei morti viventi/Fear* (1980), *Il gatto nero/Black Cat* (1981), *Quella villa accanto al cimitero/The House on the Edge of the Cemetery* (1981), *L'aldilà* (1981), *Lo squartatore di New York/New York Ripper* (1982), *L'occhio del male/Manhattan Baby* (1983), *Murderock uccide a passi di danza/Murderock* (1984) and *Il miele del diavolo* (1986) exemplify Fulci's approach to the genre, executed with Corman-style limited budgets and fast shooting, with a loyal and well-trained crew. Some are filmed on location in the US with dialogue in English for rapid foreign distribution.

Dario Argento's* *Suspiria* (1977) brought a radical change to Italian horror film. The imaginary finally breaks free from narrative and

Argento allows vision to take priority, in a kaleidoscope of glowing images which reflect an original poetry of the horrific. New directors in the genre have tended to take their cue from him. They include Bava's son Lamberto Bava, with *Macabro/Macabre* (1980), *Shark-Rosso nell'oceano* (1984), *Demoni/Demons* (1985) and *Demoni 2* (1986); the promising young Michele Soavi (*Deliria*, 1987; *La chiesa/The Church*, 1989; *La setta/The Sect*, 1991); and lesser lights such as Gianfranco Giagni (*Il nido del ragno*, 1988), Marcello Avallone (*Spettri/Specters*, 1987) and Alessandro Capone (*Streghe/Witch Story*, 1989). GVo

ITALIAN POLITICAL CINEMA (1960–94)

In the 1960s and the 1970s, by virtue of its creative vitality and variety, Italian cinema was able to compete with Hollywood productions, both at a national and a European level. The political film in particular, although sometimes derivative of Hollywood action cinema, reached the distinctiveness of a real genre. Its origins can be traced to the first Mafia movies, such as Pietro Germi's* *In nome della legge/In the Name of the Law* (1949). Since then, almost two hundred others have been made, including the television serial *La piovra/The Octopus*, started in 1983 and reaching a peak of popular success with its fifth series in 1991.

Italian cinema dealing with the Mafia is like a house with a grand reception room on the first floor, a ground floor and a bargain basement packed with comedies, parodies, cheap detective movies, etc. The most renowned tenant of the first floor is Francesco Rosi* with his masterpiece *Salvatore Giuliano* (1962), as well as *Cadaveri eccellenti/Illustrious Corpses* (1975), adapted from Leonardo Sciascia's novel *Il contesto*. With *Il caso Mattei/The Mattei Affair* (1972), *Lucky Luciano* (1973) and *Dimenticare Palermo/To Forget Palermo* (1990), Rosi presented the two Mafias (Italian and North American) as one thing ('*Cosa Nostra*'), reaching a radically pessimistic and ultimately questionable conclusion: to be a Sicilian is not just an accident of birth but an inescapable question of fate. On the same grand first floor we find Elio Petri*, the first to bring Sciascia to the screen with *A ciascuno il suo/To Each His Own* (1967), Damiano Damiani, who directed Sciascia's *Il giorno della civetta/Mafia* (1968), and Paolo and Vittorio Taviani*, who started with *Un uomo da bruciare/A Man for Burning* (1962, co-dir. Valentino Orsini), the story of a Sicilian trade unionist (Gian Maria Volonté*, the key actor of the whole genre) murdered by the Mafia. With Damiani, however, and numerous other Mafia films (such as *Perché si uccide un magistrato*, 1975, and *Pizza Connection*, 1985) and the first series of *La piovra*, we move down to the ground floor. Its original tenant was Alberto Lattuada*, whose black comedy *Il mafioso* (1962), starring an irresistible Alberto Sordi*, had one fatal flaw: the Mafia is ubiquitous, so that, as Sciascia wrote, 'the spectator is no longer led to think what is the Mafia, but rather what is not the Mafia'. The ground floor is also occupied by Florestano Vancini's *La *violenza: quinto potere/Violence: Fifth Power* (1972) and Giuseppe Ferrara's *Il sasso in bocca* (1970), a skilful 'faction' about the history of the Mafia after 1945 and its connections with the ruling political class. In 1984 Ferrara appeared to slide down to the basement with *Cento giorni a Palermo/A Hundred Days in Palermo* and, ten years later, *Giovanni Falcone* (1993). Still on the ground floor, a special place is held by Pasquale Squitieri: *Camorra* (1972), *I Guappi/Blood Brothers* (1974), and his best film, *Il prefetto di ferro* (1977). The continued power of the Mafia in Sicily and southern Italy means that younger Italian directors are also attracted to the topic; for example Emidio Greco with *Una storia semplice/A Simple Story* (1991) and Ricky Tognazzi with *La scorta* (1993).

Italian political cinema divides into four thematic groups: 1) Fascism and the Resistance; 2) the police, the judiciary, and Christian Democrat power; 3) class struggle and revolutionary utopias; 4) 1970s student revolts and terrorism. Attempts have also been made to deal with Third World and anti-imperialist issues, producing 'Spaghetti Western'-like movies [> ITALIAN WESTERNS] such as Damiani's *Quien sabe?/A Bullet for the General* (1966), Carlo Lizzani's* *Requiescant* (1967), Sergio Corbucci's *Il mercenario/A Professional Gun* (1968), and others. Gillo Pontecorvo's* *La battaglia di Algeri/The Battle of Algiers* (1966) and Giuliano Montaldo's *Sacco e Vanzetti/Sacco and Vanzetti* (1970) are other interesting examples. The first – and largest – group reached a high point with Bernardo Bertolucci's* *Il conformista/The Conformist* (1970) and the Tavianis' *La notte di San Lorenzo/The Night of San Lorenzo* (1982). It also includes, among others, Ettore Scola's* *Una giornata particolare/A Special Day* (1977), Gianni Puccini's *I sette fratelli Cervi* (1968), Giuliano Montaldo's *L'Agnese va a morire/And Agnes Chose to Die* (1976), and four documentaries on Mussolini (mainly based on the newsreels of the Istituto LUCE*). Ideologically, they range from the ambiguous right (Squitieri's *Claretta*, 1984), to the intransigent left (Pier Paolo Pasolini's* *Salò o le 120 giornate di Sodoma/Salò*, 1975). The most significant film in the second group is Petri's *Indagine su un cittadino al di sopra di ogni sospetto/Investigation of a Citizen Above Suspicion* (1969), scripted by Ugo Pirro*, who, together with Franco Solinas*, was at that time Italy's most politically committed scriptwriter. In the third group we find Francesco Maselli's* *Lettera aperta a un giornale della sera* (1970), about the crisis of left intellectuals; *Il sospetto* (1975), about the Italian Communist Party under Fascism; and Petri's *La classe operaia va in paradiso/Lulu the Tool* (1971). The fourth group includes a dozen or so films, including Rosi's *Tre fratelli/Three Brothers* (1981), although the best examples come from younger directors like Gianni Amelio* (*Colpire al cuore/Straight to the Heart*, 1983), Marco Tullio Giordana (*Maledetti vi amerò*, 1980), and Giuseppe Bertolucci (*Segreti segreti*, 1984). GVo

ITALIAN WESTERNS

Italian genre. The Italian Western, known in its home country as *'Western all'italiana'* but popularly (and slightly disparagingly) referred to abroad as the 'Spaghetti Western', emerged as a world phenomenon with the release of Sergio Leone's* *Per un pugno di dollari/A Fistful of Dollars* in 1964. Leone's film did not spring from nowhere. The preceding years had seen the making of a number of German-Yugoslav Westerns based on the popular novels of Karl May and some twenty Italian-French-Spanish co-productions in the Western genre. Between the mid-1960s and 1978, no fewer than 400 Italian Westerns (mostly co-produced) were made, involving various permutations of the formula, though as the 1970s wore on the genre went into decline. The Italian Western emerged out of the ashes of the peplum*, in which many of its first practitioners – Sergio Corbucci, Riccardo Freda*, Mario Bava* and others, including Leone himself – were trained. The crews, too, were often the same, many having also formed second units for American spectaculars shot in Rome or in Spain in the 1950s. Locations were mostly Spain (especially Almeria), but later Italy, Yugoslavia and Israel, with a brief foray into Monument Valley for Leone's *C'era una volta il West/Once Upon a Time in the West* (1968).

The Italian Western is both the most original and the most parasitic genre to emerge in Italy in the 1960s. It began as a counterfeit, not only an imitation of the foremost American genre, but under the pretence of being American, with directors, actors and technicians credited with English pseudonyms. It was bottom-drawer cinema, aimed at small-town audiences and churned out by small and medium-sized production companies, of which Alberto Grimaldi's PEA (which later used its profits to move upmarket) was the most prominent. From the beginning the genre was marked by violence, aggressivity and a fierce and hyperbolic element of male sado-masochism, pushed to the edges of parody but always with an eye to the market. Mannered and rootless, the Italian Western owed its success to its ability to function as pure, abstract, violent spectacle accessible to audiences regardless of nationality or culture, and it is no accident that it was the only form of Italian popular cinema to encounter no barriers to international diffusion. Gradually, there emerged something resembling the Western, though it was never quite *the* Western but rather a no-man's-land form of adventure. Five basic variations can be noted. First and most famous is the mannerist style pioneered in Leone's 'dollars' trilogy – *Per un pugno di dollari, Per qualche dollaro in più/For a Few Dollars More* (1965) and *Il buono, il brutto e il cattivo/The Good, the Bad and the Ugly* (1966) – and continued in films ranging from Tonino Valerii's *I giorni dell'ira/Days of Wrath* (1967) to Giulio Questi's off-the-wall *Se sei vivo, spara/If You Live, Shoot* (1967). Second, the picaresque, as exemplified by the 'Ringo' cycle starring Giuliano Gemma and directed by Duccio Tessari (such as *Una pistola per Ringo/A Pistol for*

Ringo and *Il ritorno di Ringo/The Return of Ringo*, both 1965), but also by Michele Lupo's *Arizona Colt* (1967). Third is the 'political' Western, with its ideological reading of the West and of a backward, Third-Worldist Mexico, from Damiano Damiani's *Quién sabe?/A Bullet for the General* (1967) to Carlo Lizzani's* *Requiescant* (1967, with Lou Castel and Pier Paolo Pasolini*), Sergio Corbucci's *Il mercenario/A Professional Gun* (1968) and Giulio Petroni's *Tepepa/Blood and Guns* (1969). Fourth is the macabre-funereal mode of the Sartana and Django series. And fifth are the lighter, neo-Fordian Westerns beginning with Franco Giraldi's *7 pistole per i MacGregor/Seven Guns for the MacGregors* (1966) and *Sugar Colt* (1967), and leading to the comedy cycle of the Terence Hill (Mario Girotti)/Bud Spencer (Carlo Pedersoli)/E. B. Clucher (Enzo Barboni) trio initiated by *Lo chiamavano Trinità/They Call Me Trinity* (1970).

So central was the Western to the Italian cinema of those years that it involved both specialists in popular genres and more 'serious' artists: scriptwriters Age* and Scarpelli*, Ugo Pirro*, Franco Solinas* and Franco Arcalli; writers like Ennio Flaiano*; established directors such as Tinto Brass and Gianni Puccini; emerging directors including Bernardo Bertolucci*, Gianni Amelio* and Dario Argento*; and, last but not least, composers of whom the best known is Ennio Morricone*. It also enlisted distinguished actors from outside Italy: Fernando Rey, Jean-Louis Trintignant, Yul Brynner, Charles Bronson, even Orson Welles. It made stars of Clint Eastwood, Gian Maria Volonté* and Klaus Kinski. But its own special stars were Giuliano Gemma ('Ringo'), Lee Van Cleef, Tomas Milian, Franco Nero ('Django') and the Terence Hill/Bud Spencer duo of the 'Trinity' films. With these last, the violent excesses of the classic Italian Western softened into harmless knockabout for family audiences. After 1973 the genre ran out of steam, but continued to roll on its own inertia. It was a unique example of (almost) an entire film industry turned over to the production of a single genre. It was an original cinema, with distinct and personal characteristics, which produced at least one great *auteur* in the form of Sergio Leone. GVo

L

LATTUADA, Alberto   Milan 1914

Italian director. Son of the musician Felice Lattuada, Alberto grew up in the lively cultural scene of 1920s Milan. He started as a photographer (publishing an album, *L'Occhio quadrato*, in 1941), as art critic for Fascist magazines such as *Corrente* (which was often critical of Fascism) and eventually as co-founder in 1940 (with Mario Ferreri and Luigi Comencini*) of the Cineteca Italiana, the Milan film archive. After a brief period as scriptwriter for Mario Soldati* (*Piccolo mondo antico/Old-Fashioned World*, 1941) and Ferdinando Maria Poggioli (*Sissignora*, 1942), he made his directorial debut with *Giacomo l'idealista* (1942), which initiated his reputation as a 'literary' director, with a precisely observant, at times harsh style. A number of his films were indeed based on literature: *Il mulino del Po/The Mill on the Po* (1949) on Bachelli, *Il delitto di Giovanni Episcopo/Flesh Will Surrender* (1947) on D'Annunzio, *La lupa/The She-Wolf* (1953) on Giovanni Verga, *Lettere di una novizia/Rita* (1960) on Guido Piovene, and *Don Giovanni in Sicilia* (1967) on Vitaliano Brancati. Lattuada admired Russian film-makers and writers, from whom he drew his humiliated, oppressed characters and densely pathetic, grotesque situations: for instance *Il cappotto/The Overcoat* (1952, from Gogol) and *La steppa/The Steppe* (1962, from Chekhov). Lattuada was an eclectic film-maker, but all his films, including the neo-realistic* and original *Il bandito* (1946) and *Senza pietà/Without Pity* (1948), are robustly crafted and professionally acted; he had a gift for spotting talented actresses – Giulietta Masina*, Carla Del Poggio* (later to become his wife), Silvana Mangano* and Nastassja Kinski among others. Another constant element of his work is a strong erotic and romantic vein (*La spiaggia/The Beach*, 1954; *Guendalina*, 1957; *La cicala*, 1980) and in particular relationships between young women and older men (*Le farò da padre/Bambina*, 1974). He increasingly developed a streak of bitter irony which informs two of the best-known Italian comedies, *Il mafioso* (1962) and *Venga a prendere il caffè … da noi/Come Have Coffee With Us* (1970), starring an unforgettable Ugo Tognazzi*. One the few professionals of the mid-1950s capable of adapting to technical and social change, Lattuada directed an Emmy award-winning, six-hour television film, *Cristoforo Colombo/Christopher Columbus* (1984). GVo

Other Films Include: *La freccia nel fianco* (1943–45); *La nostra guerra* (1945, doc.); *Luci del varietà/Variety Lights* (1950, co-dir. Fellini*); *Anna* (1951); *L'amore in città* (1953, ep. *Gli italiani si voltano*); *Scuola elementare* (1955); *La tempesta/The Tempest* (1958); *I dolci inganni/ Les adolescents/Sweet Deceptions* (1960); *L'imprevisto/L'imprévu* (1961); *La mandragola* (1965); *Matchless* (1967); *Fräulein Doktor* (1968); *L'amica* (1969); *Bianco, rosso e …/White Sister* (1972); *Sono stato io/I Did It* (1973); *Cuore di cane* (1975); *Oh, Serafina!* (1976); *Così come sei/Stay as You Are* (1978); *Una spina nel cuore* (1985); *Due fratelli* (1988, TV).

LEONE, Sergio

Italian director, the son of Roberto Roberti, a famous silent director (whose name Leone adapted as a pseudonym – Bob Robertson – for his first Western). Leone had a long apprenticeship as assistant director on a total of fifty-six films (including American super-productions filmed in Italy, such as *Ben-Hur*, 1959) and eventually made his debut with an unsigned peplum*, *Gli ultimi giorni di Pompei/The Last Days of Pompeii* (1959), which Mario Bonnard had abandoned for health reasons. Success came quickly, with *Il colosso di Rodi/The Colossus of Rhodes* (1961), another spectacular peplum, in which all is eventually resolved in the final catastrophe. After acting once again as a second unit director in *Sodoma e Gomorra/Sodom and Gomorrah* (1961, dir. Robert Aldrich), Leone achieved worldwide success with his 'dollar trilogy' – *Per un pugno di dollari/A Fistful of Dollars* (1964), *Per qualche dollaro in più/For a Few Dollars More* (1965) and *Il buono, il brutto e il cattivo/The Good, The Bad and the Ugly* (1966) – which inaugurated the genre of the Italian Western* (the so-called 'Spaghetti' Western), and brought instant fame to actors such as Clint Eastwood, Lee Van Cleef and Gian Maria Volonté*. The trilogy is highly mannerist (with rituals, expanded rhythms, majestic scenery, technical and linguistic exhibitionism), rich in imitations rather than citations and amplified by Ennio Morricone's* music, but it is also full of assertive vitality. *C'era una volta il West/Once Upon a Time in the West* (1968), written in conjunction with Bernardo Bertolucci* and Dario Argento*, shot no longer in Spain but in John Ford's Monument Valley, and starring Henry Fonda, attempted to produce an imaginary and mythical synthesis of the American frontier. *Giù la testa/A Fistful of Dynamite/Duck You Sucker!* (1971) is an anarchic and wittily ideological re-examination of the theme of traitors and heroes. Leone succeeded in creating a world that is both similar to the Western, yet is not the Western, a world with obscure, 'universal' roots, but which is also an exalted expression of love for, and obsession with, the cinema. When Leone returned to film-making, after more than a decade spent, among other things, launching the careers of Tonino Valerii and Carlo Verdone and directing memorable advertisements, the result was *C'era una volta in America/Once Upon a Time in America* (1983), a personal and unorthodox revisiting of the myths and archetypes of American cinema through a violent and eccentric gangster saga. GVo

LIZZANI, Carlo
Rome 1922

Italian director. Formerly a militant critic (and early theoretician of neo-realism*), and a collaborator on early neo-realist films by Aldo Vergano, Giuseppe De Santis*, Alberto Lattuada* and Roberto Rossellini*, Lizzani began his directing career with a documentary on southern Italy, followed by two films about the Resistance, *Achtung banditi!* (1951, starring Gina Lollobrigida*) and *Cronache di poveri amanti/Stories of Poor Lovers* (1954), both infused with a sincere populism. Thereafter he moved eclectically but skilfully across a variety of genres, from historical drama (*Il processo di Verona/The Verona Trial*, 1962), to Italian ('Spaghetti') Western* (*Requiescant*, 1967), comedy of manners, and literary adaptation (*Fontamara*, 1980). His best films, though, were probably his popular films inspired by journalistic *faits divers*, such as *Svegliati e uccidi/Wake up and Kill* (1966, under the pseudonym of Lee W. Beaver) and *Banditi a Milano/The Violent Four* (1968). Lizzani wrote a well-known survey of Italian cinema, *Il cinema italiano*, in 1953 and was head of the Venice film festival from 1979 to 1982. He directed *Celluloide* in 1995. GVo

LOLLOBRIGIDA, Gina   Rome 1927

Italian actress. Lollobrigida's film career began in the American-style beauty pageants that were the rage in Italy in the immediate postwar years. Though she failed to win the titles of Miss Italy, or even Miss Rome, she obtained parts in Italian films and attracted the attention of American producer Howard Hughes, who offered her a contract in Hollywood (though no film). She soon returned to Rome, in 1951, and embarked on a successful career, earning international recognition for her performances in such Franco-Italian 'tradition of quality' co-productions as Christian-Jaque's *Fanfan la Tulipe* (1952) and René Clair's *Les Belles de nuit* (1952) – both co-starring Gérard Philipe – and in Jean Delannoy's *Notre-Dame de Paris/The Hunchback of Notre Dame* (1956). At the end of Alessandro Blasetti's* episode *Il processo di Frine* in *Altri tempi/Infidelity* (1952), the concluding speech of the defence attorney (Vittorio De Sica*) gave rise to the witty designation that would come to signify a whole class of voluptuous young Italian starlets: 'If we absolve the *minorati psichici* (psychically under-endowed), why not the *maggiorate fisiche* (physically amply endowed)?' Lollobrigida's most memorable role was that of La Bersagliera – a feisty, dirt-poor, independent-minded young woman whose body may personify that of the impoverished rural South itself, but who manages to live happily ever after, in Luigi Comencini's* 'rose-tinted' realist diptych *Pane, amore, e fantasia/Bread, Love and Dreams* (1953) and *Pane, amore e gelosia/Bread, Love and Jealousy/Frisky* (1954) (both featuring De Sica as the slightly lecherous but ultimately good-hearted local police chief), two key precursors of *commedia all'italiana*. For a brief period, Lollobrigida was able to transcend her lightweight, sexy-populist persona in films which revealed some depth of dramatic talent, including Carlo Lizzani's* *Achtung banditi!* (1951) and two filmic adaptations of Moravia novels: Mario Soldati's* *La provinciale/The Wayward Wife* (1953) and Luigi Zampa's* *La romana* (1954). Aspiring to international recognition as a serious actress, Lollobrigida sought more prestigious roles as a *femme fatale*, even subsidising some productions. The titles speak eloquently of her ambitions: *La donna più bella del mondo/Beautiful but Dangerous* (1955), *Solomon and Sheba* (1959, dir. King Vidor; US), and *Vénus Impériale/Imperial Venus* (1962, dir. Jean Delannoy; Fr.).

Together with Sophia Loren*, Silvana Mangano*, Marisa Allasio and Silvana Pampanini*, Lollobrigida represented a *divismo** (stardom) of a totally physical sort. The discourse of the *maggiorate fisiche* has, as its sole sign and referent, the body itself – eloquent testimony to Italy's emergence from the devastations of war and entrance into the well-nourished arena of advanced consumer society. MMa

LOREN, Sophia
Sofia Scicolone; Rome 1934

Italian actress. Born in Rome but raised in Pozzuoli near Naples, Sophia Loren rose to stardom as one of the *maggiorate fisiche* (physically amply endowed women), along with others such as Gina Lollobrigida* and Silvana Mangano*. She soon transcended this typecasting, however, to become a fine actress and the apotheosis of idealised Italian womanhood.

Starting as an extra in Mervyn LeRoy's *Quo Vadis* (1951), Loren appeared in a series of B-movies until discovered by producer Carlo Ponti*, who married her and set about developing, safeguarding and marketing her image – which he has continued to do throughout her career. Typical of her early performances under his tutelage were her role as 'La pizzaiola' in Vittorio De Sica's* episode film *L'oro di Napoli/The Gold of Naples* (1954), and her starring role in Mario Soldati's* *La donna del fiume/Woman of the River* (1955). In 1956, a contract with producer/director Stanley Kramer took her to Hollywood where she performed in a number of films which exploited not only her beauty, but also her dramatic talent and considerable charisma. She co-starred with Cary Grant in Kramer's *The Pride and the Passion* (1957), with Alan Ladd in Jean Negulesco's *Boy on a Dolphin* (1957), with Anthony Perkins in Delbert Mann's *Desire Under the Elms* (1958), and with William Holden in Carol Reed's *The Key* (1958). Back in Italy, she resumed her collaboration with De Sica with an Oscar-winning performance as the urbanised peasant Cesira whose strength enables her and her daughter to survive wartime privation and gang rape in an adaptation of Moravia's novel *La ciociara/Two Women* (1960). Her comic talents came to the fore playing opposite Marcello Mastroianni* in two other De Sica films: in the first episode of *Ieri, oggi, domani/Yesterday, Today and Tomorrow* (1963), she is a Neapolitan who continually becomes pregnant to avoid imprisonment for selling black-market cigarettes, and in *Matrimonio all'italiana/Marriage – Italian Style* (1964) she plays a prostitute who finally gets her rich lover to marry her and legitimise their three sons.

In the 1970s and 1980s she allowed her career to slow down, acting

only in a few international productions such as De Sica's last film, *Il vi-
aggio/The Journey* (1974). Ettore Scola's* *Una giornata particolare/A
Special Day* (1977), set in Mussolini's Rome, has both her and
Mastroianni act against type: she as a frumpish middle-aged housewife
and he as a homosexual anti-Fascist intellectual. Now living in
Switzerland, she emerged from semi-retirement in 1994 to play oppo-
site Mastroianni in Robert Altman's *Prêt-à-porter*, and she and
Mastroianni were jointly chosen in 1993 to present the Oscar for
Lifetime Achievement to Federico Fellini* – who had never directed
her in a film. MMa

LUCE

Italian institution. The Istituto Nazionale LUCE (acronym for
L'Unione Cinematografica Educativa) was the earliest of the para-
state agencies created under Fascism. Its purpose was to produce
newsreels and documentaries and to monitor the production and exhibition of feature films, both foreign and domestic. LUCE was set up in
1924–25 out of a private association for the development of cinema as
a form of 'popular education'. Until 1943, it served as the most conspicuous presence of the Fascist government in film production, legislation and policy, and produced most of the official state newsreels and
documentaries. From 1926, LUCE productions were required to be
shown in all Italian cinemas, and by 1927 all other newsreels were prohibited. Throughout the 1930s, LUCE was headed by the outspoken
Luigi Freddi*. Initially located in Rome, LUCE was moved in 1940 to
its present location amid the newly constructed cinema complex on the
outskirts of Rome, next to Cinecittà* and the Centro Sperimentale*.
After World War II, the Institute's mission changed somewhat, but it
continues to be a centre for the support and archival maintenance of
Italy's national film culture. JHa

LUX

Italian production company. In 1934 Riccardo Gualino (1879–1961)
founded in Turin the Compagnia Italiana Cinematografica Lux, which
for thirty years stood out for its financial rigour and efficient organisation as well as for the cultural and technical quality of its productions.
Gualino was an efficient businessman as well as a modern art connois-
seur and promoter of avant-garde theatre. An anti-Fascist, he was involved in 1931 in an obscure financial scandal and interned by
Mussolini. From 1935 to 1938 Lux did nothing but distribute foreign
movies and it was not until 1941 that it started producing its own films
(twenty-two in 1943–45) by directors such as Alessandro Blasetti* (*La
corona di ferro/The Iron Crown*, 1941), Mario Camerini* (*I promessi
sposi/The Spirit and the Flesh*, 1941), Goffredo Alessandrini*, Mario

Soldati*, Raffaello Matarazzo*, Alberto Lattuada* and Renato Castellani*. At the end of the war, Lux supported neo-realism* by producing Giuseppe De Santis'* *Caccia tragica/Tragic Hunt* (1947) and *Riso amaro/Bitter Rice* (1949), Lattuada's *Il bandito* (1946) and *Senza pietà/Without Pity* (1948), Luigi Zampa's* *Vivere in pace/To Live in Peace* (1946) and *L'onorevole Angelina/Angelina* (1947), as well as films by Soldati, Luigi Comencini* and Pietro Germi*. At the same time it also produced popular films such as Riccardo Freda's* *I miserabili/Les Misérables* (1947) and Lattuada's *Anna* (1951). Gualino's novel production system was to choose and finance a film, and then either entrust its making to his executive producers or put it out on 'fixed-price contract' to a co-production company. Lux's activity reached its peak in 1954 with Luchino Visconti's* *Senso*, and ended with Mario Monicelli's* *I compagni/The Strikers* (1963). In 1964 it was acquired (along with other companies) by the Rovelli SIR chemicals group. Over thirty years it had produced 170 films and distributed 300, and had been involved, through associate companies, in productions worldwide. GVo

M

MACARIO, Erminio

Turin 1902–80

Italian actor. From the 1930s to his death, Macario was one of the kings of variety shows, famous for his ingenuous humour, often in dialect, and for his '*donnine*' (little women) comperes such as Wanda Osiris. With his wide eyes, kiss-curl over his forehead, Harry Langdon-like face and short stature, he evoked figures such as the innocent, 'lunar' Pierrot of *commedia dell'arte*. '*Lo vedi come sei?*' ('*Can't you see what you're doing?*') was his disarmed and disarming lullaby as well as the title of one of his best-known films, made in 1939 by Mario Mattoli, the director who understood Macario's talent better than anyone. After his debut in 1933 in the mediocre *Aria di paese*, Macario became one of the most popular comic actors of 1930s and 1940s Italian cinema, alongside Totò*, Aldo Fabrizi* and Renato Rascel. His surrealist absent-mindedness is fully represented in *Imputato, alzatevi!* (1939), a sort of *Hellzapoppin*, directed with craftsman-like precision by Mattoli and written by a team of humorists from the weekly publication *Il Bertoldo*. After the war, Macario added an element of pathos to his humour in response to the difficult period of reconstruction which Italy was going through, and gained box-office success with three films by Carlo Borghesio: *Come persi la guerra/How I Lost the* *war* (1947), *L'eroe della strada/Street Hero* (1948) and *Come scopersi l'America/How I Discovered America* (1949). Later, Macario returned to 'lowbrow' films, relying mostly on jokes, sketches and *double entendre*, frequently working with actors such as 'straight man' Carlo Campanini, Totò (for example in *Lo smemorato di Collegno*, 1962), Peppino De Filippo* and Nino Taranto. In these productions Macario once again brilliantly embodied the bewildered vagabond. Mario Soldati's* *Italia piccola* (1957) was, however, a favourite with those critics who look for the serious, 'human' side in the comic actor. GVo

MACISTE

Italian superhero. Maciste was the first, the most famous, and the most enduring in a cadre of 'muscle men' who appeared in mainstream Italian cinema virtually since its inception. Maciste was first performed by Bartolomeo Pagano, a stocky Genovese dockworker, in Giovanni Pastrone's* *Cabiria* (1914). In this historical film, set roughly on the eve of the Carthaginian wars, Pagano's Maciste accompanies a Roman patrician (Fulvio) on a mission to save a young girl who has been abducted and held captive by Numidians for their sacrificial rituals. He plays the brawn to the patrician's brain, appears shirtless throughout much of the film, and is involved in numerous physical challenges from man, beast and other forces. Largely as a result of the popularity of his character in *Cabiria*, Pagano was contracted by Pastrone to make *Maciste* in 1915 (though he had made a brief appearance as a corpulent policeman in one of the *Cretinetti** comedies). *Maciste* inaugurated a series in which the muscular hero is tested by various spectacular situations and through which the mask of Maciste became fused with the actor Pagano. Pagano's Maciste films include *Maciste alpino/Maciste in the Alpine Regiment* (1916), *Maciste atleta/Maciste the Athlete* (1918), *Maciste innamorato/Maciste in Love* (1920), a Maciste trilogy in 1920 (*Maciste contro la morte/Maciste Against Death, Il viaggio di Maciste/Maciste's Journey, Il testamento di Maciste/Maciste's Testament*), *Maciste in vacanza/Maciste on Holiday* (1921), *Maciste imperatore/Maciste Emperor* (1924) and *Maciste all'inferno/Maciste in Hell* (1926). The Maciste films opened the way for other superheroes, many with names from classical mythology, who appeared in their own film series. The most popular were Luciano Albertini's Sansone (Samson), who occasionally appeared with his wife Linda Albertini (as Sansonetta), Carlo Aldini's Ajax, Domenico Gambino's Saetta, and Alfredo Boccolini's Galaor. Most of their films were produced in Turin, and by the 1920s Albertini and Gambino had formed their own production companies (Albertini Films and Saetta Productions, respectively).

The figure of Maciste resurfaced in Italian cinema during the 1950s with the revival of the 'muscle man' epic or peplum*, performed by actors such as Kirk Morris, Alan Steel, Reg Lewis, Ed Fury, Mark Forrest and Reg Park. JHa

MAGNANI, Anna   Rome 1908–73

Italian actress. Anna Magnani, popularly known in Italy as Nannarella, was born in Rome (and not in Alexandria, as she herself claimed and is reported in many reference works), daughter of Marina Magnani and an unknown father. She began as a theatre actress in 1929, and later, in 1969, returned to the stage for *La lupa/The She-Wolf* by Giovanni Verga. She became a revue artiste from 1934, and worked with Totò* during the war. In 1935 she had married the director Goffredo Alessandrini*, but the marriage was a failure. By the time it was annulled in 1950, she had had a child (who died of polio) by the actor Massimo Serato* and entered into a relationship with Roberto Rossellini* (who then deserted her for Ingrid Bergman*). She began her film career in 1934, with bit parts, and her first success was in Vittorio De Sica's* *Teresa Venerdì* in 1941. Probably the greatest of her triumphs was Rossellini's *Roma città aperta/Rome Open City* (1945), in which she became the tragic icon of Italy's suffering during the war and German occupation, but also of its renewal, in cinema and beyond.

Magnani was the greatest and deservedly the most popular film actress in Italy, a character worthy of the great Roman dialect poet G. G. Belli. Few figures in cinema since Garbo have so powerfully overlaid personality and acting. But unlike Garbo, Magnani was an actress first and a star second. And, while Garbo embodied a middle-class myth, Magnani was the incarnation of popular passion. Her loyalty to this character remained constant, even in her most mainstream films and those in which she was called upon to play unfamiliar parts. She made four films in Hollywood – one of which, *The Rose Tattoo* (1955), won her an Oscar. She played Anita Garibaldi in *Camicie rosse/Red Shirts* (1952), directed by her ex-husband Alessandrini and finished by Franco Rossi. She was a memorable Perichole in Jean Renoir's *La carrozza d'oro/Le Carrosse d'or/The Golden Coach* (1953) and she performed a stunning monologue in *Una voce umana* (based on Jean Cocteau's play *La Voix humaine*) in Rossellini's *L'amore* (1948). Though she was a naturalistic actress, her acting was based on more than mere instinct. According to Renato Castellani*, who directed her in *Nella città l'inferno/... And the Wild, Wild Women* (1958), Nannarella's technique was so refined that she transcended technique altogether. Two of her best performances vouch for this – in Luchino Visconti's* *Bellissima* (1951) and in Pier Paolo Pasolini's* *Mamma Roma* (1962) – as do the numerous awards she received. The secret of her immense popularity was that she was passionate but never sentimental. Her energy and lust for life were acknowledged when her coffin was carried out of the Santa Maria della Minerva church in Rome, two days after her death on 26 September 1973, and an all-engulfing roar rose up from the waiting crowd, from a sustained, frenetic, extraordinary round of applause. MMo

Other Films Include: *Davanti a lui tremava tutta Roma/Tosca, Il bandito* (1946); *Siamo donne/We the Women* (1953, Visconti ep.); *Roma/ Fellini's Roma* (1972, cameo).

MANGANO, Silvana
Rome 1930 – Madrid 1989

Italian actress. After training as a dancer, working as a model and winning the Miss Rome contest, nineteen-year-old Silvano Mangano shot to international stardom with her performance in Giuseppe De Santis'* *Riso amaro/Bitter Rice* in 1949. Striding through the rice paddy with her thighs exposed she brought a breath of glamour and fleshy sensuality – welcome to some, disapproved of by others – to neo-realism*. She married the film's producer, Dino De Laurentiis*, who fostered her career throughout the 1950s, giving her starring roles in big international productions shot in Italy such as *Ulisse/Ulysses* (1954, dir. Mario Camerini*), *Jovanka e le altre/Five Branded Women* (1960, dir. Martin Ritt) and *Barabba/Barabbas* (1961, dir. Richard Fleischer). Shunning the limelight and economically secure, she let her career lapse in the mid-1960s, but re-emerged, thinner but still extraordinarily beautiful, as the showcase star of De Laurentiis' episode film production *Le streghe/The Witches* (1966) and was thereafter much sought after by art cinema directors such as Pier Paolo Pasolini* (*Edipo re/Oedipus Rex*, 1967; *Teorema/Theorem*, 1968) and Luchino Visconti* (*Morte a Venezia/Death in Venice*, 1971; *Gruppo di famiglia in un interno/Conversation Piece*, 1974). Her final starring role was in Nikita Mikhalkov's *Oci ciornie/Ochi chërnye/Dark Eyes* (1987). GNS

MARCHESI, Marcello
Milan 1912 –
S. Giovanni di Sinis 1977

and

METZ, Vittorio
Rome 1904–84

Italian scriptwriters and directors. Metz came from the theatre, worked for the weekly comic magazine *Marc'Aurelio*, and co-founded (in 1936) another magazine, *Bertoldo* – two publications which gave Marchesi and a whole generation of writers (Stefano Steno*, Age* and Scarpelli*, Frattini, Continenza and, above all, Fellini*) their training ground. He came into the cinema through scriptwriting (*Imputato, alzatevi!*, 1939) and, together with Marchesi, wrote *Il pirata sono io* (1940) and *Non me lo dire*, both starring the great comic Erminio Macario*. From then until 1968, Marchesi and Metz wrote

77

some sixty scripts for film comedies, often vehicles for such comic actors as Totò*, Macario, Renato Rascel, Walter Chiari* and Nino Manfredi. In addition, they themselves directed comedies, including *Sette ore di guai* (1951), *Mago per forza* (1952), *Lo sai che i papaveri* (1952), *Tizio, Caio e Sempronio* (1952), *Milano miliardaria* (1951) and others (on the whole less successful) in collaboration with Marino Girolami. They wrote variety shows (especially for Chiari) and musical comedies, and were prolific authors for radio and television – where Marchesi became a popular variety performer in the early 1960s. In addition, they turned out promotional slogans and hundreds of television advertisements.

Metz spent his entire career satirising political behaviour and ridiculing national fads. Marchesi published numerous books, including *Essere o malessere* (1962), *Il malloppo* (1972) and *Sette zie* (1977), in which he fully demonstrated his epigrammatic and disenchanted sense of humour. He drowned while swimming off the coast of Sardinia. He had written: 'The important thing is that death finds us alive.' MMo

MASELLI, Francesco   Rome 1930

Italian director. After studying at the Centro Sperimentale* in Rome and working as an assistant for Luigi Chiarini* and Michelangelo Antonioni* – collaborating on the script of *Cronaca di un amore/Story of a Love Affair* (1950) and *La signora senza camelie/The Lady Without Camelias* (1953) – Maselli made his directorial debut with Cesare Zavattini*, with whom he directed the episode *La storia di Caterina* in the documentary *Amore in città/Love in the City* (1953). A Communist, he told stories about bourgeois characters, analysing their problems (*Gli sbandati*, 1955), their failures (*I delfini*, 1960), their inability to make decisions (*Gli indifferenti/Time of Indifference*, 1964). He attempted, unsuccessfully, to break into comedy. In the wake of post-1968 political radicalisation, he was among the promoters of the Giornate del Cinema, the Venice* 'anti-festival' of 1973. As a filmmaker he increasingly chose more overtly political themes: the crisis of a group of Communist intellectuals in the interesting if moralistic *Lettera aperta a un giornale della sera* (1970), or the myth of the party and the exaltation of militant commitment in *Il sospetto* (1975); the latter, a thorough reconstruction of the Fascist period, remains his most rigorous film. Because of his activity as president of the ANAC (the National Association of Cinema Authors) and his alienation from new public tastes, Maselli directed few films in the 1980s. In the current apolitical climate, he decided to turn back to 'private' stories. However, with the exception of a movie exploring the world of working-class suburbs, *Storia d'amore* (1986), enlivened by the rich characterisation of the female lead (emerging actress Valeria Golino), his subsequent films have been disappointing. PM

Other Films Include: *La donna del giorno/The Doll That Took the Town* (1956); *Le italiane e l'amore* (1961, ep. *Le adolescenti/Latin Lovers*); *Fai in fretta a uccidermi … ho freddo* (1967); *Ruba al prossimo tuo/A Fine Pair* (1968); *Tre operai* (1980, TV); *Avventura di un fotografo* (1982, TV); *Codice privato* (1988); *Il segreto* (1990); *L'alba* (1990).

MASINA, Giulietta   Bologna 1920 – Rome 1994

Italian actress. Though an artist in her own right, Masina is best known for her work with Federico Fellini* (her husband), as his feminised alter ego, a human screen on to which the film-maker projected his spiritual anxieties and creative concerns.

While still a student, Masina worked in theatre, moving on to radio during the war. She enjoyed considerable success as the co-star of *Cico e Pallina*, a show about a young married couple, scripted by Fellini (writer and actress married in 1943). After the war, Masina turned exclusively to the cinema, starting with a small part in the Florentine episode of Roberto Rossellini's* *Paisà* (1946), followed by a role in Alberto Lattuada's* *Senza pietà/Without Pity* (1948) which revealed her dramatic abilities. *Luci del varietà/Lights of Variety/Variety Lights* (1950), about a troupe of itinerant entertainers, co-directed by Lattuada and Fellini, marked the beginning of Masina's function as Fellini's tutelary genius. From this point on, her physical plasticity and psychological delicacy were put to the service of Fellini's art. Gelsomina in *La strada* (1954) is a simple-minded waif whose preternatural sensitivity underscores her extraordinary gift for mime. The protagonist of *Le notti di Cabiria/Cabiria/Nights of Cabiria* (1957), prefigured in Masina's cameo in *Lo sceicco bianco/The White Sheik* (1952), is a spunky prostitute looking for redemption, which she finds neither in religion nor in romantic love, but in the world of performance and masquerade. A middle-aged, gentrified version of Gelsomina and Cabiria, the protagonist of *Giulietta degli spiriti/Juliet of the Spirits* (1965) comes to terms with her inner demons, in a feminised re-enactment of Fellini's artistic quest in *$8\frac{1}{2}$* (1963). Masina updated this character in *Ginger e Fred/Ginger and Fred* (1985), as the retired tap dancer/bourgeois matron reunited after forty years with her erstwhile dance partner and lover (Marcello Mastroianni*) for a Christmas television special.

Masina did work with other directors, including Rossellini in *Europa '51* (1952), Eduardo De Filippo* in *Fortunella* (1958), Renato Castellani* in *Nella città l'inferno/… And the Wild, Wild Women* (1958), Lina Wertmüller* in *Non stuzzicate la zanzara/Don't Tease the Mosquito* (1967), the British film-maker Bryan Forbes* in his adaptation of Giraudoux's *La Folle de Chaillot/The Madwoman of Chaillot* (1969), the Slovak Juraj Jakubisko in the children's film *Perinbaba/Frau Holle/Mother Carey* (1985), and in France with Jean-Louis

Bertuccelli in *Aujourd'hui peut-être* (1991). She appeared extensively on television, performing with great success in Tullio Pinelli's *Eleanora* (1972). With a physical expressivity reminiscent of Chaplin and Keaton, and a voice capable of conveying great ranges of emotion, Masina made an inestimable contribution to both the carnivalised exterior and the deeply serious interior of Fellini's film-making. MMa

MASTROIANNI, Marcello   Fontana Liri 1923

Italian actor. In a varied and protean career spanning nearly five decades, during which he has starred in films by Federico Fellini*, Luchino Visconti*, Michelangelo Antonioni*, Vittorio De Sica* and others, Mastroianni has come to personify the entire evolution of post-war Italian cinema. His versatility, as both dramatic and comic actor, has produced a complex persona, a cross between Latin lover and tormented modern man.

As an amateur actor after the war, he joined Visconti's theatrical company and made an early screen appearance in Riccardo Freda's* *I miserabili/Les Misérables* (1947). He drew attention to himself in a series of 'rose-tinted realist' films by Luciano Emmer*, beginning with *Una domenica d'agosto/Sunday in August* (1950), and went on to perform serious roles in Carlo Lizzani's* *Cronache di poveri amanti/ Stories of Poor Lovers* (1954) and Visconti's *Le notti bianche/White Nights* (1957). He rose to international stardom in two Fellini films, as the failed but idealistic journalist Marcello in *La dolce vita* (1960), and the film director Guido in $8\frac{1}{2}$ (1963). In the meantime he played a tormented intellectual in Antonioni's *La notte/The Night* (1961) and the scathingly satirical part of Baron Fefé Cefalù in Pietro Germi's* classic comedy, *Divorzio all'italiana/Divorce – Italian Style* (1961), and began a partnership with Sophia Loren* with two De Sica comedies, *Ieri, oggi, domani/Yesterday, Today and Tomorrow* (1963) and *Matrimonio all'italiana/Marriage – Italian Style* (1964). In the 1970s and 1980s his repertory expanded even further. The Taviani* brothers' *Allonsanfan* (1974) and Elio Petri's* *Todo modo* (1976) brought political cinema within his range [> ITALIAN POLITICAL CINEMA], and Ettore Scola* cast him in many memorable roles, most notably in *Una giornata particolare/A Special Day* (1977), where he plays Gabriele, an anti-Fascist homosexual, while Loren, in an equivalent reversal of their previous roles together, plays a frumpy housewife. As (once again) Fellini's alter ego, he found himself confronting the women's movement in *Città delle donne/City of Women* (1980) and lapsing into bitterness and nostalgia (opposite Giulietta Masina*) in *Ginger e Fred/Ginger and Fred* (1985). In the 1980s he returned to the theatre in Peter Brook's 1984 Paris production of the comedy *Cin-Cin* (filmed in 1991) and Nikita Mikhalkov's *Pianola meccanica* (1984). He appeared in Mikhalkov's film *Oci ciornie/Ochi chërnye/Dark Eyes* (1987) and was reunited with Loren in Robert Altman's *Prêt-à-porter* (1994). He received a Golden Lion for lifetime achievement at the 1990 Venice Festival. His daughter (with Catherine Deneuve) Chiara Mastroianni has begun a career as an actress in France, appearing notably in the films of André Téchiné. MMa

MATARAZZO, Raffaello   Rome 1906–66

Italian director. A film critic for the magazine *Il Tevere*, Matarazzo began working for Cines* in 1931. He made an unsuccessful debut with *Treno popolare* (1933), an unusually realist film about ordinary people, entirely shot on location. For the next ten years he devoted himself to comedies and light thrillers, from *Kiki* (1934) and *Joe il rosso* (1936) through *Sono stato io!/I Did It* (1937, where Eduardo and Titina De Filippo* played together for the first time), to *Giorno di nozze* (1942) and *Il birichino di papà* (1943). In Spain during the war he made a film with silent *diva* [> DIVISMO] Francesca Bertini (*Dora, la espia*, 1943). Back in Italy, he directed a series of extraordinarily successful torrid melodramas for Titanus*: *Catene/Chains* (1950), *Tormento/Torment* (1951), *I figli di nessuno/Nobody's Children* (1951), *Chi è senza peccato/Who Is Without Sin* (1953), *Torna!* (1954) and *L'angelo bianco/White Angel* (1955), all starring as the 'cursed' couple Amedeo Nazzari* and Yvonne Sanson, often with Folco Lulli as the bad guy. With the rediscovery of these melodramas by critics in the 1970s, Matarazzo is now acknowledged as a master of popular psychology, adept at manipulating emotions; his characters, defenceless victims of legal injustice or fate, suffer and experience the 'truth' of everyday life, with the family at the centre of their universe. More personal movies include *La nave delle donne maledette/The Ship of Condemned Women* (1953), a colourful and lyrical sea adventure, and *La risaia/Rice Girl* (1956), a popular neo-realist* tale. When public taste changed, Matarazzo was soon marginalised, though he found the opportunity to produce and direct the elegiac *Amore mio* (1964), a love story about a married man and a young woman. Although this last film, like his first, was a commercial failure, he used to say that it was only for these two that he would claim all the credit. GVo

MATTOLI, Mario   Tolentino 1898 – Rome 1980

Italian director. Mattoli came into contact with the cinema as a lawyer. In 1927 he set up an actors' company, Spettacoli Za-Bum, which worked with both dramatic theatre and music hall, bringing together the best-known actors of the period including Vittorio De Sica*. He made his directorial debut with *Tempo massimo* (1934), which fitted with a certain originality into the 'white telephone' vein of light (bourgeois) comedy. He made more than eighty films altogether, mainly in melodramatic and comic modes. An intelligent craftsman, he constructed his films by relying on his protagonists' fame outside the cinema, on stage or (later) television, never trying to impose his own authorial point of view (one critic wrote that his style was the very absence of style). Mattoli was therefore the ideal director for Totò*, with whom he made a memorable ensemble of skilful adaptations of classic stage comedies by Eduardo Scarpetta (*Un turco napoletano*, 1953; *Miseria e nobiltà*, 1954; *Il medico dei pazzi*, 1954), and intelligent evocations of the time (*Totò al Giro d'Italia*, 1948). He gained respect for his work in many genres: Camerini*-inspired comedy (*Ai vostri ordini, signora*, 1939), historical films (*Amo te sola*, 1935), 'Hellzapoppin'-type variety shows (*I pompieri di Viggiù*, 1949), neo-realist* drama (*La vita ricomincia*, 1945), musicals (*Signorinella*, 1949), juvenile comedy (*Appuntamento a Ischia*, 1960) and parody (*Fifa e arena*, 1948). PV

Other Films Include: *La damigella di Bard* (1936); *Felicita Colombo* (1937); *La dama bianca* (1938); *Il pirata sono io* (1940); *Ore 9: lezione di chimica* (1941); *Stasera niente di nuovo* (1942); *L'ultima carrozzella* (1943); *Circo equestre Za-Bum* (1944); *I due orfanelli* (1947); *Cinque poveri in automobile* (1952); *Tipi da spiaggia* (1959); *Sua eccellenza si fermò a mangiare* (1961); *Per qualche dollaro in meno* (1966).

METZ, Vittorio – see MARCHESI, Marcello

MINGOZZI, Gianfranco   Bologna 1932

Italian director. A distinguished documentarist and also a maker of feature films. The career of Gianfranco Mingozzi is emblematic of the difficulties facing independent filmmakers in Italy. Commissioned by Dino De Laurentiis* to make a low-budget film about the Mafia in Sicily, Mingozzi saw the project aborted by order of the producer. He managed nevertheless to extract enough material to make the 30-minute *Con il cuore fermo, Sicilia*, which won a Golden Lion in Venice for best documentary in 1965. Asked by RAI* in 1988 to re-edit his footage into a three-part documentary mini-series he again had the rug pulled from under him, with the resultant film, *La terra dell'uomo*, shown at festivals but never screened on television. In the meantime he had made a number of independent features, but his sharpness of vision and uncompromising stance in dealing with political and sexual themes led to difficulties with the censor. *La vita in gioco*, made in 1973, was held up for two years before being released in a cut version retitled *Morire a Roma*, while *Flavia, la monaca musulmana/Flavia the Heretic* (1974) also suffered cuts. Less controversial have been his documentaries on the cinema, notably *Michelangelo Antonioni, storia di un autore* (1966), *Francesca Bertini, l'ultima diva*, his tribute to the *dive* of early Italian cinema (1982), and *Bellissimo* (1985). GNS

Carmine Gallone's *Scipione l'africano* (1937).

Massimo Girotti with Luisa Ferida in Alessandro Blasetti's
La corona di ferro (1941).

Barbara Steele in Mario Bava's trend-setting Italian horror film,
La maschera del demonio (The Mask of the Demon, 1960).

Clara Calamai in Ferdinando Maria Poggioli's comedy
Le sorelle Materassi (1943).

Giulietta Masina in *Luci del varietà*, jointly directed by
Alberto Lattuada and Frederico Fellini in 1950.

Clint Eastwood
and Eli Wallach
in Sergio Leone's
*The Good, the Bad
and the Ugly* (1966).

Gina Lollobrigida in Luigi Comencini's proto-typical comedy Italian-style, *Pane, amore e fantasia (Bread, Love and Dreams*, 1953).

Bartolomeo Pagano, the original Maciste, in *Maciste all'inferno* (1926).

Sophia Loren

Anna Magnani with Aldo Fabrizi in the film which made her an international star, Roberto Rossellini's *Rome Open City* (1945).

Silvana Mangano in Guiseppe De Santis's *Bitter Rice* (1949).

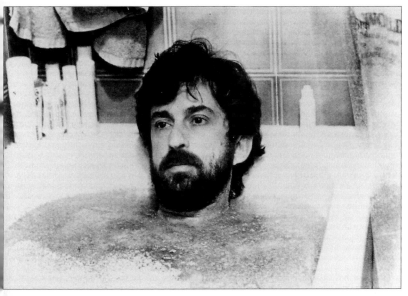

Nanni Moretti in his autobiographical *Dear Diary* (1994).

The young Franco Interlenghi and Rinaldo Smordini behind bars
in Vittorio De Sica and Cesare Zavattini's early neo-realist classic
Sciuscià (1946).

Silvana Pampanini

MIRANDA, Isa
Inès Isabella Sampietro;
Milan 1909 – Rome 1982

Italian actress. The elegant Isa Miranda, whose beauty recalled that of Marlene Dietrich, was one of Italy's most celebrated film stars in the 1930s and 1940s. She appeared in several Italian films before her first lead role in Guido Brignone's *Tenebre* (1934). That same year she was launched into stardom by Max Ophuls' *La signora di tutti*, which the German director made in Italy. Significantly, Ophuls' film drew upon her relative anonymity as an actress in a story that recounts the rise to stardom and eventual destruction of a film star. Between 1934 and 1937 Miranda was cast in five more Italian films – *Come le foglie/Like the Leaves* (1934), *Passaporto rosso/Red Passport* (1936), *Il fu Mattia Pascal/The Late Mathias Pascal* (1937; Miranda also appeared in the French version, *L'Homme de nulle part*, 1936), *Scipione l'africano/ Scipio Africanus* (1936) and *Una donna fra due mondi/Between Two Worlds* (1937) – before signing a contract with Paramount in Hollywood, where she made two films, *Hotel Imperial* (1939, a remake of a 1927 silent film) and *Adventure in Diamonds* (1940). Back in Italy she appeared in three films directed by her husband, Alfredo Guarini – *Senza cielo* (1940), *È caduta una donna* (1941) and *Documento Z 3* (1942) – and starred in Mario Soldati's* critically acclaimed *Malombra* (1942), based upon Antonio Fogazzaro's classic nineteenth-century novel, and in the title role of another turn-of-the-century romance, Renato Castellani's* *Zazà* (1942). After the war, Miranda appeared in many international co-productions, including René Clément's *Au-delà des grilles/Le mura di Malapaga/The Walls of Malapaga* (1949), co-starring Jean Gabin, and Max Ophuls' *La Ronde* (1950). One of her last appearances was in Liliana Cavani's* *Il portiere di notte/The Night Porter* (1974). JHa

MONICELLI, Mario

Italian director. Brought up and trained in Milan in the 1930s, Monicelli made a precocious start as a film-maker when he won a prize at the 1935 Venice Festival as co-director of an amateur film, *I ragazzi della via Paal*. After apprenticeship with Mario Camerini* and Augusto Genina*, he made his professional debut in the late 1940s in partnership with Stefano Vanzina (Steno), with whom he made a large number of films as vehicles for the great comedian Totò* (notably *Totò cerca casa/Totò Wants a Home*, 1949; *Guardie e ladri/Cops and Robbers*, 1951; *Totò e Carolina*, 1953). He then made a key contribution to what became known as *commedia all'italiana**, starting with the brilliantly funny *I soliti ignoti/Persons Unknown* (1958). His most important films, while flattering audiences' tastes, were also moved by an acute – even fierce – critical spirit. In 1959 *La grande guerra/The*

Great War shared the Golden Lion at the Venice Festival with Roberto Rossellini's* *Il generale Della Rovere* – the first time a popular and partly comic film was admitted to the ranks of art cinema. *I compagni/The Strikers* (1963) was an ambitious attempt to reclaim the history of the workers' and socialist movements in turn-of-the-century Turin. The film enjoyed some art-house success, especially abroad, but the general public in Italy was confused by its insertion of socio-political commitment into a basically entertainment genre. Monicelli had more success with a series of episode films, in particular *L'armata Brancaleone* (1965), starring an extraordinary Vittorio Gassman*. If *I soliti ignoti* had signalled the beginning of *commedia all'italiana**, *Amici miei/My Friends* (1975), a nihilistic critique of the years of consumerism and modernisation in Italy, is the swansong of the genre. The next chapter in Monicelli's life was *Un borghese piccolo piccolo/ An Average Man* (1977), starring the comic actor Alberto Sordi*, whose tragic potentiality Monicelli had guessed in much the same way as twenty years before he had inspired a comic talent in dramatic actor Gassman. In *Speriamo che sia femmina/Let's Hope It's a Girl* (1985) – one of the many projects Monicelli inherited from someone else – he achieved a happy balance between traditional Tuscan 'malice' and an appealing sentimentality, and demonstrated an acute observation of new patterns of behaviour. PDA

Other Films Include: *È arrivato il cavaliere* (1950); *Totò e le donne* (1952, co-dir.); *Proibito* (1954); *Un eroe dei nostri tempi* (1955); *Donatella* (1955); *Padre e figli/The Tailor's Maid* (1956); *Risate di Gioia* (1960); *Boccaccio 70* (1962, ep. *Renzo e Luciana*); *Casanova 70* (1965); *Capriccio all'italiana* [ep. *La Bambinaia*], *La ragazza con la pistola/The Girl with a Pistol* (1968); *Toh, è morta la nonna* (1969); *Brancaleone alle Crociate* (1970); *La mortadella/Lady Liberty* (1971); *Vogliamo i colonnelli* (1973); *Romanzo popolare* (1974); *Caro Michele* (1976); *I nuovi mostri/Viva Italia* (1977, co-dir.); *Viaggio con Anita/ Lovers and Liars* (1978); *Temporale rosy* (1980); *Camera d'albergo* (1981); *Il marchese del Grillo* (1981); *Amici miei atto II* (1982); *Bertoldo, Bertoldino e Cacasenno* (1984); *Le due vite di Mattia Pascal* (1985); *I picari* (1987); *Il male oscuro* (1990); *Rossini! Rossini!* (1991); *Parenti serpenti* (1992).

MORETTI, Nanni   Brunico 1953

Italian director and actor. Moretti sprang precociously to fame in 1976 with a Super-8 film, *Io sono un autarchico/I Am an Autocrat* (literally 'I am an autarchic', meaning something between anarchist, autonomist and autarkic in the old – and historically also Fascist – sense of self-sufficient), a witty, ironic immersion into the unreal feelings of a generation. This was followed by *Ecce bombo* (1978) and *Sogni d'oro/ Golden Dreams* (1981), and a series of films throughout the 1980s which marked him out as an *auteur* with a highly personal approach and original style. Moretti's anti-naturalistic narrative discourse is an assault on the banality of the world and of the cinema, a desperate search for meaning in a violent and fragmented universe. His characters are paradoxical (the professor in *Bianca*, 1984, kills out of moralism); disturbing (the priest in *La messa è finita/The Mass is over*, 1985, renounces his calling out of his inability to help others); or bewildered (the amnesiac water-polo-playing Communist in *Palombella rossa/Red Lob*, 1989). His narration is disjointed, tending increasingly towards open-ended structures and a great economy of means, and making use of his own body as actor. *Caro diario/Dear Diary* (1993), a film in three episodes based on his own experience, is a light yet profound picture of contemporary Italy illuminated by the harsh gaze of a solitary humorist. In recent years Moretti has used his growing reputation to promote the work of talented newcomers such as Carlo Mazzacurati and Daniele Luchetti and has acted in their films (such as Luchetti's *Il portaborse/The Bagman*, 1991) as well as in his own. He has become a major public figure in Italy and a contributor to cultural and political debate – not least through his documentaries: *La cosa/The Thing* (1990), about Communist militants at the time the Party was changing its name, and the collective *L'unico paese al mondo/The Only Country in the World* (1994), a violent assault on Prime Minister and television entrepreneur Silvio Berlusconi and his 'telly-ocracy'. GVo

MORRICONE, Ennio   Rome 1928

Italian composer. One of the most influential and respected composers working in contemporary cinema, Morricone has provided music for an extraordinary 400 or so films in Europe and internationally. He has worked regularly with a host of renowned directors, including Bernardo Bertolucci*, Brian De Palma, Roland Joffé, Pier Paolo Pasolini* and Gillo Pontecorvo*. It was Morricone's innovative scores for the Italian Westerns* (or 'Spaghetti' Westerns) of Sergio Leone*, however, which brought the composer to prominence and which are seen as his trademark. The celebrated 'Man With No Name' trilogy – *Per un pugno di dollari/A Fistful of Dollars* (1964), *Per qualche dollaro in più/For a Few Dollars More* (1965), *Il buono, il brutto e il cattivo/ The Good, the Bad and the Ugly* (1966) – is marked by Morricone's original use of instrumentation, including cracking whips, bells, the jew's harp, and most strikingly, human whistling and chanting. His Western scores are also notable for their strong characterisation of individuals, whether Clint Eastwood's loner in the trilogy or Charles Bronson's stranger in *C'era una volta il West/Once upon a Time in the West* (1968), defined by a simple but haunting harmonica solo.

Classically trained at the Conservatorio di Santa Cecilia in Rome, Morricone has proved he can turn his hand to virtually any musical style. His range is easily demonstrated by comparing the rich pastorale score of Terrence Malick's *Days of Heaven* (1978, US) to the ragtime numbers, 'Prohibition Dirge' and 'Speakeasy', in *C'era una volta in America/Once Upon a Time in America* (1983). Morricone won British Academy Awards for his work on *Days of Heaven*, *The Mission* (1986, UK), *C'era una volta in America* and *The Untouchables* (1987, US), and four Oscar nominations. The score for *The Mission*, in which Morricone claims to take most pride, was awarded a Golden Globe in 1986. Morricone somehow manages to find time for work outside the cinema, writing, among other things, 'El Mundial', the official theme of the 1978 football World Cup in Argentina, as well as 'Chi Mai', the best-selling theme tune of the 1981 BBC television series *The Life and Times of David Lloyd George*. SH

Other Films Include: *Prima della rivoluzione/Before the Revolution* (1964); *I pugni in tasca/Fists in the Pocket* (1965); *Uccellacci e uccellini/Hawks and Sparrows* (1966); *La battaglia di Algeri/The Battle of Algiers* (1966); *Faccia a faccia/Face to Face* (1967); *Two Mules for Sister Sara* (1970, US); *Il Decamerone/The Decameron* (1971); *Giù la testa/A Fistful of Dynamite/Duck You Sucker!* (1971); *Novecento/1900* (1976); *La Cage aux folles* (1978, Fr./It.); *The Thing* (1982, US); *Ginger e Fred/Ginger and Fred* (1985); *Good Morning Babilonia/Good Morning Babylon* (1987); *Frantic* (1988, US); *Nuovo Cinema Paradiso/Cinema Paradiso* (1988); *Casualties of War* (1989, US); *Atame!/Tie Me Up! Tie Me Down!* (1989, Sp.); *Hamlet* (1990, UK); *Bugsy* (1991, US); *In the Line of Fire* (1993, US); *La Scorta* (1993); *Wolf* (1994, US); *Disclosure* (1994, US).

N

NAZZARI, Amedeo
Cagliari 1907 – Rome 1979

Italian actor. Arguably Italy's most popular male screen star in the late 1930s, Nazzari was often compared to Errol Flynn because of his undaunted coolness as adventure or romantic leading man and because his characters' trim moustaches or goatees bore some resemblance to Flynn's. His screen image was, however, quite complex. In Goffredo Alessandrini's* *Luciano Serra pilota/The Pilot Luciano Serra* (1938) he only becomes a 'Fascist hero' late in the film, having previously been a cynical expatriate living in South America. In *Montevergine/La grande luce/The Great Light* (1939) and *Harlem* (1943) he has underworld connections, while in *La cena delle beffe* (1941) and *Caravaggio, Il pittore maledetto/Caravaggio, Painter with a Curse* (1941) he is cast as a character whose heroic exploits seem driven, directly or indirectly, by madness. Meanwhile he also appeared, in sunnier guise, in light romances.

After the war his image was recast to suit the prevailing neo-realist* mode. He plays a partisan in Alessandro Blasetti's* *Un giorno nella vita/A Day in the Life* (1946), a returning P.O.W. in Alberto Lattuada's* *Il bandito* (1946), and a naval officer reduced to working on a dredger along the Tiber in *Fatalità* (1947). As he explains in *Fatalità* to his female co-star: 'The war is over. So many things have changed. Even I have changed.' In the early 1950s he starred in a series of hugely popular melodramas directed by Raffaello Matarazzo*, starting with *Catene/Chains* (1950). By the mid-1950s, however, he had lost his status as a leading man, though he continued to work in film until the 1970s. JHa

NEO-REALISM

Italian film movement. Neo-realism is a generic term applied to the cinema which emerged in Italy in the years immediately following the liberation of Italy in 1943-45 and is associated with the names of Roberto Rossellini*, Luchino Visconti* and the director-writer team of Vittorio De Sica* and Cesare Zavattini*. Although the expression has been understood in many different ways, the core characteristics of neo-realism can be defined in terms of method (a preference for location filming and the use of non-professional actors), attitude (a wish to get close to everyday reality), subject matter (the life of the popular classes in the aftermath of war), and ideology/politics (the expression first of a hope of political renewal after the years of Fascist dictatorship and Nazi occupation, and then of a certain disillusionment when many aspects of the renewal failed to materialise). Not all neo-realist films necessarily shared all these characteristics, and neo-realism in the strong sense petered out in the early 1950s, its death knell sounded by the box-office disaster of De Sica and Zavattini's *Umberto D.* in 1952. Its main protagonists drifted away into other styles, while some of the attributes of the original neo-realism were taken up, in softer form, in the so-called *neo-realismo rosa* (rosy, or rose-tinted, neo-realism) of the 1950s. Curiously it was after neo-realism had already more or less died in Italy that it became a worldwide influence on film-makers as far apart as Spain, India – *Ladri di biciclette/Bicycle Thieves* (1948) was shown in Calcutta in 1951 – and Latin America, where its simplicity and directness of means were greatly admired and widely imitated. [> EUROPEAN ART CINEMA] GNS

NEW ITALIAN COMICS

In the late 1970s a new type of Italian film comedy emerged, which owed very little to the *commedia all'italiana** of the previous two decades or to any other comic tradition. The spur to the emergence of the 'new comics' ('*i nuovi comici*') was the ideological crisis provoked by the wave of terrorism of the 1970s and the intensification of government corruption scandals.

The new comics are a loose grouping of actors, directors and actor-directors, of whom the first to emerge were Roberto Benigni*, Massimo Troisi* and Nanni Moretti*. Moretti's Super-8 film *Io sono un autarchico/I Am an Autocrat* (1976) and his *Ecce bombo* (1978) have been cited as paving the way to the new comics, but Moretti is not typical. A director more than a performer, he owes nothing to cabaret and television, so important for the other comics (for example, the extraordinary television show *Non Stop*). However, Moretti does embody some characteristics of the new comics, especially the ability to connect with current cultural reality. The new comics created characters, situations and languages which constitute both a repertory and a synthesis of local slangs and sub-cultures: Moretti's apathetic youngsters of the 1960s, Troisi's young and up-and-coming Neapolitans, Paolo Villaggio's white-collar workers, Benigni's surrealist peasant Tuscany, Carlo Verdone's Alberto Sordi*-like Rome, Abantantuono's southern dialect, Maurizio Nichetti's cartoon-like figures, and, finally, a whole 'bestiary' of character actors. The new comics also shared a search for new narrative modes, often 'contaminated' by other forms: cabaret, mime, animation, comic strips, and the verbal games of television entertainers and disc-jockeys, and it was this original mixture of performing modes that unified them for the audience throughout the 1980s. Emerging along the axis Naples–Rome–Milan (with some incursions into Tuscany), their wild and exhibitionist films constituted the leading edge of Italian cinema in terms both of 'quality' and of box-office. Throughout the 1980s the films of the new comics, usually released around Christmas, monopolised the national market and often out-performed Hollywood mega-productions. After the triumph in the late 1970s of the films of former rock singer Adriano Celentano, Troisi's *Ricomincio da tre/Starting Again at Three* (1981), Benigni and Troisi's *Non ci resta che piangere* (1984), Benigni's *Il piccolo diavolo/ The Little Devil* (1988) and *Johnny Stecchino* (1991) were all major box-office hits. The success of Renzo Arbore's *Il pap'occhio* (1980) served as a powerful catalyst for many sub-cultures, opening up a space for Villaggio's *Fantozzi* series, Verdone's existential comedies (*Io e mia sorella*, 1987; *Maledetto il giorno che ti ho incontrato*, 1992), the surrealist games of Nichetti, the light-headed mime from Milan (*Ladri di saponette/Icicle Thief*, 1989, and *Volere Volare*, 1991), and Francesco Nuti's movies (*Io, Chiara e lo Scuro*, 1983, *Donne con le gonne*, 1991). There were also blatantly commercial spin-offs: Renato Pozzetto's *Culo e camicia* (1981), Abantantuono, Celentano, Enrico

Montesano and Verdone's *Grand Hotel Excelsior* (1982), Jerry Cala and Christian De Sica's *Vacanze di Natale* (1983), Massimo Boldi, Cala, Ezio Greggio and De Sica's *Yuppies 2* (1986). The new comics seem to have lost their originality around the early 1990s, becoming either more radically personal (Troisi), or more abstract and self-indulgent. Some were absorbed into art cinema (like Benigni and Villaggio, the protagonists of Federico Fellini's* *La voce della luna/The Voice of the Moon*, 1990), though they continued to enjoy wide popular success. GVo

NORIS, Assia
Anastasia Noris von Gerzfeld; St Petersburg, Russia 1912

Italian actress. Noris became a popular figure in Italian cinema during the 1930s and early 1940s. She most often appeared in romantic comedies, particularly those directed by Mario Camerini*, to whom she was married between 1940 and 1943. The films she made with Camerini include *Giallo* (1933), *Darò un milione* (1935), *Ma non è una cosa seria/But It's Nothing Serious* (1936), *Il Signor Max/Mr Max* (1937), *Batticuore* (1938), *Grandi magazzini* (1939), *Centomila dollari* (1940), *Una romantica avventura* (1940), and *Una storia d'amore* (1942). Her persona in these and other films from the 1930s was that of a wholesome, shy, idealistic, middle-class heroine struggling to find romance and career opportunity in contemporary urban Italy. Her screen image was also developed through her frequent pairing with Vittorio De Sica*. Declared best actress of 1939–40 by *Cinema* magazine, she was appropriately cast as a star in Mario Soldati's* *Dora Nelson* (1939). Her image, however, was anathema to the postwar neorealist* cinema, and she emigrated to Egypt, making only two more films. JHa

NOTARI, Elvira
Elvira Coda; Naples 1895–1946

Italian director and producer. The earliest and most prolific woman director in Italy, Notari made about sixty feature films, one hundred documentaries and numerous shorts for her own production house, Dora Film, between 1906 and 1930. She chose the stories, wrote the scripts, directed and co-produced all films at Dora. Her name was cancelled out of history, and her contribution to the history and development of Italian and world cinema has long remained unacknowledged.

Although not uneducated, Elvira Notari was of modest social origin. She founded Dora Film with her husband Nicola Notari, and the use of her husband's last name has added to the lack of acknowledgment of her authorship. Dora Film was a family enterprise, but it was unquestionably Elvira who wrote and directed all films, while Nicola

89

worked as cameraman. The couple jointly supervised the whole production process from financing to editing. Their son Edoardo played
'Gennariello', an ever-present character whom scriptwriter Elvira
kept modifying as he grew up. Her obscured contribution to the development of cinema presents several questions to the history of film,
including that of the novelty and 'uniqueness' of Italian neo-realism*.
In opposition to the contemporary Italian 'super-spectacles', Elvira
Notari's cinema prefigures the aesthetic of neo-realism in its manner
of direction, *mise-en-scène*, and subject matter. From the 1910s, her fic-
tions were shot on location, in the streets and dwellings of Naples,
often with non-professional actors. They documented, with stark realism, the conditions of urban living for the underclass. The suppression
of female authorship is intertwined with that of historical forms of
popular culture. Notari drew the subjects of her dark melodramas
from the repertoire of Neapolitan popular culture, nineteenth-century
popular novels as well as Italian popular romantic fiction directed at
female audiences and centred on female characters. Her films offer in-
sights into female viewpoints, desires and transgressive social behav-
iours. Dora Film 'silent' production specialised in colour and 'talking
pictures'. Films were hand-painted frame by frame and synchronised
'live' with singing and music. Notari's films were distributed nationally
as well as internationally, reaching Italian immigrants abroad. Some of
the documentaries were produced specially for, and even commissioned by, such immigrants.

   Notari's films encountered difficulties with Fascist censorship, which
opposed her cinema's criticism of the law, its display of poverty and
crime, and its use of regional popular culture and dialect. The coming
of sound, together with Fascist censorship, put an end to her work. (A
complete filmography can be found in the book below.) GB

Bib: Giuliana Bruno, *Streetwalking on a Ruined Map: Cultural theory
and the city films of Elvira Notari* (1993).

OLMI, Ermanno   Bergamo 1931

Italian director. Unusual among Italian directors in being of working-
class (originally peasant) origin, Olmi started his film career as a
maker of in-house documentaries for the Edison Volta electric
company of which he was an employee. After making documentaries
in the 1950s he wrote and shot his first feature, *Il tempo si è fermato/*

Time Stood Still, a delicate study of two men trapped in the mountains, in 1959. Still in the same documentary-influenced style he made *Il posto/The Job* (1961) and *I fidanzati/The Engagement* (1963), establishing himself as a sensitive and careful observer, not afraid to use a deliberately undramatic narrative rhythm. Another facet to his character – his Catholicism – emerged with *E venne un uomo/A Man Named John* (1965), a biopic of Pope John XXIII narrated by Rod Steiger. After a relatively fallow period in the mid-1970s he returned to prominence with *L'albero degli zoccoli/The Tree of Wooden Clogs*, a peasant family saga which won the Palme d'or at Cannes in 1978 and was widely interpreted as a Catholic and politically right-of-centre (so by implication Christian-Democrat) response to Bernardo Bertolucci's* Marxist epic *Novecento/1900* (1976), though a more pointed contrast could be made between the full-blown rhetoric of Bertolucci and Olmi's gentle understatement. In the 1980s Olmi obtained commissions mainly from Italy's state-owned RAI* television network and reverted to documentary, but a deal struck with RAI, the producer Mario Cecchi Gori* and a French company enabled him to make a foray into international film with *La leggenda del santo bevitore/The Legend of the Holy Drinker* (1988), an adaptation of Joseph Roth's novel, enlivened by a marvellous performance by Rutger Hauer as the eponymous drinker. A full-length documentary, *Lungo il fiume/Down the River* (1992), about the ecology of the Po valley, rich in pious sentiment but short on analysis, revealed his limitations as a film-maker, but his early unpretentious films will secure his place in film history. He directed *Il segreto del bosco vecchio* in 1993 and *Genesi: la creazione e il diluvio* in 1994. GNS

P

PAMPANINI, Silvana   Rome 1925

Italian actress. Silvana Pampanini studied singing and piano at the Santa Cecilia Conservatory. In 1946 she was runner-up in the first postwar Miss Italy competition and was promptly offered her first (small) screen roles. She became one of the most popular actresses of the generation immediately preceding the so-called '*maggiorate fisiche*' ('physically amply endowed' women) actresses, such as Gina Lollobrigida* and Sophia Loren*. A lively and imposing brunette, she played vamps, courtesans and elegant ladies in a series of B-quality films churned out at the rate of about ten a year. Deploying a seemingly irrepressible sensuality, she had a talent for both dramatic roles

(Luigi Zampa's* *Processo alla città*, 1952; Giuseppe De Santis'* *Un marito per Anna Zaccheo*, 1953; Abel Gance's *La Tour de Nesle/La torre di Nesle*, 1955) and comedy (Mario Soldati's* *O.K. Nerone*, 1951; Luigi Comencini's* *La bella di Roma*, 1955). In 1958 she directed a twenty-minute documentary on Giuseppe Verdi, and in her honour the actor Totò* wrote one his most beautiful songs, 'Malafemmina' ('wicked woman'). Although still enjoying success abroad, especially in Spain, her popularity in Italy suddenly declined at the end of the 1950s; she returned as the ex-*diva* in Dino Risi's* *Il gaucho* (1964) and made a brief comeback appearance in Alberto Sordi's* *Il tassinaro* (1983). MMo

PASOLINI, Pier Paolo   Bologna 1922 – Ostia 1975

Italian director and writer. Pasolini spent most of his childhood in Friuli in the far north-east of Italy. As a young man he joined the Communist Party, but was expelled from it in 1949 for alleged homosexuality. In spite of his expulsion and his many subsequent public disagreements with the Party and with the rest of the left he continued proudly to regard himself as a Communist to the end of his life. In 1950 he set out for Rome, where he soon established a reputation with two volumes of poetry, *Le ceneri di Gramsci* (1957) and *La religione del mio tempo* (1961), and two novels making creative use of Roman dialect and slang, *Ragazzi di vita* (1955) and *Una vita violenta* (1959). His skill with vernacular dialogue brought him work in the film industry, notably on the script of Federico Fellini's* *Le notti di Cabiria/Cabiria/ Nights of Cabiria* (1957).

Pasolini's first two films as director – *Accattone* (1961) and *Mamma Roma* (1962) – had Roman low-life themes, but were distinguished by a strong utopian current. A short film, *La ricotta* ('Curd-cheese' – episode of the 1963 compilation film *RoGoPaG/Laviamoci il cervello*), featured a hilarious but far from malicious parody of the Deposition from the Cross which led to charges of blasphemy. By contrast *Il Vangelo secondo Matteo/The Gospel According to Saint Matthew* (1964) was a stark and sober retelling of the Gospel according to Matthew, which earned him the inaccurate label of Catholic-Marxist – in fact his Marxism was as heterodox as his attitude to religion was ambivalent. He was interested in what he called 'the sacred' (*sacrale*), but increasingly located this quality in primitive religion and myth. In his 'unpopular' films of the late 1960s – *Edipo re/Oedipus Rex* (1967), *Porcile/Pigsty* (1969) and *Medea* (1970) – he explored mythic notions of the transition from primitivism to civilisation, to the implied disadvantage of the latter. His own utopias were located as far away as possible from the modern, capitalist, bourgeois world of which he felt himself a member and a victim – either downwards (among the peasantry and sub-proletariat), outwards (in southern Italy, Africa, the

Arab world, India), or backwards in time (in the Middle Ages or pre-classical Greece).

In the 1960s his longstanding interest in language drew him to semiotics, and he attempted to theorise his approach to cinema in a number of essays (available in English in *Heretical Empiricism*, 1988). He argued that film language has a natural base in reality, which is endowed with meaning when the film-maker turns it into signs. But his own film work is far from naturalistic. Eschewing narrative continuity, Pasolini concentrates on single, powerful images whose expressivity seems independent of 'reality' as ordinarily conceived. What underlies them, however, is a desperate search for a pre-symbolic emotional truth which modern man can no longer grasp. From the mid-1960s onwards Pasolini's films were mostly set either in the past or, in the case of *Appunti di viaggio per un film sull'India* (1968) and *Appunti per un'Orestiade africana* (1970), in far-off places. The exceptions are *Teorema/Theorem* (1968), a brutal dissection of the bourgeois family, the 'modern' section of *Porcile*, and a few shorts. In 1970 he embarked on a series of films based on medieval tales – *Il decamerone/The Decameron* (1971), *I raconti di Canterbury/The Canterbury Tales* (1972), and *Il fiore delle mille e una notte/The Arabian Nights* (1973). Though all three films (especially *The Canterbury Tales*) have their darker side, this so-called 'trilogy of life' was widely interpreted as a celebration of a lost world of joyful and innocent sexuality. Pasolini, however, repudiated this interpretation and indeed the films themselves. Increasingly convinced that 'sexual liberation' (including gay liberation) was a sham, he turned in his journalism to a fierce denunciation of contemporary sexual mores. Having courted unpopularity on the left for his criticisms of the radical students of 1968, he compounded it with his opposition to the liberalisation of Italy's archaic abortion law, though he had to beat a hasty retreat. Then in 1975 he made *Salò o le 120 giornate di Sodoma/Salò*, setting de Sade's novel in the last years of Fascism in Italy, explicitly linking fascism and sadism, sexual licence and oppression. *Salò* was to be his last film. On the morning of 2 November 1975, his battered body was discovered on waste ground near the seaside resort of Ostia (a site revisited in Nanni Moretti's* *Caro diario/Dear Diary*, 1993), outside Rome. Controversy continues to surround this brutal murder, for which a young male prostitute was tried and convicted in 1976. GNS

Bib: Sam Rohdie, *The Passion of Pier Paolo Pasolini* (1995).

Other Films Include: *La rabbia* (1963); *Comizi d'amore, Sopralluoghi in Palestina* (1964); *Le streghe/The Witches* (ep. *La terra vista dalla luna*), *Uccellacci e uccellini/The Hawks and the Sparrows* (1966); *Capriccio all'italiana* (ep. *Che cosa sono le nuvole?*), *Amore e rabbia* (1968, ep. *La sequenza del fiore di carta*); *12 Dicembre* (1972).

PASTRONE, Giovanni Piero Fosco; Asti 1883 – Turin 1959

Italian director and producer. Starting his career in 1905 on the administrative and technical side of the film industry in Turin, Pastrone was one of the moving spirits of the Itala film company. In 1908 he went to Paris and enticed the successful Pathé comedian André Deed to join Itala, under the name Cretinetti*. Graduating to production and direction, he scored a hit with the early spectacular *La caduta di Troia/The Fall of Troy* (1912) and an even greater one with *Cabiria* (1914), the film in which the character of Maciste* made his first appearance in Italian cinema. He went on to direct a number of other films, including *Tigre reale* (1916), adapted from the story by Giovanni Verga, and a sonorised version of *Cabiria* (1931). But it was as producer and studio organiser that he made his greatest impact. From 1910 onwards he rationalised production at Itala, kept its finances in order by balancing safe successes such as *Cretinetti* comedies with more ambitious productions, experimented with colour, and hired Segundo de Chomón from Pathé to develop the company's special effects department. Even Pastrone's gift for management, however, could not save Itala from the crisis which ensued in the early 1920s, and the company went into liquidation until resurrected by Stefano Pittaluga* at the end of the decade. GNS

PEPLUM

Italian genre. The peplum was a cycle of internationally successful Italian adventure films running from *Le fatiche di Ercole/The Labours of Hercules/Hercules* in 1958 to c. 1965. There had been a comparable cycle from *Quo Vadis?* (1912) to c. 1926, and Italian cinema has produced historical spectaculars throughout its history. The term refers to the short skirt worn by the heroes. These heroes are drawn from the ancient world: Hercules, Spartacus, Samson and, most popular of all, Maciste*, invented for *Cabiria* (1914). Peplum heroes range freely, and without explanation, from classical antiquity to prehistoric times (for example *Maciste l'uomo più forte del mondo/Maciste the Strongest Man in the World/The Mole Men Battle the Son of Hercules*, 1961), through non-Western ancient worlds (Aztec civilisation in *Ercole contro i figli del sole/Hercules versus the Sons of the Sun*, 1964) to more recent history (such as seventeenth-century Scotland in *Maciste all'inferno/Maciste in Hell/The Witch's Curse*, 1962). They are played by body-builders, who either were from the US (notably Steve Reeves) or appeared to be so (Adriano da Venezia, for instance, became Kirk Morris). The peplum affirmed the worth of male physical strength in a rapidly industrialising society and addressed the fascist imagery of the superhero, often condemning totalitarian societies while asserting the need for strong, white male leadership. The cycle's comic-book qualities (one-dimensional imagery, freedom to range in time and space), its energy and fun, continue to give it a cult status. RD

Bib: Domenico Cammarota, *Il cinema peplum* (1987).

PETRI, Elio   Rome 1929–82

Italian director. After a stint as a junior official in the Italian Communist Party, Petri worked for the Communist daily *L'Unità*, where his functions included that of assistant film critic. He found his way into cinema thanks to Giuseppe De Santis*, for whom he carried out the investigation that was to serve as a basis for *Roma ore 11* (1952), and with whom he worked as scriptwriter. He also co-wrote scripts with Carlo Lizzani*, Puccini and Dino Risi* (*I mostri/The Monsters*, 1963). In 1961 he directed his first film, *L'assassino*, an anti-realist thriller with an acid – even Kafkaesque – vein. The same taste for mixing genres (in particular realism and Antonioni*-style symbolism) can be found in his following film, *I giorni contati* (1962), starring the excellent stage actor Salvo Randone. Petri was less successful with 'fantastic' plots (*La decima vittima/The 10th Victim*, 1965) or manifestly metaphysical ones (*Un tranquillo posto di campagna/A Quiet Place in the Country*, 1968). With scriptwriter Ugo Pirro*, however, he found the perfect blend of allegory and politics. Together they made *A ciascuno il suo/To Each His Own* (1967), a story of the Sicilian mafia adapted from a Leonardo Sciascia novel, and *Indagine su un cittadino al di sopra di ogni sospetto/Investigation of a Citizen Above Suspicion* (1969, Oscar for best foreign film), about a petit-bourgeois character (skilfully played by Gian Maria Volonté*) who gives authoritarian vent to his sexual inhibitions and bureaucratic conformism. But after *La classe operaia va in paradiso/Lulu the Tool* (1971, Palme d'or at Cannes) and *La proprietà non è più un furto* (1973), Petri's work degenerated into a compendium of all the vices of Italian 'leftist cinema', whether in their tendency towards increasingly stylised and mannered characters, or in their unnecessarily virulent pessimism, as can be seen in his last films, *Todo modo* (1976, again from Sciascia) and *Buone notizie* (1979, also known as *La stanza delle buone notizie*). PM

Other Films Include: *Il maestro di Vigevano* (1963); *Alta infedeltà* (ep. *Peccato nel pomeriggio*, 1964).

PIETRANGELI, Antonio   Rome 1919 – Gaeta 1968

Italian director. After studying medicine, Pietrangeli wrote for the film journals *Bianco e nero* and *Cinema*, becoming an important theorist and advocate of neo-realism*. As a scriptwriter, he contributed to some of the most significant films of the period: Luchino Visconti's* *Ossessione* (1942) and *La terra trema* (1948), Alberto Lattuada's* *Senza pietà/Without Pity* (1948), and Roberto Rossellini's* *Europa '51* (1952) and *Viaggio in Italia/Voyage to Italy* (1953). Although still within the external framework of neo-realism, his debut film, *Il sole negli occhi/Celestina* (1953), was remarkable for its ideological acuteness and sensitive psychological analysis and for the almost unprecedented significance attached to women, a recurrent theme in almost all his later works. This theme was touched upon in varying degrees by *Nata di marzo* (1958), a somewhat bitter middle-class marital comedy; *Adua e le compagne/Love à la Carte* (1960); and *Lo scapolo/Alberto il conquistatore* (1955) and *Souvenir d'Italie* (1957), all reflecting a shift towards comedy. It was, however, in the magnificent trilogy made up of *La parmigiana* (1963), *La visita* (1964) and *Io la conoscevo bene/I Knew Her Well* (1965) that the director portrayed three unforgettable female figures while at the same time refining a distinctly personal film language. An original but always somewhat marginal figure, Pietrangeli created through the tender, provocative and highly intelligent *Fantasmi a Roma/Phantom Lovers* (1961) a new fusion of the imaginary and comedy, a combination generally regarded with suspicion in Italian culture. Pietrangeli died in an accident on the set of *Come, quando, perchè* (1968), which was completed by Valerio Zurlini*. PV

Other Films Include: *Amori di mezzo secolo* (1954, ep. *Girolanda 1910*); *Il magnifico cornuto* (1964); *Le fate* (1966, ep. *Fata Marta*).

PIRRO, Ugo   Salerno 1920

Italian scriptwriter. Starting his career as a journalist, Pirro first worked in the cinema with Carlo Lizzani* (*Achtung banditi!*, 1951), sharing his idea of a cinema midway between commitment and entertainment. For twenty years he was one of the most significant scriptwriters of an Italian cinema centred on political, historical and social themes [> ITALIAN POLITICAL CINEMA]. Lizzani's *Il processo di Verona/The Verona Trial* (1962) and *Svegliati e uccidi/Wake Up and Kill* (1966), Gianfranco Mingozzi's powerful Sardinian picture *Sequestro di persona/Kidnap* (1968), Pasquale Squitieri's colourful *I guappi* (1974), Elio Petri's* *A ciascuno il suo/To Each His Own* (1967), Damiano Damiani's *Il giorno della civetta/Mafia* (1968), Mario Bolognini's *Metello* (1970) and *L'eredità Ferramonti/The Inheritance* (1976) and Gillo Pontecorvo's* *Ogro* (1979) are the most important stages in Pirro's artistic career. He adapted his own novels to provide scripts for Martin Ritt's *Jovanka e le altre/Five Branded Women* (1960) and Valerio Zurlini's* *Le soldatesse/The Girl Soldiers* (1965), and transposed Giorgio Bassani for Vittorio De Sica's* *Il giardino dei Finzi-Contini/The Garden of the Finzi-Continis* (1970). In his own words, 'half hunter, half voyeur', Pirro elaborated the notion that cinematic ideas 'act and advance within the movie like an underground river'. His relationship with Elio Petri is precisely the expression of such a complexity, especially in *Indagine su un cittadino al di sopra di ogni sospetto/Investigation of a Citizen Above Suspicion* (1969), with its description of the interior mechanisms of power, and *La classe operaia va in paradiso/Lulu the Tool* (1971), where reality becomes expression, metaphor, hyper-reality, but is never merely 'repeated'. GVo

PITTALUGA, Stefano
Campomorone 1887 – Rome 1931

Italian entrepreneur. Originally an exhibitor, Pittaluga played a crucial role in the revival of the Italian film industry after its collapse in the aftermath of World War I. In order to acquire product to supply his rapidly expanding chain of theatres (concentrated in northern Italy), he moved into film distribution in the mid-1920s. Then, faced with a continuing lack of suitable Italian films and with the stranglehold exercised by the American majors, he took the next logical step and became a producer. He resurrected Itala Film and Cines*, and constructed Italy's first sound stages; he was also responsible for the production of two of Italy's most famous early sound films, Alessandro Blasetti's* *Sole/Sun* (1929) and Mario Camerini's* *Rotaie/Rails* (1929–31). He successfully lobbied a previously indifferent government for help for film production and distribution. After his early death in 1931, Cines became Italy's most important and innovative production company, while his theatre chain served to structure the government's ENIC – a state-sponsored system of film distribution. GNS/JHa

PONTECORVO, Gillo
Gilberto Pontecorvo; Pisa 1919

Italian director. Pontecorvo started his career as an unwilling student of chemistry. However, a change of residence to Paris as a result of racial discrimination enabled him to continue his music studies (he wrote the music for all his films), to sign up for a journalism course and later to find his way into the world of cinema. During the war he joined the Italian Communist Party and played an important part in the Resistance. He was an assistant to Yves Allégret and Joris Ivens after the war and made some short films. His first feature, *La grande strada azzurra/The Wide Blue Road* (1957), is a condensed version of a 'social' novel by Franco Solinas*, his favourite scriptwriter. *Kapò* (1960) was an uneasy amalgam of crude description of the Nazi death camps with a melodrama of love and redemption (and as such was fiercely criticised by Jacques Rivette in *Cahiers du cinéma*). *La battaglia di Algeri/Battle of Algiers* (1966), his most famous film, awarded a Golden Lion at the Venice Festival, revealed his mastery of a political cinema capable of explaining rather than judging. Produced almost entirely with Algerian government money, the film adopts a quasi-documentary style to describe the struggle and suffering of a whole country rather than identifying individual heroes. The success of this film (except in France, where it was banned for a long time and is even now rarely shown) paved the way for his Hollywood debut, directing Marlon Brando in *Queimada!/Burn!* (1969), a somewhat schematic treatise on capitalism and colonialism. Ten years later, *Ogro* (1979), about Basque terrorism, proved too unfocused to be of genuine interest. In 1992 Pontecorvo was appointed Director of the Venice* Film Festival, where he used his international prestige to organise the 'Assise degli Autori' (an annual meeting held in defence of artistic liberty) and to entice Hollywood productions to Italian film festivals away from the hegemony of Cannes. PM

PONTI, Carlo   Magenta 1910

Italian producer. A lawyer, Ponti entered cinema in the early 1940s, working for Lux*. In 1950 he left Lux to found Ponti-De Laurentiis with Dino De Laurentiis*, setting in motion an industry combine characterised by high investment and cultural profile. Their productions spanned the range from art films – Roberto Rosselllini's* *Europa '51* (1952) and Federico Fellini's* *La strada* (1954) – to popular comedies: Mario Monicelli's* *Guardie e ladri/Cops and Robbers* (1951), Totò* films, and many others. After breaking with De Laurentiis, Ponti migrated to the US with Sophia Loren*, whom he married in 1957 and whose stardom provided him with many successful productions. An expert player of the international market, and a shrewd businessman, he worked in the US as an independent producer, masterminding complex operations which culminated with *Doctor Zhivago* (1965). At the European end, in between Italy (where he encountered some legal and tax-related problems) and France (whose citizenship he acquired in 1964), Ponti's company Champion produced some high-quality movies like Vittorio De Sica's* *La ciociara/Two Women* (1960) starring Loren, Jean-Luc Godard's *Une Femme est une femme/A Woman is a Woman* (1961, Fr.), Elio Petri's* *La decima vittima/The 10th Victim* (1965), Michelangelo Antonioni's* *Blowup* (1966, UK/It.), *Zabriskie Point* (1969, US), and *Professione: Reporter/The Passenger* (1975), Ettore Scola's* *Una giornata particolare/A Special Day* (1977), as well as films by Roman Polanski, Claude Chabrol and Agnès Varda among others. Although he never attended the set during the shooting of a film, he claimed the last word on it, sometimes asking for substantial changes, as he did for Godard's *Le Mépris/Contempt* (1963, Fr./It.) and Marco Ferreri's* *Break-up* (1965), reduced to a single episode (an uncensored version was released in 1969). Before retiring, Ponti produced Maurizio Ponzi's *Qualcosa di biondo/My Three Loves* (1984), built entirely around Sophia Loren. GVo

R

RAI (Radio [subsequently Radiotelevisione] Italiana)

Italian broadcaster and production house. RAI, Italy's public broadcasting service, held a monopoly in radio and (from 1955) television broadcasting until the mid-1970s. In terms of film production, for many years it supported both famous and unknown *auteurs*. With a series including *L'età del ferro/The Iron Age* (1964) and *Atti degli apostoli/Acts of the Apostles* (1969), Roberto Rossellini* was the first to be given the chance to work free of commercial constraints. Whereas this first phase was characterised by low-cost, independent made-for-television productions, a second phase aimed at more ambitious projects. In the 1970s, despite a climate of ideological intolerance and political censorship, RAI played a fundamental role in Italian cinema, both culturally and economically. It achieved great success with the Taviani* brothers' *Padre padrone/Father Master* (1977) and Ermanno Olmi's* *L'albero degli zoccoli/The Tree of Wooden Clogs* (1978); it offered Fellini the opportunity to shoot *I clowns* (1970) and *Prova d'orchestra/Orchestra Rehearsal* (1978); it allowed Antonioni to experiment with documentary (*Chung-Kuo*, 1972) and electronics (*Il mistero di Oberwald/The Oberwald Mystery*, 1980) and produced some of the finest work by Liliana Cavani*, Nelo Risi, Bernardo Bertolucci*, the Taviani brothers, Olmi, Marco Bellocchio* and many others, including Vittorio Cottafavi*, Pier Paolo Pasolini* and Pupi Avati*. With Francesco Rosi's* *Cristo si è fermato a Eboli/ Christ Stopped at Eboli* (1979), RAI started making two versions of each title: a feature-length one for theatrical release and a longer one for television. More recently, RAI has played, albeit decreasingly, an important role in promoting experimental film, in association both with Olmi's school in Bassano and with Nanni Moretti's* company Sacher, and has financed the work of young *auteurs* such as Gianni Amelio*. Since the early 1980s film production in Italy would have ground to a halt without the intervention of television, although RAI's proportion has been largely eclipsed in the last few years by the massive investment by companies associated with Berlusconi's Fininvest*. GVo

Italian director, who graduated in medicine (specialising in psychiatry), before working as an assistant to Alberto Lattuada* and Mario Soldati*. After the war and emigration to Switzerland, he returned to the cinema, shooting documentaries, writing on film and working as a scriptwriter, an enthusiastic participant in the creative climate of the northern Italian cities of the time. Before finding his vocation as the sceptic and ironic castigator of contemporary mores, Risi, like many others, went through 'social' neo-realism* (he took part in the collective film inspired by Cesare Zavattini*, *Amore in città/Love in the City*, 1953) and then 'rose-tinted' neo-realism (*neo-realismo rosa*), of which he was one of the creators with his enormously successful *Poveri ma belli/Poor But Beautiful* (1956). Risi became the perfect screen interpreter of the greed and arrogance of the 1950s and 1960s, and a master of the caustic comedy of manners [> COMMEDIA ALL'ITALIANA], helped by the producer Mario Cecchi Gori* and a brilliant team of comedy scriptwriters and actors, including his favourite star, Vittorio Gassman*. He directed Gassman in *Il mattatore/Love and Larceny* (1959) and in the masterly *Il sorpasso/The Easy Life* (1962), a skilful description of Italy's and his own transition from youthful euphoria to utilitarian cynicism; Gassman with Ugo Tognazzi* in *La marcia su Roma/The March to Rome* (1962) and *I mostri/The Monsters* (1963); and Gassman again in *Il tigre/The Tiger and the Pussycat* (1967), *In nome del popolo italiano/In the Name of the Italian People* (1972) and *Profumo di donna/Scent of a Woman* (1974). One of his most successful films was *Una vita difficile/A Difficult Life* (1961), which gave Alberto Sordi* the chance to prove his capability as a dramatic actor. Risi's later work became increasingly melancholy (with a few notable exceptions such as *Straziami ma di baci saziami/Hurt Me, But Cover Me with Your Kisses*, 1968), to the detriment of the more trenchant side of his talent, which had made him an undisputed master of Italian caustic comedy. PDA

Other Films Include: *Pane, amore e .../Scandal in Sorrento* (1955); *Belle ma povere/Beautiful But Poor* (1957); *Venezia, la luna e tu/Venice, the Moon and You* (1958); *Poveri milionari/Poor Millionaires, Il vedovo/The Widower* (1959); *A porte chiuse/Behind Closed Doors* (1961); *Il gaucho/The Gaucho* (1964); *L'ombrellone/The Parasol/Weekend, Italian Style, Operazione San Gennaro/Treasure of San Gennaro* (1966); *Vedo nudo/I See Everybody Naked* (1969); *La moglie del prete/The Priest's Wife* (1970); *Noi donne siamo fatte così/Women: So We Are Made* (1971); *Mordi e fuggi/Bite and Run, Sessomatto/How Funny Can Sex Be?* (1973); *Telefoni bianchi/White Telephones/The Career of a Chambermaid, Anima persa/Lost Soul* (1976); *La stanza del vescovo/The Bishop's Room, I nuovi mostri/Viva Italia* [co-dir.] (1977); *Primo amore* (1978); *Caro papà* (1979); *Sono fotogenico* (1980); *Fantasma d'amore/Ghost of Love* (1981); *Sesso e volentieri/Sex* and *Violence* (1982); *Scemo di guerra* (1985); *Il commissario Lo Gatto/Inspector Lo Gatto* (1986); *Teresa* (1987); *Tolgo il disturbo* (1990); *Giovani e belli* (1996).

RISI, Marco   Milan 1951

Italian director. The son of Dino Risi* and nephew of the poet and director Nelo Risi, he started his apprenticeship within the family circle as assistant and scriptwriter for his father's film *Caro papà* (1979), and worked with Alberto Sordi*, Duccio Tessari and Carlo Vanzina. Marco Risi directed his first film in 1983, *Vado da vivere da solo*, followed by *Un ragazzo e una ragazza* (1984) and *Colpo di fulmine* (1985), all starring comic actor Jerry Calà. From the start his work met with popularity. With *Soldati, 365 all'alba* (1987), about military life, he tried a new theme and a new genre, together with a more personal style. Similarly, *Mery per sempre* (1989) and *Ragazzi fuori* (1990), both depicting events from the lives of young Sicilian delinquents, seemed to initiate a new current of 'neo-neorealism'. More journalistic was *Il muro di gomma* (1991), the reconstruction of the 'Ustica case' (an unexplained air crash) in which he denounced the serious military and political responsibilities for this tragic event. In *Nel continente nero* (1992), Risi tried to resurrect the satiric vein of the *commedia all'italiana** of the 1960s, of which his father's masterpiece *Il sorpasso/The Easy Life* (1962) was an archetype. He directed *Nel continente nero* in 1993 and *Branco* in 1994. PDA

RIZZOLI, Angelo   Milan 1889–1970

Italian producer. A publishing tycoon, Rizzoli first ventured into the cinema in the early 1930s with the publication of popular weekly magazines such as *Novella Cinema*, followed by the creation of a company which produced Max Ophuls' *La signora di tutti* (1934) and Mario Camerini's* *Darò un milione* (1935). His next involvement came in the 1950s with the creation of Cineriz and other joint-stock companies (Dear, Riama, Rizzoli Film). Rizzoli was an unusual producer, the cinema representing only one of his many activities. He possessed a strong sense of the 'popular', leading to huge success with the Don Camillo comedy series, starring Fernandel and Gino Cervi*, 'film operas' (Carmine Gallone's* *Puccini*, 1953), melodramas and sensationalist documentaries (Gualtiero Jacopetti's *Mondo cane*, 1962). The producer of a very large range of titles (more than forty films between 1952 and 1955 alone), he was a pioneer of international co-productions, including René Clair's *Les Belles de nuit* (1952, Fr./It.) and *Porte des Lilas* (1957, Fr./It.), Joseph Mankiewicz's *The Barefoot Contessa* (1954, US/It.), Fritz Lang's *Der Tiger von Eschnapur/The Tiger of Bengal* and *Das indische Grabmal/The Hindu Tomb* (1959, both

Ger./It./Fr.). He gave *carte blanche* to his *auteurs*, relying on his ability to choose the right director in the first place, with some justification since he produced, among other films, Roberto Rossellini's* *Francesco giullare di Dio/The Flowers of St Francis/Francis, God's Jester* (1950), Vittorio De Sica's* *Umberto D.* (1952), Michelangelo Antonioni's* *L'eclisse/The Eclipse* (1962), and Federico Fellini's* *La dolce vita* (1960), $8\frac{1}{2}$ (1963) and *Giulietta degli spiriti/Juliet of the Spirits* (1965). After Rizzoli's death, Cineriz still found some success with Nino Manfredi's *Per grazia ricevuta* (1970) and popular films starring Paolo Villaggio and former rock star Adriano Celentano. Cineriz came to an end in the early 1980s when it was involved in the intricate financial, political and legal vicissitudes of Angelo Rizzoli Jr's RCS and of the daily *Corriere della Sera*; it was eventually sold to emerging television tycoon Silvio Berlusconi. GVo

ROSI, Francesco   Naples 1922

Italian director. Rosi's apprenticeship began in 1948, when he was assistant director to Luchino Visconti* on *La terra trema* – a film whose uncompromising neo-realism* and dedication to the Sicilian proletariat were to influence Rosi's own investigative approach to filmmaking and his perennial return to the 'Southern Question'. Rosi was Visconti's assistant again on *Bellissima* (1951) and *Senso* (1954), while working with other postwar directors, including Michelangelo Antonioni*, Goffredo Alessandrini*, Luigi Zampa* and Mario Monicelli*. His directorial debut was *La sfida/The Challenge* (1958), a film about the *camorra* (the Neapolitan Mafia), which won a prize at the Venice* festival. By 1962, the year of *Salvatore Giuliano*, Rosi had perfected his technique of *cine-inchiesta*, or investigative cinema, about cases involving power relationships between charismatic individuals, corporations, criminal organisations, and the state. Refusing to sensationalise his subject matter and adopting a dispassionate view that was nonetheless partisan, Rosi labelled his approach 'a second phase of neo-realism', characterised by a new 'critical realism of overt ideological intentions' and anticipating the cinema of Costa-Gavras and Elio Petri* in the late 1960s and the 1970s [> ITALIAN POLITICAL CINEMA]. *Salvatore Giuliano* best exemplifies Rosi's investigative filmmaking, with its inquiry into the death of the Sicilian bandit turned political hero turned right-wing terrorist. The prize-winning *Le mani sulla città/Hands Over the City* (1963), starring Rod Steiger, concerned a scandal in the Neapolitan construction industry, while *Il caso Mattei/The Mattei Affair* (1972, starring Gian Maria Volonté*, like several other Rosi films) probed the mysterious death of an oil magnate. *Lucky Luciano* (1973), like *Salvatore ·Giuliano*, applied Rosi's anti-spectacular approach to a flamboyant criminal character; Rosi was more interested in how American and Italian authorities used Luciano to further their own agendas.

The year 1975 signalled Rosi's turn to literary (and in the case of *Carmen*, operatic) sources, though this did not imply a withdrawal from committed film-making. Leonardo Sciascia's all too topical novel *Il contesto* provided the model for *Cadaveri eccellenti/Illustrious Corpses* (1976), about the serial assassinations of magistrates presiding over politically and criminally sensitive trials in Sicily, while Edmonde Charles Roux's text inspired Rosi's exposé of Mafia links between Sicily and New York in *Dimenticare Palermo/To Forget Palermo* (1990). Even the adaptation of Carlo Levi's *Cristo si è fermato a Eboli/Christ Stopped at Eboli* (1979), set in 1935–36, was topical in its treatment of the seemingly irresolvable Southern Question. Andrei Platonov's short story *The Third Son* was transformed into an allegory of the internal Italian diaspora in *Tre fratelli/Three Brothers* (1981), in which a mother's funeral brings together the three sons who had strayed, both geographically and ideologically, from their southern roots. As well as being a leading exponent of political cinema, Rosi is an emblematic figure in his attempt to negotiate powerful realist experiences within an exploration of the medium's own spectacular properties. MMa

Other Films Include: *I magliari* (1959); *Il momento della verità/The Moment of Truth* (1965); *C'era una volta/More Than a Miracle* (1967); *Uomini contro* (1970); *Cronaca di una morte annunciata/Chronicle of a Death Foretold* (1987).

ROSSELLINI, Roberto   Rome 1906–77

Italian director. Roberto Rossellini is generally regarded, alongside Vittorio De Sica* and Luchino Visconti*, as one of the great masters of postwar Italian neo-realism*. Yet his neo-realist work was only a small part, and in some ways an anomalous one, of a long and varied career that included many types of artistic experiment both in cinema and television.

Rossellini began his film career in the late 1930s as a maker of short films and as scriptwriter and assistant director on Goffredo Alessandrini's* *Luciano Serra pilota/The Pilot Luciano Serra* (1938), a film conceived and supervised by Mussolini's son Vittorio. His first feature as director was *La nave bianca* (1941), a narrativised documentary about a hospital ship, which was followed by two more conventionally fictional war films, *Un pilota ritorna* (1942) and *L'uomo dalla croce* (1943). Rossellini's next film, *Roma città aperta/Rome, Open City*, is generally considered a founding work of neo-realism and, along with his following two films, comprises his 'neo-realist trilogy'. Although the documentary look of some sequences of *Roma città aperta*, filmed in part during the nine-month Nazi occupation of Rome, conveys the sense of happening 'on location', the film's narrative is firmly rooted in the conventions of Italian family and religious melodrama. *Paisà*, his next film, explores the ironies pervading the Allied 'liberation' of Italy. It intercuts newsreel footage of the Allied advance with staged vignettes occurring across Italy, with many of these scenes shot on location amid the recently transformed landscape of postwar Italy. The third of the trilogy, *Germania anno zero/Germany Year Zero* (1947), through a studio-set narrative and location shots of war-devastated Berlin, examines the plight of defeated Germany. Thereafter Rossellini increasingly separated himself from the neo-realist mainstream. By the late 1940s, with *Una voce umana* (based on Jean Cocteau's play *La Voix humaine*), *Il miracolo* (based on a story by Federico Fellini*) [the two films released as *L'amore/Love*, 1948] and *La macchina ammazzacattivi/The Machine that Kills Bad People* (made in 1948, released in 1952), about a man who turns a camera into a killing machine, the projection and construction of reality became central concerns to Rossellini. The first two films, with central per-formances by Anna Magnani*, also explored a woman's social alien-ation and consequent psychic unravelling. These are themes that Rossellini developed further in his films with Ingrid Bergman, with whom he was by then identified in the public mind, and who was to star in *Stromboli, terra di Dio/Stromboli* (1950). Their much publicised off-screen romance and the fact that in the film the Bergman charac-ter leaves her husband led to public scandal and the film's release by RKO (who had commissioned it) in a cut and modified version. Rossellini's subsequent films with Bergman – now his wife – were com-mercial failures though critically praised; *Viaggio in Italia/Journey to Italy* (1954) in particular was much admired in France by André Bazin and the future New Wave directors.

To revive his career Rossellini made a number of more mainstream films, notably *Il generale Della Rovere* (1959, starring Vittorio De Sica*). But after *Anima nera* (1962) he abruptly abandoned the cin-ema, to return to it only in 1974 with *Anno uno/Italy Year One* (a biopic of Christian Democrat leader Alcide De Gaspari). Instead he turned to television, for which he directed a long series of dramatised historical documentaries tracing the development of Western civilis-ation from Ancient Greece to the present day. Of these the (deserv-edly) most famous is *La Prise de pouvoir par Louis XIV/The Rise to Power of Louis XIV*, made for French television in 1966. Most, how-ever, were made by Rossellini's own company in association with RAI*, with a view to worldwide sales which were rarely forthcoming. In spite of the limited impact of his television work, Rossellini was not discouraged and at the time of his death he was working on a tele-vision biography of Karl Marx. JHa

Bib: Peter Brunette, *Roberto Rossellini* (1987).

Other Films: **Shorts**: *Daphne* (1936); *Prélude à l'après-midi d'un faune* (1938); *Fantasia sottomarina, Il tacchino prepotente, La vispa teresa* (1939); *Il ruscello di ripasottile* (1941). **Features**: *Desiderio* (1943, completed by Marcello Pagliero in 1946); *Francesco giullare di Dio/The Flowers of St Francis/Francis, God's Jester* (1950); *I sette peccati capitali/The Seven Deadly Sins* (1951, ep. *L'invidia*); *Europa '51* (1952); *Siamo donne/We, the Women* [ep. *Ingrid Bergman*]; *Dov'è la libertà?* (1953); *Amori di mezzo secolo/Mid-Century Loves* [ep. *Napoli '43*], *Giovanna d'Arco al rogo/Joan of Arc at the Stake, La paura/Fear* (1954); *India* (1958); *Era notte a Roma/Escape By Night, Viva l'Italia/Garibaldi* (1960); *Vanina Vanini* (1961); *RoGoPaG/Laviamoci il cervello* (1963, ep. *Illibatezza*). **Television**: *Torino nei cento anni* (1961); *L'età del ferro/The Iron Age* (1964); *La lotta dell'uomo per la sua sopravvivenza, Idea d'un isola* (1967); *Atti degli apostoli/Acts of the Apostles* (1969); *Socrate* (1970); *Intervista con Salvador Allende* (1971); *Blaise Pascal, Agostino d'Ippona, L'età di Cosimo de' Medici* (1972); *Cartesius/Descartes* (1974); *The World Population, Il messia* (1975); *Concerto per Michelangelo, Beaubourg, Centre d'art et de culture Georges Pompidou* (1977).

ROTA, Nino   Nini Rinaldi; Milan 1911 – Rome 1979

Italian composer. Although he composed nearly 150 scores for film and television, Nino Rota is mostly remembered for his close collaboration with Federico Fellini*, director and composer having worked together from *Lo sceicco bianco/The White Sheik* (1952) to *Prova d'orchestra/Orchestra Rehearsal* (1978). Rota's music has been described as a 'consistently sympathetic musical alter ego for Fellini in his quixotic leaps in style', and it is undoubtedly an essential constituent of the film-maker's best work, whether this be the haunting theme from *La strada* (1954), the circus band from $8\frac{1}{2}$ (1963) or the hypnotic synthesised score which structures much of *Casanova* (1976). Because of this celebrated partnership, there is a danger of overlooking Rota's work with other major directors both in and outside Europe. Rota scored important films for, among others, Luchino Visconti* – notably *Rocco e i suoi fratelli/Rocco and His Brothers* (1960) and *Il gattopardo/The Leopard* (1963) – and Francis Ford Coppola. The lush melodic score which Rota composed for Coppola's *The Godfather* (1972, US) received a BAFTA Award and an Oscar nomination, and his work for *The Godfather, Part II* was awarded an Oscar in 1974.

A child musical prodigy (composing his first oratorio aged eleven), Rota leaves an impressive body of concert music which spans the range of classical genres from chamber music to opera. Rota was also director of the Bari Conservatory from 1950 until 1978. SH

ROTUNNO, Giuseppe

Rome 1923

Italian cinematographer. After a lengthy period of activity as a camera operator, Rotunno made his debut as director of photography in the final part of *Senso* (1954), taking over the work of the great G. R. Aldo*, who had died in a road accident. Other important stages in his career, in the US and Italy, were: Mario Monicelli's* *La grande guerra/The Great War* (1959), where he reproduced old-fashioned colours, as he did for the newsreels in Federico Fellini's* *E la nave va/And the Ship Sails On* (1983); *On the Beach* (1959, US), about post-atomic desolation, with extensive use of filters and backlighting; *All That Jazz* (1980, US), and *The Adventures of Baron Munchausen* (1989, US/Ger.). Although such films as Huston's *La Bibbia/The Bible in the Beginning* ... (1966), Fred Zinnemann's *Five Days One Summer* (1982, US), and *Regarding Henry* (1991, US) are – among others – indicative of his high standards of professionalism, it was with Fellini and Luchino Visconti* that he was most creative. For Visconti he was eminently successful in heightening the poetic effects of *Le notti bianche/White Nights* (1957) through widespread use of gauzes and the mixing of two different types of film stock. He continued in the same vein in *Rocco e i suoi fratelli/Rocco and His Brothers* (1960) and *Il gattopardo/The Leopard* (1963). For Fellini, he orchestrated the brilliant colours of *Fellini-Satyricon* (1969) and the funereal setting of *Casanova* (1976), especially the scene of the empty theatre, regarded by many as a masterpiece, and went through a whole range of approaches for *Roma/Fellini's Roma* (1972), *Amarcord* (1973) and *La città delle donne/City of Women* (1980), sincerely convinced, like Fellini, that 'truth can be recreated'. GVo

S

SANDRELLI, Stefania

Viareggio 1946

Italian actress. The winner of a beauty contest, Stefania Sandrelli was noticed by Pietro Germi*, who gave her the role of the adolescent who drives the Baron (Marcello Mastroianni*) to uxoricide in *Divorzio all'italiana/Divorce – Italian Style* (1961). Characterised by an androgynous beauty, graceful gestures and a vivacious expression, she stood out immediately for her charming self-confidence before the camera. After this dazzling debut, Sandrelli's artistic success reached its height in Antonio Pietrangeli's* masterpiece *Io la conoscevo bene/I Knew Her Well* (1965). She plays the unforgettable Adriana, a frail, alienated woman of the boom years, uprooted and adrift in the greedy and hostile city, a character that was to fix her 'type' for a while. In her rich but discontinuous career certain roles stand out, such as the narrow-minded wife in Bernardo Bertolucci's* *Il conformista/The Conformist* (1970), the southern worker in Luigi Comencini's* *Delitto d'amore* (1974) and the washer of dishes who finds liberation in marriage and militancy in Ettore Scola's* *C'eravamo tanto amati/We All Loved Each Other So Much* (1974). After the success of Tinto Brass' *La chiave/The Key* (1984) she entered a phase dominated by sexually explicit films, although this was soon followed by some impressive characterisations, particularly in 'choral' films such as Mario Monicelli's* *Speriamo che sia femmina/Let's Hope It's a Girl* (1986) and Scola's *La famiglia/The Family* (1987). PV

Other Films Include: *La bella di Lodi* (1962); *Sedotta e abbandonata/Seduced and Abandoned* (1963); *L'immorale/The Climax* (1966); *Partner, L'amante di Gramigna* (1968); *Brancaleone alle Crociate* (1970); *Alfredo Alfredo* (1972); *Novecento/1900* (1976); *L'ingorgo/Bottleneck, La terrazza* (1979); *Segreti segreti* (1984); *Mignon è partita* (1984).

SCARPELLI, Furio – see AGE, Agenore Incrocci

SCOLA, Ettore   Trevico 1931

Italian director and scriptwriter. After a period as a comic journalist, the young Scola was instrumental, as a scriptwriter, in the emergence of *commedia all'italiana**, working on Steno's* *Un americano a Roma* (1954) and Dino Risi's* *Il sorpasso/The Easy Life* (1962) and *I mostri/The Monsters* (1963), the last two co-written by Ruggero Maccari. With Maccari again he co-scripted a number of films directed by Antonio Pietrangeli*, including *Nata di marzo* (1958), *Fantasmi a Roma/Phantom Lovers* (1961), *La parmigiana* (1963) and, best of all, *Io la conoscevo bene/I Knew Her Well* (1965). Scola quickly rose to prominence as a director of comedies of manners informed by social criticism, with *Se permettete parliamo di donne/Let's Talk About Women* (1964), *La congiuntura* (1965, starring Vittorio Gassman*), *Il commissario Pepe* (1969, with Ugo Tognazzi*), *Dramma della gelosia: tutti i particolari in cronaca/The Pizza Triangle* (1970) and *Permette? Rocco Papaleo* (1972, starring Marcello Mastroianni*). A complete change of direction came with *Trevico-Torino, viaggio nel Fiat-Nam* (1973), depicting, in *cinéma-vérité* style, the migration of southern workers to the Fiat factories of the north. From this point onwards, he alternated different styles and sensitivities. On the one hand, he took on the legacy of *commedia all'italiana*, in particular with *C'eravamo tanto amati/We All Loved Each Other So Much* (1974), *Brutti, sporchi* *e cattivi* (1976), *La terrazza/The Terrace* (1979), *Maccheroni* (1985) and the ambitious *La famiglia/The Family* (1987). On the other hand, he looked abroad with *La nuit de Varennes* (1982, Fr.) and *Le Bal* (1983, Fr.), which brought him international recognition. Scola reached his peak with *Una giornata particolare/A Special Day* (1977), a close confrontation between a man and a woman (Mastroianni and Sophia Loren*, both cast against type) marginalised by Fascism yet capable of relating to each other; the film represents a particular aspect of Italian cinema at its best, with its combination of clearly defined milieu and humanism. Scola was an active member of the former Communist Party (PCI) and in charge of its cultural activities. He dedicated *Mario, Maria e Mario* (1992) to the PCI's recent crisis (which led to a change of name, from PCI to PDS – Partito Democratico della Sinistra). PDA

Other Films Include: *Thrilling* (1965, ep. *Il vittimista*); *L'arcidiavolo/ The Devil in Love* (1966); *Riusciranno i nostri eroi a ritrovare l'amico misteriosamente scomparso in Africa?* (1968); *Signore e signori, buonanotte* (1976, co-dir.); *I nuovi mostri/The New Monsters/Viva Italia* (1977, co-dir.); *Passione d'amore/Passions of Love* (1981); *Splendor* (1988); *Che ora è?/What Time is It?* (1989); *Il viaggio del capitan Fracassa* (1990); *Romanzo di un giovane povero* (1995).

SERATO, Massimo   Oderzo 1916 – Rome 1989

Italian actor. After leaving the Centro Sperimentale* in Rome, Serato walked straight into cinema as Alida Valli's* co-star in *Piccolo mondo antico/Old-Fashioned World* (1941). His handsome profile made him the favourite young actor of the 'calligraphic' directors of the period, including Alberto Lattuada* (*Giacomo l'idealista*, 1942), Ferdinando Poggioli (*Le sorelle Materassi*, 1943) and Mario Soldati* (*Quartieri alti*, 1944). During the war he also worked in variety shows alongside Anna Magnani* (with whom he had a son). In the postwar period, he specialised in charming scoundrels, and won a Silver Ribbon for his Nazi officer in *Il sole sorge ancora* (1946). He attracted attention for his ironic Don Juan in *Una domenica d'agosto/Sunday in August* (1950), for the cynical protagonist of *Febbre di vivere* (1953), and for *Il magistrato* (1959). Like Rossano Brazzi* a durable 'eternal masculine' type, he starred in all popular genres: melodrama, swashbuckler, peplum* and Italian Westerns*, historical film and science-fiction, costarring with Hedy Lamarr and Martine Carol. Until the early 1970s he appeared as 'guest star' in American super-productions filmed in Europe, although he also contributed some good characterisations in films by Elio Petri*, Carlo Lizzani*, Nicholas Ray and Nicolas Roeg. In De Crescenzo's *32 dicembre* (1987) he embodied a character who, though no longer young, was still full of vitality. MMo

SOLDATI, Mario Turin 1906

Italian director and writer. A well-known writer of both fiction and non-fiction (*America primo amore/America – First Love*, 1935), Soldati studied for a while at Columbia University in New York. Unable to obtain US citizenship, he returned to Italy and joined Cines* in 1931, soon becoming an assistant director and a leading scriptwriter. He scripted films for Alessandro Blasetti* (*La tavola dei poveri/The Poor Men's Table*, 1932), for Walther Ruttmann (*Acciaio/Arbeit macht Frei/Steel*, 1934), and for Augusto Genina* (*Castelli in aria/Ins blau leben/Castles in the Air*, 1939, Ger./It.). But his most famous collaboration was with Mario Camerini*, for whom he worked as assistant director and scriptwriter. His first full feature as director was *Dora Nelson* (1939), a comedy of mistaken identity starring Camerini's wife Assia Noris*. He then went on to direct a number of successful adventure films and light comedies throughout the 1940s and 1950s. Sceptical of the cinema's potential as an art, he claimed that he only made films because they brought in more money than writing. Nevertheless he achieved distinction with his adaptations of nineteenth-century novels, notably Antonio Fogazzaro's *Piccolo mondo antico/Old-Fashioned World* (1941) and *Malombra* (1942), which aligned him with the so-called 'calligraphic' school of film-makers who concentrated on visual refinement and elegance as a deliberate withdrawal from Fascist culture. Unlike others in the calligraphic school, however, Soldati did not wholeheartedly embrace neo-realism* after the war, preferring to make popular genre films for producers such as Carlo Ponti* and Dino De Laurentiis*, for instance *La donna del fiume/Woman of the River* (1954), which gave Sophia Loren* one of her early starring roles. JHa

Other Films as Director Include: *Tutto per la donna/Anything for the Lady* (1940); *Quartieri alti* (1943, released 1945); *Le miserie del signor Travet/His Young Wife* (1945); *Eugenia Grandet* (1947); *Her Favourite Husband* (1950, UK); *O.K. Nerone/OK Nero* (1951); *I tre corsari/Three Pirates* (1952); *Jolanda – la figlia del Corsaro Nero* (1953); *Policarpo, ufficiale di scrittura/Policarpo, Master Writer* (1959).

SOLINAS, Franco Cagliari 1927 – Fregene 1982

Italian scriptwriter, possibly the most important and most coherent Marxist writer in European cinema during the 1960s and 1970s. After apprenticeship with Steno and with Mario Monicelli*, he turned his novel *Squarciò*, about Sardinian poachers, into the script for *La grande strada azzurra/The Wide Blue Road* (1957), directed by Gillo Pontecorvo*, with whom he had already worked on *Giovanna* (1957, an episode of *Die Windrose*, Ger.). His association with Pontecorvo continued for *Kapò* (1960), *La battaglia di Algeri/The Battle of Algiers* (1966) and *Queimada!/Burn!* (1969), all of which present civilian suffering with documentary rigour in their uncompromising rejection of totalitarianism. Solinas showed a particular interest in ambiguous anti-heroes animated by some sort of historical awareness. It was in this spirit that he wrote *Salvatore Giuliano* (1962, dir. Francesco Rosi*), *Etat de siège/State of Siege* (1973, Fr./It./Ger., dir. Costa-Gavras) and *Il sospetto* (1975, dir. Francesco Maselli*) [> ITALIAN POLITICAL CINEMA], as well as *Mr. Klein* (1977, Fr./It., dir. Joseph Losey). Solinas also made a significant contribution to the Itallian Western* with *Quién sabe?/A Bullet for the General* (1966), *La resa dei conti/The Big Gundown* (1967), *Il mercenario/A Professional Gun* (1968) and *Tepepa/Blood and Guns* (1969). Before his death Solinas wrote a splendid script for Losey on *Ibn Saud* (1969), the unifier and first king of Saudi Arabia. It was never made into a film but was published posthumously as *La battaglia* (1984). MMo

Other Films Include: *Persiane chiuse/Behind Closed Shutters* (1950); *Ombre bianche/The Savage Innocents* (1960, It./Fr./US); *Vanina Vanini* (1961); *Una vita violenta* (1962); *Le soldatesse* (1965); *Hanna K.* (1983).

SONEGO, Rodolfo   Florence 1921

Italian scriptwriter, an important contributor to neo-realism* with scripts for *Achtung banditi!* (1951, dir. Carlo Lizzani*), *Roma ora 11* (1952, dir. Giuseppe De Santis*), and two films by Alberto Lattuada*, *Anna* (1952) and *La spiaggia/The Beach* (1954). His own comic vein emerged in the mid-1950s. He was one of the scriptwriters on *Totò e Carolina* (1953), one of the best of the many (often mediocre) films starring Neapolitan comedian Totò*. But what finally brought Sonego into the world of *commedia all'italiana*, and marked a turning point in his career, was his encounter with Alberto Sordi*, for whom he wrote scripts for many years. *Il seduttore* (1954) is a landmark of the genre, both a mature version of earlier dialect farces and the introduction of new themes, social milieux (the emerging middle classes) and modes of thinking. Further films included *Il marito* (1958), *Il moralista* (1959), *Il vedovo/The Widower* (1959), *Il vigile/The Cop* (1960) and *Il diavolo* (1963), all depicting the hypothetical 'average' Italian on which Sordi successfully built his image. Sonego's masterpiece – and the best of Sordi's many roles – was undoubtedly *Una vita difficile/A Difficult Life* (1961), an exemplary parable of an ex-partisan who refuses the 'liberal' yet conformist new moral thinking of Italy's economic miracle. The success of this film was also due to skilful direction by Dino Risi*, for whom Sonego also provided the story for *Il sorpasso/The Easy Life* (1962). The collaboration with Sordi continued through the 1970s, producing two more films of note: *Detenuto in attesa di giudizio* (1971) and *Lo scopone scientifico* (1972). PDA

SORDI, Alberto   Rome 1920

Italian actor and director. Though less well-known internationally than some of his compatriots, such as Marcello Mastroianni* and Vittorio Gassman*, Sordi is one of the funniest and most successful postwar Italian actors. His career began in the early 1940s in variety. For the cinema he dubbed Oliver Hardy's voice and on the radio (in the late 1940s) he developed a pair of successful characters – Mario Pio and Conte Claro – who became the basis of his screen persona. After he appeared in Federico Fellini's* *Lo sceicco bianco/The White Sheik* (1952) and *I vitelloni/The Spivs* (1953), a character was created for him in Steno's episode film *Un giorno in pretura* (1953). This character, based on the new lifestyle imported into Italy by the 'liberators', and further elaborated in Steno's *Un americano a Roma*, initiated a long and prosperous career. Sordi was the new young suburban Roman, voluble and uninhibited in his way of dressing. This exhilarating character ran through more than twenty years of Italian cinema and society, maturing as he went along, and generating a counter-history 'from the bottom' of Italy's profound changes from Fascism to the *'anni di piombo'* (literally 'leaden years', of terrorism) and up to the 1980s. In the late 1980s and early 1990s, Sordi's prime concern has been a series of television programmes significantly entitled *Storia di un italiano*, 'The story of an Italian'. But the best of his work, under the guidance of talented scriptwriters (Age* and Scarpelli*, Sonego*) and directors, was in the 1950s and 1960s. With Mario Monicelli's* *La grande guerra/The Great War* (1959), Luigi Comencini's* *Tutti a casa/Everybody Go Home!* (1960) and Dino Risi's* *Una vita difficile/A Difficult Life* (1961), Sordi added dramatic weight and stature to his comic acting without sacrificing the 'antihero' image which has become, for better or worse, a model of Italianness. Beginning with *Fumo di Londra/London Smoke* (1966), Sordi also directed himself in a number of films. Although he rarely found again the balance of his golden years, he has continued to enjoy success with some excellent roles, such as the tragic father figure in Monicelli's *Un borghese piccolo piccolo/An Average Man* (1977). PDA

Other Films as Actor Include: *Mamma mia, che impressione!* (1951); *Il seduttore* (1954); *Un eroe dei nostri tempi* (1955); *Il conte Max* (1957); *Fortunella, ladro lui, ladro lei* (1958); *Il moralista* (1959); *I magliari* (1959); *Il giudizio universale/The Last Judgment* (1961); *Il commissario, Il mafioso* (1962); *Il boom* (1963); *Il medico della mutua* (1968); *Nell'anno del signore/In the Name of the Lord* (1969); *Lo scopone scientifico* (1972); *L'ingorgo/Bottleneck* (1979); *Il marchese del Grillo*

(1981). **As Director**: *Amore mio aiutami* (1969); *Polvere di stelle/
Stardust* (1973); *Finchè c'è guerra c'è esperanza* (1974); *Il comune
senso del pudore* (1976); *Le vacanze intelligenti* (1978); *Io e Caterina*
(1980); *Io so che tu sai che io so* (1982); *In viaggio con papà* (1982); *Il
tassinaro* (1983); *Tutti dentro* (1984); *Un tassinaro a New York* (1987);
Assolto per avere commesso il fatto (1992); *Nestore – l'ultima corsa*
(1994).

SPAGHETTI WESTERNS – see ITALIAN WESTERNS

STEELE, Barbara   Liverpool 1938

British actress, who became a cult icon of Italian horror films* in the
1960s. After seeing her in a small role in one of her British films, Mario
Bava* hired her for the lead in his directorial debut, *La maschera del
demonio/Mask of the Demon/Black Sunday* (1960). Steele has always
maintained that anyone could have played the role, but the film is
structured around her physical presence, as were the horror films she
subsequently made in Italy. Her operatic, gestural style of performance brought back the figure of the silent film *diva* [> DIVISMO], but it
was her face in close-up that inspired a unique fetishistic fascination.
With her chalky skin, high cheekbones and flowing black hair, she became the paradoxical image of a living-death mask, a head of the
Medusa which the camera could never fix or penetrate as completely
as the mask of the title does when its spikes are hammered into her.
This snuff-movie aesthetic (similar to that of Michael Powell's *Peeping
Tom*, released the same year) is crucial to Steele's films, whose narra-
tives perpetually suspend her as a figure of life-in-death. Steele made
a few films in Hollywood and appeared in such art films such as
Federico Fellini's* $8\frac{1}{2}$ (1963) and, later, Louis Malle's *Pretty Baby*
(1978, US), but her career slowed down considerably after the mid-
1960s and she remains indelibly associated with a short but intense
phase of the Italian horror film. CJ

Other Films Include: *L'orribile segreto del Dottor Hichcock/The
Terror of Doctor Hichcock* (1962); *Danza macabra/Castle of Blood, I
lunghi capelli della morte/The Long Hair of Death* (1964).

STENO   Stefano Vanzina; Rome 1915–88

Italian director and screenwriter. Stefano Vanzina, who signed almost
all his films simply as Steno, was one of the most prolific Italian directors of the postwar period, often functioning as co-screenwriter. At
first in collaboration with Mario Monicelli* and then on his own, he directed a stream of starring vehicles for the great comedian Totò* in

112

the 1950s, including the brilliant *Totò a colori* (1952). Although he also directed films in other genres, it was as a writer and director of comedy that he was most successful. GNS

STORARO, Vittorio   Rome 1940

Italian cinematographer. A graduate of the Centro Sperimentale* (1960) and of Camillo and Luigi Bazzoni's school, Storaro made his debut as director of photography with Franco Rossi's *Giovinezza, giovinezza* (1969), his only black-and-white film. This creative *'metteur en lumière'* is linked first and foremost with Bernardo Bertolucci*, having been in charge of photography on all but one of his films from *Strategia del ragno/The Spider's Stratagem* (1970) to *Little Buddha* (1993). For Bertolucci, Storaro is 'the hand of the painter which I am not and never will be', the artist who miraculously manages to 'give physical form to an idea of light or colour'. A theorist of 'photographic ideology', he produced two very different versions of Paris in *Il conformista/The Conformist* (1970) and *Ultimo tango a Parigi/Last Tango in Paris* (1972), worked with natural light in *Novecento/1900* (1976) and with symbolic and tonal effects in *La luna* (1979), followed by the inventiveness of *The Last Emperor* (1987) and *The Sheltering Sky* (1990), in which he fully demonstrated his ability to 'write' with light. The only European cinematographer to win three Oscars, Storaro found new critical and professional recognition in America for his work with Francis Ford Coppola on *Apocalypse Now* (1979), especially in the extensive night scenes; *One from the Heart* (1982), in which he experimented with electronics and used different colours to portray different characters; *Tucker: The Man and His Dream* (1988); and the Coppola episode of *New York Stories* (1989). Also notable were his contributions to Warren Beatty's *Reds* (1981) and *Dick Tracy* (1990). Among other directors for whom he produced innovative work were: Salvatore Samperi (*Malizia*, 1973, and *Scandalo*, 1976); Dario Argento* (*L'uccello dalle piume di cristallo/The Gallery Murders*, 1970); and Giuseppe Patroni Griffi (*Addio fratello crudele/Tis a Pity She's a Whore*, 1971, and *Identikit*, 1973). Mention should also be made of Storaro's television work, from Rossi's serial *Eneide* (1970) to *Orlando Furioso* (1972), a complex adaptation by the great theatre director Luca Ronconi, and from the high-definition experiments of Giuliano Montaldo's *Arlecchino a Venezia* to Marvin J. Chomsky's *Peter the Great* (1985, for NBC). MMo

T

TAVIANI, Paolo	San Miniato 1931
and	
TAVIANI, Vittorio	San Miniato 1929

Italian directors. The first films of the Taviani brothers were made with their long-standing friend, Valentino Orsini. Together they experimented in a documentary mode in an attempt to go beyond neo-realism* while preserving certain realist imperatives. They succeeded with the intelligently constructed *Un uomo da bruciare/A Man for Burning* (1962), which retraces the life and death of a Sicilian trade unionist murdered by the Mafia, but rather less well with the incoherent *I fuorilegge del matrimonio/Outlaws of Marriage* (1963). The two brothers on their own then directed *I sovversivi* (1967), an ambitious attempt to combine several stories of personal or political crisis against the background of the funeral of Communist leader Palmiro Togliatti, and the cryptic *Sotto il segno dello Scorpione/Under the Sign of Scorpio* (1969), which initiated their characteristic cinema of utopia, eclectic in style but held together by a consistent Marxism. A sense of stylistic maturity emerged in *San Michele aveva un gallo/St Michael Had a Rooster* (1971), an apologia for a latter-day anarchist. Then, after the grotesque *Allonsanfan* (1974), they made the harsh and sober *Padre padrone/Father Master* (1977), the story of an ultimately victorious struggle against oppressive patriarchal power, and the film which brought them to international attention. Another breaking point was the 'peasant fresco' *La notte di San Lorenzo/The Night of San Lorenzo* (1982), which used a combination of reportage and fantasy, epic and elegy to depict the struggle against Fascism. Since then the Tavianis have distanced themselves somewhat from the political-existentialist tension of their earlier films, concentrating on the pleasures of story-telling and elegant *mise-en-scène*. *Kaos* (1984), a retelling of some Sicilian stories by Luigi Pirandello, is their most successful film in this vein. GVo

Other Films Include: *Il prato/The Meadow* (1980); *Good Morning Babilonia/Good Morning Babylon* (1987); *Il sole sorge anche di notte* (1990); *Fiorile* (1993).

TITANUS

Italian production company. The history of Titanus is closely identified with the Lombardo family. The father, Gustavo, moved from Naples to Rome and in 1928 founded Titanus, initially a distribution

114

company with just a few in-house productions: between 1932 and 1935 it produced thirteen run-of-the-mill films. When Gustavo's son Goffredo (born Naples, 1920) joined the company, Titanus went more systematically into production: it enlarged its Farnesina studios, bought the Scalera theatre chain, and created an integrated distribution and exhibition circuit. It developed a balanced strategy for the production of popular films – by such directors as Raffaello Matarazzo* and Dino Risi* – and *auteur* cinema, with film-makers like Giuseppe De Santis* (*Roma ore 11*, 1952), Alberto Lattuada* (*La Spiaggia/The Beach*, 1954) and Federico Fellini* (*Il bidone/The Swindlers*, 1955). Goffredo Lombardo put a personal stamp on his films and influenced the course of Italian cinema as much as the *auteurs* he produced. In the late 1950s he stood out as a remarkable pioneer of a technically and culturally 'European' cinema, producing Luchino Visconti's* *Rocco e i suoi fratelli/Rocco and His Brothers* (1960) as well as films by Vittorio De Sica*, Mario Monicelli*, Valerio Zurlini*, Elio Petri*, and many others. Titanus experienced a severe crisis in the early to 1960s, mostly because of two super-productions in which it invested enormous funds: Visconti's *Il Gattopardo/The Leopard* (1963) and the disastrous *Sodoma e Gomorra/Sodom and Gomorrah* (1961, dir. Robert Aldrich). But it survived and managed more successful productions, including the 'discovery' of Giuseppe Tornatore* (*Il camorrista/The Camorra Member*, 1986). However, the company's main assets were acquired by the Romagnoli construction group, and ten years later Titanus disappeared. Only a small production house survived, controlled by Goffredo Lombardo and mainly devoted to occasional television productions. GVo

TOGNAZZI, Ugo   Cremona 1922 – Rome 1990

Italian actor. Unlike Vittorio Gassman* or Marcello Mastroianni*, Tognazzi had to wait until his mature years before his talent was fully recognised. He served a long apprenticeship in variety shows and cheap comic television programmes (together with Raimondo Vianello) before finding his way to the cinema. In film, he worked with directors such as Luciano Salce (*Il federale/The Fascist*, 1961), Dino Risi* (*La marcia su Roma/The March to Rome*, 1962) and especially Marco Ferreri*, who made repeated use of him from *L'ape regina/The Conjugal Bed* (1963) onwards. Ferreri was the first to recognise Tognazzi's special talent, particularly his covert sense of humour, which made him more flexible than, for example, the standard Alberto Sordi* character. Tognazzi was one of the key figures in *commedia all'italiana**, whose remarkable flexibility inspired a range of *auteurs* to create non-comic roles for him: Bernardo Bertolucci* (*La tragedia di un uomo ridicolo/The Tragedy of a Ridiculous Man*, 1981, which won Tognazzi an award for best actor at the Cannes film festival), Pier Paolo Pasolini* (*Porcile/Pigsty*, 1969), Alberto Bevilacqua (*La califfa*,

1970). The films for which he will be best remembered include Antonio Pietrangeli's* *Io la conoscevo bene/I Knew Her Well* (1965), Ettore Scola's* *Il commissario Pepe* (1969) and Risi's *In nome del popolo italiano/In the Name of the Italian People* (1972). In all these he specialised in the predicaments of masculinity in the context of provincial or metropolitan despair. A very skilled actor, he gained the esteem of his directors, was encouraged by the critics and adored by the public (yet he bitterly criticised the cinema shortly before he died). His considerable range overlapped with that of other great comic actors of his generation: he could be Sordi's mean 'average' Italian, Gassman's ostentatious braggart, Nino Manfredi's well-behaved 'everyman', and Mastroianni's tormented bourgeois, but he always succeeded in adding some qualities of his own. PDA

Other Films Include: *I cadetti di Guascogna* (1950); *Una bruna indiavolate* (1951); *Noi siamo due evasi* (1959); *La voglia matta* (1962); *Le ore dell'amore/The Hours of Love, I mostri/The Monsters* (1963); *La donna scimmia/The Ape Woman* (1964); *Marcia nuziale* (1966); *Barbarella* (1967, Fr.); *La bambolona, Straziami ma di baci saziami/Hurt Me, But Cover Me with Your Kisses* (1968); *Venga a prendere il caffé da noi/Come Have Coffee With Us* (1970); *L'udienza* (1971); *La Grande Bouffe/La grande abbuffata* [Fr./It.], *Vogliamo i colonnelli* (1973); *Touche pas la femme blanche/Non toccare la donna bianca* [Fr./It.], *Amici miei/My Friends* (1975); *La Cage aux folles/Il vizietto* (1978, Fr./It.); *La terrazza/The Terrace* (1979); *Dagobert* (1984); *Bertoldo, Bertoldino e Cacasenno* (1984).

TORNATORE, Giuseppe   Born 1956

Italian director. On the strength of a promising first film, *Il camorrista/The Camorra Member* (1986), starring Ben Gazzara and produced for Silvio Berlusconi's Fininvest* group, Giuseppe Tornatore went on in 1988 to write and direct *Nuovo Cinema Paradiso/Cinema Paradiso*, the story of a young boy who takes over as projectionist in a cinema in Sicily in the 1930s (the film co-stars Philippe Noiret). After an unsuccessful first release, *Nuovo Cinema Paradiso* was cut and radically reshaped under the supervision of its producer, Franco Cristaldi*, and went on to win the Palme d'or at Cannes and international art-house success in Europe and the United States. He was unable to repeat this success with his next film, *Stanno tutti bene/Everybody's Fine*, about an aged Sicilian patriarch (played by Marcello Mastroianni*) who goes to see his five children who have emigrated to mainland Italy and finds that, contrary to the film's title, they are not doing fine at all. GNS

TOTÒ Antonio de Curtis; Naples 1898 – Rome 1967

Italian actor. Although the quality of the films in which he appeared is sometimes debatable, there is no questioning Totò's status as one of the greatest European comics. He made his name as a variety artist, and entered films at the end of the 1930s. His first films were in the gently absurdist tradition of late 1930s Italian humour. After *Fermo con le mani* (1937, dir. Gero Zambuto), roles were scripted for him by Achille Campanile (*Animali pazzi*, 1939, dir. Carlo Ludovico Bragaglia) and Cesare Zavattini* (*San Giovanni Decollato*, 1940, dir. Amleto Palermi). But that whimsical mode was unsuited to Totò's aggressive character – perpetually hungry for food, for sex, for a place in the sun – which he had created for himself on stage and was to establish in his postwar films. This character had its roots in popular tradition, going as far back as Pulcinella in the *commedia dell'arte* and indeed beyond.

Throughout the postwar period, Totò dominated Italian film production, churning out film after film, most of them written and directed as vehicles for his distinctive talent and persona. The films directed for him by Mario Mattoli, which include *I due orfanelli* (1947), *Totò al giro d'Italia* (1948), the involuntary masterpiece *I pompieri di Viggiù* (1949), *Totò Tarzan* (1950), *Un Turco napoletano* (1953), and *Miseria e nobiltà/Poverty and Nobility* (1954), are probably the most typical. But the first films directed by Steno* and Mario Monicelli* (*Totò cerca casa/Totò Wants a Home*, 1949; *Totò e i re di Roma*, 1951), or Carlo Ludovico Bragaglia (*Totò cerca moglie*, 1950), Luigi Comencini* (*L'imperatore di Capri*, 1949), Camillo Mastrocinque (*Siamo uomini o caporali?*, 1955 – the film Totò most thought of as his own), Sergio Corbucci, Lucio Fulci and Mario Amendola follow much the same path. Heir to the acrobatic '*buffi*' of variety, Totò carried over to the screen his most famous sketches (an anthology of which can be found in Steno's *Totò a colori*, 1952, a minor classic). Totò typically would burst out in a set of frenzied variations, helped by a limitless capacity for improvisation and a disjointed physique which he used like a surreal puppet. The Totò persona, ultimately larger and more 'human' than his characters, was located between the sub-proletariat and the lower middle class; it was resentful, vulgar, aggressive, intolerant of convention and in constant struggle for survival – an ambivalent breath of freedom in the suffocating Italy of the 1950s. The encounter with neo-realism* gave rise to a compromise which humanised the character but fortunately without losing any of its craziness or vitality, as shown by his performances in Eduardo De Filippo's* *Napoli milionaria/Side Street Story* (1950), Steno and Monicelli's *Guardie e ladri/Cops and Robbers* (1951) and the (censored) *Totò e Carolina* (1953), and above all as the madcap hero of Vittorio De Sica's* *L'oro di Napoli/The Gold of Naples* (1954). The Totò persona was exploited by other prestigious directors, including Roberto Rossellini* (*Dov'è la libertà?*, 1953), Alberto Lattuada* (as the villainous priest in *La man-*

dragola, 1965) and Pier Paolo Pasolini*, who constructed around it the figure of the itinerant sub-proletarian of *Uccellacci e uccellini/The Hawks and the Sparrows* (1966) and the extraordinary Iago of *Che cosa sono le nuvole?* (1967, an episode of *Capriccio all'italiana*).

Right until the end of his long career (and even when his eyesight began to fail) Totò remained the consummate professional, true to his roots in Neapolitan popular comedy. Impervious to high-art influence (except perhaps Pirandello) or to that of other screen comics, he was prized by the Italian public for his timelessness, a film personality to add to the great stage ones of Harlequin and Pulcinella. GF

TROISI, Massimo   Naples 1953 – Rome 1994

Italian actor and director. Troisi is the most southern of the young actors/*auteurs* known as the 'new Italian comics'* who entered Italian cinema in the 1970s and 1980s. Coming out of cabaret and television, Troisi broke box-office records with his first film, *Ricomincio da tre/Beginning with Three* (1981). Although still within the framework of classic stage comedy, Troisi's shy and clumsy Gaetano was the first male character in Italian cinema who showed the extent of the revolution brought about by feminism. Using monologue, gestures, frequent pauses and interruptions, Troisi established himself with *Scusate il ritardo/Sorry I'm Late* (1983) as a worthy exponent of the Neapolitan theatre of which Eduardo De Filippo* was both master and model. *Non ci resta che piangere* (1984), co-directed and co-acted with Roberto Benigni*, is a disconnected journey to a past Tuscany, in the year 'almost 1500'. In *Le vie del signore sono finite* (1987) Troisi moved once again to the past (Fascist Italy of the 1920s and 1930s), and tackled the theme of illness. *Pensavo fosse amore... invece era un calesse* (1991), like earlier films written with Anna Pavignano, is a reflection on the impossibility of marriage and relationships; the interest of their work lies in its roots in both a generation and a city (Naples). In addition to acting in all his own films, Troisi distinguished himself as an actor in Gasparini's *No, grazie, il caffè mi rende nervoso* (1982) alongside Lello Arena, with whom, together with Enzo Decaro, Troisi formed the theatre group 'La Smorfia'. Troisi also made his mark in Ettore Scola's* *Splendor* (1988) and *Che ora è?/What Time is It?* (1989) alongside Marcello Mastroianni*, and in *Il viaggio del capitan Fracassa* (1990). He is a very fine mailman in Radford's *Il postino/The Postman*, whose final scene was shot just a few days before his death from heart disease. MMo

V

VALLI, Alida

Alida Maria Altenburger;
Pola [now Croatia] 1921

Italian actress. One of the most famous actresses of Italian cinema in the 1940s, Valli later appeared in many international productions. Her striking beauty, with her extraordinary, slanted eyes, has been put to many different uses during her long career: from youth idol in the 1940s, to seductress in the 1950s and horror film heroine in the 1970s.

A teenage student at the newly formed Centro Sperimentale* in Rome, Valli appeared as a supporting actress in several films in 1936–38 before being cast as the female lead in five films directed by Max Neufeld: *La casa del peccato/The House of Shame* (1938), *Assenze ingiustificata/Absent Without Leave* (1939), *Manon Lescaut* (1939), *Mille lire al mese/A Thousand Lire a Month* (1939), and *Ballo al castello/The Castle Ball* (1938). By the early 1940s, having barely turned twenty, she had become one of the Italy's most famous stars, receiving laudatory reviews as the lead in such critically acclaimed literary adaptations as Carmine Gallone's* *Oltre l'amore/Beyond Love* (1940), Mario Soldati's* *Piccolo mondo antico/Old-Fashioned World* (1941), Goffredi Alessandrini's* *Noi vivi/We the Living* (1942), and in Mario Camerini's* remake of his 1930s success, *T'amerò sempre/I'll Always Love You* (1943). Her image was closely tied, in part because of her youth and the success of school films such as *Ore 9 – lezione di chimica* (1941), with that of a serious student.

Both because of her fame and because of the neo-realist* cinema's tendency to eschew prewar stars, Valli signed a contract with David Selznick to make films in Hollywood, where she was billed simply as 'Valli'. Her most noteworthy films for Selznick include Alfred Hitchcock's *The Paradine Case* (1948, US) and Carol Reed's *The Third Man* (1949, UK). In the 1950s, after her contract with Selznick expired, she returned to Europe and appeared in Italian and international co-productions, notably Luchino Visconti's* sumptuous *Senso* (1954) and Michelangelo Antonioni's* *Il grido/The Cry* (1957). Her career suffered a temporary setback in 1954 when she was involved in a drugs, sex and murder scandal. She later founded a theatrical company and kept working in film co-productions, especially in France. The mature Valli was cast by Bernardo Bertolucci* in *Strategia del ragno/The Spider's Stratagem* (1970) and *Novecento/1900* (1976) as, respectively, the former mistress of an anti-Fascist hero who holds the key to his past and a matriarch landowner whose world is transformed with the onset of Fascism. After appearing in several French horror films, she was cast as the leader of a coven of witches in Dario Argento's* *Suspiria* (1977). JHa

VENICE

Italian film festival. The 'Mostra Internazionale d'Arte Cinematografica' in Venice is the world's oldest film festival. It was first held at the Lido in Venice in 1932 as a touristic and cultural promotional event by the hotel industry and the Biennale degli Arti. It was declared an annual event (with prizes) in 1934. The Palazzo del Cinema was completed in 1937 (and is still in use today), while the introduction of major retrospectives in 1938 signalled the recognition of cinema as an art. Embraced by the Fascist government as a social event and political status symbol, and directed until 1942 with those objectives by Ottavio Croze, Venice was throughout the 1930s a showcase for the best of world cinema, irrespective of ideology. In 1939, however, American films were withdrawn, and in 1940 and 1941 the Festival became an Italo-German Film Week. Suspended for the rest of the war, it was revived in 1946 under the direction of Elio Zorzi, and soon recovered its international prestige, despite new competition from Cannes. However, after the 1948 election it came under political pressure from the Christian Democrat government, which appointed a series of placemen directors, badly compromising its cultural role and interfering with the prize-giving process (though not so much with the selection of films, which remained of quality). Increasing pressure in support of the Festival's independence led to the appointment of the prestigious film-maker and critic Luigi Chiarini* as director. From 1963 to 1968 under Chiarini's direction the Festival pursued a rigorous policy in favour of artistic quality and a '*politique des auteurs*'. But the student protests of 1968, and those of the film-makers in 1972–73, created a new turmoil which lasted throughout the 1970s. Between 1979 and 1983, under the direction of Carlo Lizzani*, and in a context radically altered by the emergence of new and competing festivals, Venice pursued a more flexible and lively policy, open to the tastes of younger *cinéphiles* and to a mingling of European and American, art and popular cinema, an approach which remained in place throughout the 1980s. Gillo Pontecorvo* was nominated director in 1992. GVo

VISCONTI, Luchino   Milan 1906 – Rome 1976

Italian director. Born into a distinguished patrician family, Visconti developed an early interest in music which would resurface later in his films and operatic work. At the age of thirty he moved to Paris, immersed himself in international film culture, and assisted Jean Renoir on *Une Partie de campagne* (1936). After a brief visit to Hollywood, he returned to Rome, where he became part of the goup around the journal *Cinema* which was beginning to lay the theoretical groundwork for a new realism based on the literature of nineteenth-century *verismo*, typified by the novels and stories of Giovanni Verga. When his pro-

120

posal for an adaptation of Verga's story *L'amante di Gramigna* was rejected by the Fascist censors, Visconti turned instead to an adaptation of James Cain's thriller *The Postman Always Rings Twice*. The resulting film, *Ossessione* (1942), shot on location in the Po valley, was subsequently hailed as a precursor of neo-realism* in its location shooting and naturalistic treatment of ordinary men and women. In 1944, his anti-Fascism earned Visconti a short spell in a Gestapo prison. After the war he went to work in the theatre before accepting funding from the Italian Communist Party to make what was planned to be a series of three films about the fishermen, miners and peasantry in Sicily. In the event, only the 'Episode of the Sea' was made under the title *La terra trema* (1948). Based on Verga's novel *I Malavoglia*, *La terra trema* was a paragon of neo-realist purity in its location shooting and use of non-professional actors speaking a local dialect so incomprehensible that it had to be supplemented by a voice-over narration in standard Italian. The film's disappointing performance at the box office forced Visconti to accept a less than congenial script by Cesare Zavattini* for the film *Bellissima* (1951). The opportunity of working with Anna Magnani*, however, overrode his distaste for the screenplay and the film emerged as both a fine satire of Cinecittà* and a convincing portrait of a working-class woman.

Visconti's first colour film, *Senso* (1954), triggered a storm of controversy in its exploitation of the star system (Farley Granger and Alida Valli*), its recourse to historical reconstruction (the Risorgimento), and its lush, aristocratic milieu. Against those who called *Senso* a betrayal of neo-realist populism, the influential Guido Aristarco defended the film as the logical progression of neo-realism towards a critical realism based on a rethinking of the nineteenth-century origins of the Italian state. Visconti's 1963 adaptation of Giuseppe Tomasi di Lampedusa's *Il Gattopardo/The Leopard* deepens his critique of the Risorgimento by filtering events through the consciousness of a Sicilian prince who is aware that his class is doomed and is resigned to accept change. It is this character, played with great subtlety by Burt Lancaster, who best expresses Visconti's own plight as a man temperamentally bound to the old order but ideologically committed to its demise. Visconti's command of spectacle – his power to reconstruct in glorious detail a lost aristocratic world and to direct hundreds of extras with naturalness and grace – is admirably displayed in the film's hour-long ball sequence, mutilated by US distributors but fortunately restored to its full splendour in the film's 1983 re-release. In *La caduta degli dei/The Damned* (1969) – a chronicle of the Krupp family whose steel empire supported Hitler's rise to power – Visconti takes to decadent extremes his fondness for recreating privileged worlds on the verge of extinction. Class demise is also the theme of his adaptation of the Thomas Mann novella *Morte a Venezia/Death in Venice* (1972), where Gustav von Aschenbach's (masterfully played by Dirk Bogarde) fatal bondage to aesthetic purity and homoerotic desire allegorises the aristocracy's inertia in the face of historical obliteration. The protagonist of *Ludwig* joins Gustav as an autobiographical projection of Visconti's own tormented aestheticism. The badly cut (from 246 to 150 minutes) 1972 version of the film regained its integrity on its re-release in 1980 as an epic account of the Bavarian king more given to art than politics. *Gruppo di famiglia in un interno/Conversation Piece* (1974), made during Visconti's last illness, stars Burt Lancaster again as an intellectual confronted with a revolution (this time, the sexual and political revolution of 1968) into which he is unwillingly drawn. The aristocratic protagonist of Visconti's last film, *L'innocente/The Innocent* (1976), an adaptation of Gabriele D'Annunzio's novel, chooses withdrawal through suicide as a commentary both on his own interpersonal failure and that of the *belle époque* whose end is both merited and mourned.

Forerunner and practitioner of neo-realism, Visconti was instrumental in transcending its limitations by incorporating influences from the other arts (primarily literature, but also opera and theatre) as well as legitimising forays into historical subject matter. He had an enormous impact on successive generations of film-makers, including Bernardo Bertolucci*, Franco Zeffirelli*, Francesco Rosi*, Liliana Cavani*, and Stanley Kubrick. MMa

Bib: Elaine Mancini, *Luchino Visconti: A Guide to References and Resources* (1986); Geoffrey Nowell-Smith, *Visconti* (1973).

Other Films Include: *Siamo donne/We the Women* [ep. *Anna Magnani*], *Le notti bianche/White Nights* (1957); *Rocco e i suoi fratelli/Rocco and His Brothers* (1960); *Boccaccio '70* (1962, ep. *Il lavoro*); *Vaghe stelle dell'orsa/Sandra* (1965); *Le streghe/The Witches* [ep. *La strega bruciata viva*], *Lo straniero/The Stranger* (1967).

VITTI, Monica   Maria Luisa Ceciarelli; Rome 1931

Italian actress, remarkable in her ability to incarnate such antithetical film-making modes as *auteur* cinema and *commedia all'italiana**, and in her power, as a woman, to penetrate cinematic terrain previously restricted to men. As the privileged vehicle for Michelangelo Antonioni's* exploration of modernist consciousness in the 1960s, Vitti became intimately associated with the auteurist movement in Italy. Later, as the 'queen' of *commedia all'italiana*, she helped break the all-male hold on the genre through the creation of her own, enormously successful comic-grotesque persona.

Vitti attended the Accademia Nazionale d'Arte Drammatica and enjoyed early success in the theatre. She made her cinematic debut in Mario Amendola's *Le dritte* (1958), but it was Antonioni's tetralogy *L'avventura* (1960), *La notte/The Night* (1961), *L'eclisse/The Eclipse* (1962) and *Deserto rosso/The Red Desert* (1964) that won her international acclaim and established her reputation as an actress of con-

122

siderable talent. In her portrayal of deeply troubled middle-class women, unable to establish satisfying relationships and incapable of connecting with their environment, the glamorous blonde Vitti came to embody the modernist dilemma in all its complexity and angst. 'The female consciousness', claimed Antonioni, 'is the best filter of reality I know', and Vitti, with her intensely cerebral performance style, provided the perfect vehicle for the film-maker's own alienated, highly abstract vision of the real. Vitti's image underwent a sea-change in the late 1960s with her award-winning performance in Mario Monicelli's* comedy *La ragazza con la pistola/The Girl with a Pistol* (1968). In Ettore Scola's* proletarian tragi-comedy *Dramma della gelosia: tutti i particolari in cronaca* (1970), ingeniously entitled *The Pizza Triangle* in English, Vitti played the common love object of Marcello Mastroianni* and Giancarlo Giannini and established her international reputation as comedienne. Just as Vitti came to feel constrained by her role as alienated woman in the 1960s, however, so she began to chafe at the limitations imposed by her type-casting in *commedia all'italiana*. The late 1970s were a time of reassessment and experimentation – she accepted Michael Ritchie's invitation to perform a different type of role in *An Almost Perfect Affair* (1979, US), then rejoined Antonioni in the critically disappointing *Il mistero di Oberwald/The Oberwald Mystery* (1980), and reappeared on screen, after a hiatus of two years, in the first directorial effort of photographer Roberto Russo, *Flirt*. 1986 marked her return to the theatre, both as teacher and actress. In recent years, Vitti has performed and directed for television, and has sponsored the careers of such young directors as Francesca Archibugi and Massimo Guglielmi. Vitti's debut as a film director came in 1990 with *Scandalo segreto/Secret Scandal* (starring Elliott Gould and Catherine Spaak), which was well received critically but met with limited box-office success. MMa

VOLONTÉ, Gian Maria   Milan 1933 – Florina, Greece 1994

Italian actor. After studying at the Accademia Nazionale d'Arte Drammatica, Volonté embarked on a theatrical career, including appearances in radical theatre. It was in the cinema, however, that he gained remarkable popularity. His first success was in Italian Westerns*, displaying his histrionic talent and ability to express cold 'post-expressionist violence' as the bad guy in Sergio Leone's* *Per un pugno di dollari/A Fistful of Dollars* (1964) and *Per qualche dollaro in più/For a Few Dollars More* (1965) and in Damiano Damiani's 'political' Western *Quién sabe?/A Bullet for the General* (1966). Before that he had played a trade union representative murdered by the Mafia in the Taviani* brothers' *Un uomo da bruciare/A Man to Burn* (1962) and a terrorist in Gianfranco De Bosio's *Il terrorista* (1963), and over the years it is this 'political' image which he became associated with. Nationally and internationally, he became the star of the 'Italian political cinema'* of the 1960s and 1970s. Landmarks in this 'genre' include his power-hungry police inspector in Elio Petri's* *Indagine su un cittadino al di sopra di ogni sospetto/Investigation of a Citizen Above Suspicion* (1969), and the tragic Lulu, the working-class protagonist of *La classe operaia va in paradiso/Lulu the Tool* (1971). He became especially associated with a series of films directed by Francesco Rosi*: he was the anti-militarist official of *Uomini contro* (1970), the government official of *Il caso Mattei/The Mattei Affair* (1972), the emigrant gangster of *Lucky Luciano* (1973), and later the novelist Carlo Levi discovering the South in *Cristo si è fermato a Eboli/Christ Stopped at Eboli* (1979). He twice played the role of the Christian Democrat prime minister Aldo Moro, in Petri's *Todo modo* (1976) and in Giuseppe Ferrara's *Il caso Moro/The Moro Affair* (1986), the latter made after Moro's death at the hands of the Red Brigades.

A modern follower of the naturalist tradition, Volonté had extraordinary presence and expressiveness. He increasingly developed an interiorised and melancholic mode (particularly after a long period of illness) as can be seen in his portrayal of the embittered and laconic protagonist of Claude Goretta's *La mort de Mario Ricci/The Death of Mario Ricci* (1983) and his stoic and thoughtful judge in Gianni Amelio's* *Porte aperte/Open Doors* (1990). He died of a heart attack a few days before the end of the shooting of Thodoros Angelopoulos' *To vlemma tou Odissea/Le Regard d'Ulysse/Ulysses' Gaze* (released 1995), the story of a film-maker from Belgrade in search of the archives of early Greek cinema. GVo

Other Films Include: *Vent d'Est, Le Cercle rouge/The Red Circle* (1970, Fr.); *Sacco e Vanzetti* (1971); *Giordano Bruno* (1973); *Svegliati e uccidi/Wake Up and Kill* (1966); *Banditi a Milano/The Violent Four* (1968); *Il sospetto* (1975).

W

WERTMÜLLER, Lina
Arcangela Felice Assunta
Wertmüller von Elgg Spanol von Braueich;
Rome 1928

Italian writer and director. A disciple of Federico Fellini*, Wertmüller soon developed her own original blend of carnivalesque style and scathing social satire which took the critical establishment by storm and enjoyed tremendous box-office success in many countries in the 1970s.

Wertmüller graduated in 1957 from the Accademia Teatrale directed by Pietro Sharoff and worked intensively as assistant director and scriptwriter for vaudeville as well as legitimate theatre. She entered the film world as Fellini's assistant director on $8\frac{1}{2}$ (1963) and shot a documentary of the film's making. At the completion of $8\frac{1}{2}$ Wertmüller wooed away most of Fellini's crew to Sicily, where she filmed her own first feature, *I basilischi/The Lizards* (1963), a critique of middle-class life in a small Italian town. Her next three films were blatantly commercial ventures: *Questa volta parliamo di uomini/Let's Talk About Men* (1965), a film in four episodes, *Rita la zanzara/Rita the Mosquito* (1966), and *Non stuzzicate la zanzara/Don't Tease the Mosquito* (1967). These last two works, made under the pseudonym of George Brown, were musical comedies starring the popular singer Rita Pavone, along with Giancarlo Giannini, who became Wertmüller's leading man through the 1970s. Upon returning to theatre, she met and married Enrico Job, her future art director and the person responsible for the set and costume design so integral to her filmic universe.

The year 1972 marked the beginning of Wertmüller's golden age: for a while she made at least one hit annually, most of them starring the remarkably versatile and expressive Giannini, teamed up three times with the equally powerful Mariangela Melato. In this couple, Wertmüller found the perfect vehicle for exploring her preferred theme: the tangle of political and sexual passions that link personal stories to public history during moments of revolutionary social change. Thus the Sicilian Mimi (Giannini), politically enlightened and sexually liberated by his mistress Fiore (Melato), turns into a Mafioso caveman when confronted with his wife's infidelity in *Mimì metallurgico ferito nell' onore/The Seduction of Mimi* (1972); the anarchist Tunin (Giannini), pledged to assassinate Mussolini, abdicates his free will to prostitutes, one of them his comrade, Salome (Melato), in *Film d'amore e d'anarchia ovvero*: '*Stamattina alle 10 in Via dei Fiori nella nota casa di tolleranza ...'/Love and Anarchy* (1973); and the proletarian male supremacist Gennarino (Giannini) capitulates to his bourgeois love-slave, Raffaela (Melato), in *Travolti da un insolito destino/ Swept Away* (1974). With *Pasqualino Settebellezze/Seven Beauties* (1975), based on the true experiences of a concentration camp inmate who abdicated his humanity for survival, Wertmüller launched Giannini to international stardom. The actor performed in two more Wertmüller films, playing a brooding intellectual opposite Candice Bergen in *La fine del mondo nel nostro solito letto in una notte piena di pioggia/Night Full of Rain* (1978) and a sleazy Mafioso in *Fatto di sangue fra due uomini per causa di una vedova, si sospettano moventi politici .../Blood Feud* (1978), but the intensity of the early 1970s collaborations had dissipated by then. Wertmüller's 1980s films have all been topical in focus: high-tech security goes awry in *Scherzo del des-*

tino in agguato dietro l'angolo come un brigante da strada/Joke of Destiny (1983), lesbian desire complicates marital relations in Sotto ... sotto ... strapazzato da anomala passione (1984), drugs and organised crime are attacked in Un complicato intrigo di donne, vicoli e delitti/Camorra (1985), environmentalism and kidnapping converge in Notte d'estate con profilo greco, occhi a mandorla e odore di basilico/ Summer Night (1986), and the fear of AIDS takes over In una notte di chiaro di luna/Crystal or Ash, Fire or Wind, as Long as It's Love (1989). Wertmüller also made sporadic returns to the theatre, including the writing and directing of Amore e magia nella cucina di mamma, performed in Spoleto in 1979 and New York in 1980. She added opera to her repertory in 1987 with a production of Carmen at the prestigious San Carlo theatre in Naples. In 1988 she was appointed Commissario Straordinario at the Centro Sperimentale*.

Wertmüller's powerful 1970s films combined the intense energy and physicality of the commedia dell'arte tradition with the high emotionalism of her theatrical training, and applied them to the post-1968 political consciousness. Her achievement was not met without controversy, however – critical discomfort ran high, especially in feminist circles. Wertmüller's resolve to communicate her political messages to mass audiences through hyperbolic and grotesque comic techniques raised serious questions about whether or not the regional, gender and class stereotypes which sustain her cinema do not reinforce the public's most regressive prejudices. If such polemics are an index of success, then Wertmüller's 1970s production fully achieved its goals. MMa

Other Films Include: Tutto a posto e niente in ordine/All Screwed Up (1974); Sabato, domenica e lunedì (1990).

Z

ZAMPA, Luigi   Rome 1905–91

Italian director. A typically exuberant and cultured Roman, Zampa emerged as a scriptwriter and director from the Fascist cinema of the 'white telephones'. Also a writer of comic plays and novels, he left his mark above all in the field of film comedy. He achieved success with Vivere in pace/To Live in Peace (1946), a rural variation on the Allied Occupation theme, mixing pathos and farce. Highly regarded abroad as a masterpiece of neo-realism*, the film was voted Best Foreign Feature of 1947 by New York film critics. Zampa continued in a similar vein in *L'onorevole Angelina/Angelina* (1947), with Anna Magnani* as a popular village leader. He shifted focus somewhat with a trilogy of satirical films written by the Sicilian novelist Vitaliano Brancati: *Anni difficili/Difficult Years* (1948), *Anni facili/Easy Years* (1953) and *L'arte di arrangiarsi* (1954). The last of these, the portrait of a man whose opinions change to fit different regimes, remains one the best performances of Alberto Sordi*, with whom Zampa made a dozen or so films. These include very successful films like *Il vigile/The Cop* (1960) and *Il medico della mutua* (1968), whose indictment of the Italian health system is continued in a more melodramatic mode in *Bisturi, la mafia bianca* (1973). This vein of denunciatory films, in a direct and pithy style, sometimes tending towards demagogy, includes *Il magistrato/The Magistrate* (1959), *Una questione d'onore/A Question of Honour* (1965), *Gente di rispetto* (1975) and *Il mostro* (1977). In the course of his career Zampa made some three dozen films of uneven quality, but none of them entirely without merit. His best is probably *Processo alla città/The City Stands Trial* (1952), in which the inquiry by the judge played by Amedeo Nazzari* reveals a tough network of power and racketeering in Naples at the turn of the century. MMo

Other Films Include: *L'attore scomparso, Fra Diavolo* (1941); *Signorinette, C'è sempre un ma ...* (1942); *L'abito nero da sposa* (1943); *Un americano in vacanza/A Yank in Rome* (1945); *Campane a martello/Children of Change* (1949); *È più facile che un cammello ...*, *Guerra o pace/Cuori senza frontiere* (1950); *Signori, in carrozza!* (1951); *Siamo donne/We the Women* (1953, fourth episode); *Questa è la vita* [ep. *La patente*], *La romana* (1954); *Ragazze d'oggi* (1955); *Tempo di villeggiatura* (1956); *La ragazza del palio/The Love Specialist* (1957); *Ladro lui, ladra lei* (1958); *Anni ruggenti/Roaring Years* (1962); *Frenesia dell'estate* (1963); *I nostri mariti* (1966, ep. *Il marito di Olga*); *Le dolci signore* (1967); *Contestazione generale* (1970); *Bello, onesto, emigrato Australia sposerebbe compaesana illibata* (1971); *Letti selvaggi* (1979).

ZAVATTINI, Cesare   Luzzara 1902 – Rome 1989

Italian scriptwriter and novelist. One of the most prolific scriptwriters of Italian cinema (with over a hundred scripts), Zavattini is particularly well-known as the theoretician of neo-realism*, an advocate of a realist, anti-illusionist cinema steeped in the quotidian, best exemplified by *Umberto D.* (1952), directed by Vittorio De Sica*.

A law graduate, Zavattini went straight into journalism, working first for a minor provincial paper and then for some of the most important magazines of the period. He moved to Milan, where he worked for the publishers Rizzoli, Mondadori and Bompiani and published his first two great novels, the extraordinary *Parliamo tanto di me* (1931) and *I poveri sono matti* (1937). He collaborated with the humorist Giaci Mondaini on a script called *Buoni per un giorno*, which was directed by Mario Camerini* in 1935 under the title *Darò un milione*. The film was so successful that it was remade in Hollywood as *I'll Give a Million* (1938). As a result of this activity Zavattini moved to Rome, where he made an essential contribution to Alessandro Blasetti's* important film *Quattro passi fra le nuvole/Four Steps in the Clouds* (1942). His fruitful collaboration with Vittorio De Sica* led to a first film of considerable interest, *I bambini ci guardano* (1943), after which Zavattini spent the postwar years working on what are now considered to be the milestones of neo-realism*: *Sciuscià/Shoeshine* (1946), *Ladri di biciclette/Bicycle Thieves* (1948), *Miracolo a Milano/Miracle in Milan* (1951) and *Umberto D*. Of great significance also are his contributions to Luchino Visconti's* *Bellissima* (1951), Blasetti's *Prima comunione/Father's Dilemma* (1950), Giuseppe De Santis'* *Roma ore 11* (1952), and the works of an impressive number of other directors (of both art and popular films), from Alberto Lattuada* to Domenico Paolella, Renato Castellani* and Mario Mattoli*. The 1950s saw a puzzling decline in his scriptwriting activities as he became involved in increasingly routine projects. Nonetheless, in other respects he continued to row against the tide, as was his custom, with a series of ingeniously utopian – and partially abortive – projects: popular episode films – *L'amore in città* (1953), *Siamo donne/We the Women* (1953), *Le italiane e l'amore* (1961) and *I misteri di Roma* (1963) – the committed 'Newsreels for peace' and 'Freedom Newsreels', protests at the Venice* film festival in 1968, cultural animation, impromptu live broadcasts in the 1980s. In 1982, at over eighty years of age, he directed his first and only film, *La veritàaaa*, a distinguished though outlandish digest of his deeply felt pacifism.

To mention only Zavattini's (albeit crucial) scriptwriting and theoretical contributions to neo-realism, as is often the case, would be to paint an incomplete picture. He was also one of the best Italian novelists of the twentieth century, a very fine poet, a humorist, the author of comic-strip texts, a painter of recognised talent, a publishing and general media mandarin. He inhabited half a century of Italian culture and marked it profoundly. PV

Other Films as Scriptwriter Include: *I nostri sogni* (1943); *La porta del cielo* (1944); *Caccia tragica/Tragic Hunt* (1946); *Una domenica d'agosto/Sunday in August* (1950); *È primavera/It's Forever Springtime* (1949); *Il cappotto/The Overcoat* (1952); *Un marito per Anna Zaccheo* (1953); *L'oro di Napoli/The Gold of Naples* (1954); *Il segno di Venere* (1955); *Il tetto* (1956); *La ciociara/Two Women* (1960); *Cuba baila* (1961, Cuba); *Historias de la revolucion* (1961, Cuba); *Il giudizio universale/The Last Judgment* (1961); *Boccaccio '70* (1962); *Un mondo nuovo/A Young World* (1966); *Una breve vacanza/A Brief Vacation* (1977).

ZURLINI, Valerio

Bologna 1926 – Verona 1982

Italian director. Trained as a lawyer with a deep and abiding interest in art, Zurlini made his feature debut with a screen adaptation of Vasco Pratolini's novel *Le ragazze di San Frediano* (1954). His sense of the fragility of human life and emotion was further explored in *Estate violenta/Violent Summer* (1959), *La ragazza con la valigia/Girl With a Suitcase* (1961) and especially in *Cronaca familliare/Family Diary* (1962), again adapted from Pratolini, and widely considered his masterpiece. His subsequent films were all honourable but on the whole unsuccessful. *Le soldatesse* (1965) examined the guilt of Italians in wartime Greece; *Seduto alla sua destra/Out of Darkness* (1968) combined a meditation on divine grace with a reflection on the assassination of Patrice Lumumba, while a deep philosophical pessimism informs *La prima notte di quiete* (1972). His last production was *Il deserto dei tartari*, an international co-production based on Dino Buzzati's novel, which allowed him the resources to develop his filmmaking in a manner inspired by the classics of science-fiction and by surrealist painting. PV

ITALIAN CINEMA IN EUROPE

Key European cinema concepts, genres and institutions

Avant-garde cinema in Europe
Emigration and European cinema
European art cinema
European cinema and Hollywood
European Community [now European Union] and the cinema
European film awards [FELIX]
Festivals
Heritage cinema in Europe
Lesbian and gay cinema in Europe
Sexuality, eroticism and pornography in European cinema

Key European cinema concepts, genres and institutions

This section gathers entries commissioned for the *Encyclopedia of European Cinema* on pan-European concepts, genres and institutions. They are included here as a useful and relevant background to the information contained in the preceding sections. The authors of these entries are named at the end of each one of them.

AVANT-GARDE CINEMA IN EUROPE

From our present postmodern vantage point, the concept of the avant-garde might appear as simultaneously archaic and elitist, now that it is behind us historically and seemingly beyond us politically. Two factors recur: the relationship of film to the other arts, and of aesthetics to politics, with the term 'avant-garde' breaking into the following registers of aspiration – experimentation and abstraction, independence and opposition.

Soviet montage, German expressionism, French impressionism and surrealism are traditionally considered the 'historical avant-gardes' of European cinema and the overlap of film with fine arts is characteristic of each of these founding moments. At its most militantly innovative and highly theorised in the work of Sergei Eisenstein and Dziga Vertov, Soviet montage was wrought from the combination of a modernist consciousness of the revolutionary moment – 1917, Bolshevism – and a fertile cross-pollination of film with Constructivist design, Futurist sound poetry [> FUTURISM] and Suprematist experimentation with form. In France, impressionism and surrealism lacked the political impetus of the Soviets, but endorsed cinema as the manifestation of the Wagnerian idea of the *Gesamtkunstwerk*, the means of synthesising all the arts in the new, unique art of film, termed by Ricciotto Canudo 'the seventh art'.

The encounter between film and the fine arts has persistently characterised the abstract tendency of the European avant-garde. And while recent work in video-art can be seen as maintaining this tradition, it might equally be seen in the Structuralist/Materialist films of the 1970s. Malcolm Le Grice, one of the leading British exponents of such work, has identified abstract work as taking place as early as 1910–12 in the experiments of Bruno Corra and Arnaldo Ginna. Corra's theoretical text, *Abstract Cinema – Chromatic Music*, serves as an early indication of the enduring tendency in abstract film to seek aesthetic alliances with painting and music. This example predates the work of abstract animators Walther Ruttmann, Viking Eggeling, Hans Richter and Oskar Fischinger, often seen as inaugurating this aesthetic tendency. Richter gave perhaps the best summary of the abstract film position when he wrote: 'Problems in modern art lead directly into the film. The connection to theatre and literature was completely severed. Cubism, Expressionism, Dadaism, Abstract Art, Surrealism found not only their expression in film, but a new fulfilment on a new level.'

Two words serve to encapsulate the motivation of this first, historical phase of the European avant-garde: silence and 'specificity'. It is noticeable that this experimental phase ended with the coming of sound. While for the Soviet directors this can in part be attributed to Stalin's cultural policies of the late 1920s and early 1930s, the termination was also informed by the anti-realist agendas common to all the avant-gardes, with sound representing a decisively realist 'supplement' to the image. The change in the mode of production from the artisanal/patronage-based one enjoyed by the avant-garde to the labour and capital intensive base demanded by the new sound cinema also had a part to play in the end of the silent avant-gardes. The search for cinematic 'specificity' was polemical and separatist on the one hand – against theatrical and narrative models – synthesising and hybridising on the other, with models from painting and music.

The notion of the avant-garde in film was constructed around the idea of its oppositional status vis-à-vis the established cinematic order both generally and specifically in European cinema. This tendency can be defined in terms either of opposition or of independence, the former being predicated along militant political lines, the latter a means of constructing an alternative space for independent production, distribution and exhibition. This taxonomy works usefully in respect of the works of the 1960s and 1970s that best illustrate the bifurcation of European avant-garde practice into what Peter Wollen christened in 1975 'the Two Avant-Gardes', one concerned with a politically oriented 'politics of form', the other with a formalist 'politics of perception'. The strand of European practice that came to be known as Counter-Cinema, while having its immediate origins in the political revolt of May 1968 in France, nevertheless took its conceptual and aesthetic leads from a longer European tradition of radical, oppositional aesthetic practices, drawing on ideas from Brechtian dramaturgy – distanciation, the *Verfremdungseffekt* – and lauding Vertov over Eisenstein in the 'second discovery' of Soviet cinema of the mid- to late 1960s. While Jean-Luc Godard is most commonly associated with the counter-cinematic turning away from what he dubbed 'the Hollywood-Mosfilm' and towards a didactic cinema of '*films tableaux noirs*' (blackboard films), he was by no means alone in opting for this radical strategy. Chris Marker in France, Rainer Werner Fassbinder and Werner Schroeter in Germany, Věra Chytilová in Czechoslovakia and Dušan Makavejev in Yugoslavia experimented with a Brechtian challenge to narrative transparency against the perceived stylistic – hence ideological – hegemony of Hollywood cinema.

The other more Formalist/Structuralist-Materialist strand of avant-garde film-making rooted itself in an opposition to conventional narrative that owed much to the abstract cinema of the 1920s, although it

132

might be said that the master-text of both the Structuralist-Materialist and counter-cinematic movements of the 1960s and 1970s remains Vertov's remarkable *Chelovek s kinoapparatom/The Man with the Movie Camera* (1929). The Co-op movements of the 1970s, particularly the London Film-makers Co-op, represented the pursuit of a radical, independent practice both aesthetically and institutionally. Film-makers such as Malcolm Le Grice and Peter Gidal participated in a cinema of minimal effects concerned with the material properties of film – grain, emulsion, flicker, qualities of light – and in the spectatorial experience, experimenting with duration and performance-art styled interventions during projection. This strand arguably had more in common with the North American and Canadian avant-garde of Brakhage, Sharits and Snow than with the militancy of European counter-cinema. Godard himself attempted, in *Tout va bien* (1972), a Brechtian cinema-with-stars (Jane Fonda and Yves Montand), while other art cinema directors such as Yvonne Rainer and Chantal Akerman employed avant-garde strategies to question the sexual politics of cinematic representation, notably in Akerman's *Jeanne Dielman 23 Quai du Commerce 1080 Bruxelles* (1975), with its experimentation with duration.

With the advent of video technologies in the mid-1960s one would have imagined a revival of the European avant-gardes. However, in the hands of Godard and Marker, video has been used as a means of thinking cinema and of expressing an analytic relationship with the image. Marker's *Sans soleil/Sunless* (1983) and Godard's *Scénario du film Passion* (1982) are most representative of this application of video, the Marker film also being an eloquent piece of mourning-work for the lost illusions of 1960s political radicalism and so-called 'guerrilla film-making', while fully and euphorically exploiting the possibilities of video. European video-art *per se* has yet to achieve the international visibility of North American and Canadian video-artists such as Bill Viola, Gary Hill and Nam June Paik. However, the avant-garde has been – and, in the example of video-art, remains – an international, exportable phenomenon that cuts across both national, cultural and artistic boundaries, addressing a wide set of disparate art/film constituencies, in contrast to European popular cinemas that remain more firmly embedded in specific national traditions and hence export less effectively. (Chris Darke)

Bib: Peter Wollen, 'The Two Avant-Gardes', in *Readings and Writings: Semiotic Counter-Strategies* (1982).

EMIGRATION AND EUROPEAN CINEMA

The phenomenon of emigration both within Europe and from Europe greatly affected the cinema throughout its first century. Social factors (poverty and racism, especially anti-semitism) and historical events such as wars, revolutions and totalitarian regimes drove people from their home countries, usually west, towards Germany and the Netherlands, then France and the UK, and massively to the US. Economic and cultural factors specific to the film industry have also repeatedly drawn European film personnel to North America. There has been a small movement in the opposite direction, with American directors such as Joseph Losey and Jules Dassin, and stars like Eddie Constantine and Paul Robeson making a career in Europe.

Many Hollywood pioneers and movie moguls came from central Europe. Subsequently, Hollywood attracted film people who went either of their own volition or as a result of the studios' systematic policies of talent-scouting. Some made a first or second career there (Charlie Chaplin, Mihály Kertész [Michael Curtiz], Jean Negulescu [Negulesco], Ernst Lubitsch, Greta Garbo, Ingrid Bergman, Douglas Sirk [Detlef Sierck]) while for others Hollywood was a – more or less extended and more or less successful – episode: Victor Sjöström, Mauritz Stiller, Max Ophuls, Fritz Lang, René Clair, Julien Duvivier, Jean Renoir, S. M. Eisenstein, Louis Malle, Nestor Almendros and many others. The country most affected has been Germany. While directors, actors, scriptwriters, art directors and cameramen were forced to leave Germany when the Nazis came to power in 1933, others had already left. Those tempted, apart from Lubitsch, Sirk and Lang, included F. W. Murnau, William Dieterle, E. A. Dupont, Paul Leni, Ludwig Berger, Emil Jannings, Marlene Dietrich, Robert Siodmak, Pola Negri, Lya de Putti, Erich Pommer, Carl Mayer, Karl Freund, Joe May, Richard Oswald, Otto Preminger, Billy Wilder and Reinhold Schünzel. From 1 April 1933, Jews were systematically excluded from public life in Germany and consequently almost a third of Germany's film industry personnel fled to neighbouring countries and the US. France and Britain were especially important for émigré film-makers, since their film industries were then experiencing a period of dramatic growth. Consequently, producers like Pommer, Seymour Nebenzal and Alexander Korda set up new production companies which provided work for fellow émigrés. Between 1933 and 1940, Lang, Siodmak, Ophuls, Kurt Bernhardt, G. W. Pabst, Anatole Litvak and others made nearly fifty films in France, including box-office hits such as *Mayerling* (1936), *Carrefour* (1938) and *Pièges* (1939), while in Britain Korda and Max Schach produced highly successful costume films for the international market.

Most émigrés resettled in the US, though few of those who arrived in Hollywood between 1933 and 1938 had a studio contract. After 1938–39, the number of refugees to the US increased dramatically. Altogether, about 500 German film-makers lived in Hollywood. In the 1920s–30s the German émigrés in Hollywood worked on films with a 'European flavour' and from the early 1940s film-makers such as Wilder, Siodmak and Lang contributed greatly to the development of *film noir* with such films as *Double Indemnity* (1944), *Phantom Lady* (1944), *Scarlet Street* (1945) and many others. German émigrés are also known for the sub-genre of the anti-Nazi film, of which about 180 were produced between 1939 and 1945 in the US, transmitting an anti-fascist message in traditional genre films such as spy thrillers (*Confessions of a Nazi Spy*, 1939), melodramas (*The Mortal Storm*, 1940) and comedies (*To Be or Not to Be*, 1942). In addition, German actors and their accents were much sought-after, ironically often to play Nazis (or their victims) in anti-Nazi films; Schünzel, Peter Lorre and Conrad Veidt were particularly successful in this respect. Only a handful of film-makers returned to Germany after World War II; most had settled permanently in the US and, furthermore, the German film industry was still run by those who had been successful in the Third Reich. Though it is impossible to speculate on what might have happened otherwise, there is no doubt that German film production suffered incalculably from this drain of talented film personnel.

Less visible because of the shared language has been the drain from the British film industry. Among the most famous British émigrés (or British personnel who worked substantially in Hollywood), apart from Chaplin, are: Julie Andrews, Cecil Beaton, Ronald Colman, Alfred Hitchcock, James Mason and David Niven. The important migrations mentioned above slowed down somewhat in the postwar period, as Hollywood itself went through a crisis and started investing in European productions [> EUROPEAN CINEMA AND HOLLYWOOD]. Since the 1980s, however, a renewed migration has taken place, with European film-makers seeking work abroad as their own national cinemas weaken; examples include Andrei Mikhalkov-Konchalovsky, Miloš Forman, George Sluizer, Wolfgang Petersen, Paul Verhoeven, Roman Polanski and Bernardo Bertolucci*, as well as actors such as Rutger Hauer.

During the same period many other film-makers have turned to France, following another long tradition. In the 1920s, the French cinematic avant-garde was international, with film-makers such as Alberto Cavalcanti, Carl Theodor Dreyer and Luis Buñuel among others [> AVANT-GARDE CINEMA IN EUROPE]. A significant group of émigrés had already arrived from Russia in the wake of the October revolution. The old Pathé studios in Montreuil became the centre of an active community. Iosif Yermolev [Joseph Ermolieff in France], an ex-Pathé employee, founded Ermolieff-film in 1920, with a team of prestigious directors including Yakov Protazanov [Jacob Protazanoff], Alexandre Volkov [Volkoff], Vjačelav Turžanskij [Victor Tourjansky], actor Ivan Mozzhukhin [Mosjoukine], set designers and cinematographers. Yermolev produced a dozen films before leaving for Berlin in 1922, and Ermolieff-film became Les Films Albatros, specialising in literary adaptations of French and Russian classics, with emphasis on nostalgia and exoticism, and producing prestigious films by Marcel L'Herbier, Jacques Feyder, René Clair, and others. Other firms, such as Ciné-France-Film, had a strong Russian contingent and produced French films, including Abel Gance's *Napoléon* (1926) and Volkov's *Casanova* (1927, starring Mosjoukine). The Russian influence con-

135

tinued in the 1930s when personnel included directors Fyodor Otsep [Fédor Ozep], Nicolas Farkas and Tourjansky and many others, as well as gifted cinematographers and set designers, generating the popular French genre of the 'Slav melodrama'. Lazare Meerson revolutionised set design and taught other designers such as Alexander Trauner and Georges Wakhevitch. New directors from Russia emerged, such as Litvak, and Władysław Starewicz [Ladislav Starevitch]. There were, during the same period, significant exchanges between France and Italy. Franco-Italian bilingual films were made, and several Italian directors worked in France: Mario Bonnard, Carmine Gallone* and Augusto Genina*.

Meanwhile, despite the threatening political climate, the attraction of better conditions in German studios remained strong, and French stars and directors became frequent travellers between Paris, Berlin and Munich. The coming of sound also contributed to the acceleration of cross-European journeys, with the making of multi-language versions by Ufa in Germany, Paramount in Paris and British International in London, between 1929 and 1932. Films were made in sometimes as many as a dozen versions (especially at Paramount) but more often in two or three, with German, French and English the most common languages, usually using the same decor but native stars (it was also at that time that Hollywood initiated the practice of remaking European films, especially French films, a phenomenon renewed with particular vigour in the 1980s and 1990s). As mentioned above, Paris in the 1930s also saw a major influx of German and central European personnel, the result of both economic and political emigration. During World War II, while some French film personnel left for Hollywood (Renoir, Duvivier, Jean Gabin, Michèle Morgan and others), French cinema lived in virtual autarchy.

In the postwar period, emigration to France took an individual character, with a wide range of personnel (Buñuel, Luis Mariano, Roman Polanski, Walerian Borowczyk, Eddie Constantine) working in Paris, though two strands can be detected. First, the intense programme of co-productions (especially with Italy) in the 1940s and 1950s brought many actors to France: Antonella Lualdi, Lea Massari, Gina Lollobrigida*, Raf Vallone, Romy Schneider and Maria Schell among others. Secondly, the combination of generous French aid and of the break-up of the Eastern block, has produced another wave of eastern Europeans in France, among them Andrzej Wajda, Krzysztof Kieślowski and Otar Iosseliani and, from other countries, directors such as Pedro Almodóvar and Manoel de Oliveira. No doubt the increasing 'Europeanisation' of European cinema, through co-productions and EU-backed projects, will further increase this transnational movement of personnel [> EUROPEAN COMMUNITY AND THE CINEMA]. (Ginette Vincendeau and Joseph Garncarz)

EUROPEAN ART CINEMA

We think we know what we mean by 'art cinema'. Yet in the European cinema of the 1990s, when directors as diverse in their preoccupations and styles as Krzysztof Kieślowski, Leos Carax and Pedro Almodóvar can be united by the same term, it would be more accurate to talk of 'art cinemas' to indicate the national and historical plurality concealed by the term. While being a means of defining and marketing a certain kind of European film, art cinema is also the institutional and aesthetic space into which the work of directors from beyond Europe has been integrated: for example, Kenji Mizoguchi from Japan, Satyajit Ray from India and, more recently, Zhang Yimou from China. Art cinema operates as a means of merging aesthetic and national 'difference', and of encouraging both.

Two moments can be loosely identified as having contributed to the formation of what Peter Lev calls 'a continuing impulse in film history', and to its association with Europe: the European avant-gardes of the 1920s and the New Waves that flourished from the late 1950s to the early 1970s [> AVANT-GARDE CINEMA IN EUROPE]. The first of these moments includes the schools of Soviet montage, surrealism, French impressionism and German expressionism, all sharing a common search for creative and conceptual liaisons between the then silent medium and painting, music and poetry. In its earliest incarnation, then, art cinema implied an aesthetic project based in formal experimentation and innovation. Equally, as Steve Neale has observed, the concept of art cinema as an institutional space was developed by the national cinemas of Europe from the 1920s as 'attempts to counter both American domination of their indigenous markets in film and to foster a film industry and a film culture of their own'. The second, postwar, flourishing of art cinema can thus be seen as a consolidation of characteristics established in the 1920s.

The crucial role of Italian neo-realism* in the development of postwar European art cinema is, as David Bordwell notes, in its being 'a transitional phenomenon' between the prewar and wartime national cinemas and those that were to develop after the war. The demise of the American studio system and the Paramount anti-trust decrees of 1948 created a shortage of films for international distribution. Equally, television was emerging both as a competitor for audiences and as a new market for films. This combination of factors meant that, from the mid-1950s onwards, films were increasingly made for international distribution. Italian neo-realism, then, can be seen as the forerunner of the art cinemas of the 1950s and 1960s, wherein the themes, styles and authorial address specific to a national cinema would find international audiences. 'The fullest flower of the art cinema paradigm', as Bordwell has called the postwar New Waves, 'occurred at the moment that the combination of novelty and nationalism became the marketing device it has been ever since'. The late 1950s/early 1960s thus brought the cinematic 'shocks' of the French New Wave, of Michelangelo

Antonioni's* *L'avventura* (1960), Federico Fellini's* *La dolce vita* (1960) and the international discovery of Ingmar Bergman, for many the archetypal European art cinema director.

The stylistic modes of art cinema – as opposed to Hollywood popular genres – traditionally privilege realism and ambiguity, two registers generally unified through the appeal to authorial expressivity. The notion of the *auteur* director as developed in *Cahiers du cinéma* in the 1950s, and then modified by Andrew Sarris in the US during the 1960s, speaks both of the critical support system that comes into being around art cinema and of the complexity of art cinema's internationalism. After all, the French New Wave defined itself positively in relation to American cinema and negatively in relation to the French cinema of the 1950s. Similarly, the New German Cinema of the late 1960s and 1970s established the *auteur* as 'public institution' in order to mark out a space for a national cinema founded on a combination of art cinema precepts: an aesthetics of personal expressivity supported by state funding. This tendency to 'institutionalise' the idea of the *auteur*, and with it an idea of a national art cinema, reached its apogee in the cultural policies of the French Minister for Culture, Jack Lang, in the 1980s when French *auteur* cinema was regarded as a significant part of the national cinematic patrimony. Perhaps the most high-profile example of this particular strategy is the French co-production of the French/Swiss/Polish *Trois couleurs/Three Colours* trilogy: *Bleu/Blue*, *Blanc/White* (both 1993) and *Rouge/Red* (1994) directed by Kieślowski, who represents the paradigm of the European *auteur*.

While Kieślowski, Carax and Almodóvar serve as significantly different versions of contemporary European art cinema directors, the specificity of European art cinema is increasingly unclear. Since the 'New American Cinema' of De Palma, Scorsese and Cimino took part of its inspiration from the European cinema of the 1960s, the idea of the *auteur* has become a critical/industrial commonplace. Yet since its heyday in the 1960s, art cinema has been understood, in some European film industries at least, as both a generic and an institutional option that, if no longer guaranteeing international visibility, at least preserves some of the cultural cachet associated with its past. (Chris Darke)

Bib: David Bordwell, *Narration in the Fiction Film* (1985).

EUROPEAN CINEMA AND HOLLYWOOD

Before 1914, France and Italy were the two main exporters of film. Between 1913 and 1925, however, American exports of film to Europe increased fivefold. If Hollywood secured its position as the world leader in film exports at the expense of a war-ravaged Europe, there was little American production involvement in Europe until 1945. European concern over the extent of the influx of American films began to take shape in the 1920s, with Germany the first major industry to take action against American films in the form of the Film Europe initiative spearheaded by Erich Pommer. Following the German example – whereby distributors were issued a permit to release a foreign film each time they financed and distributed a German one – France and Italy began to impose import restrictions, quotas, tariffs and quid pro quo conditions that sought to secure screen time for domestic production. In the UK, the 1927 Cinematograph Films Act instituted a quota on foreign film imports, which resulted in a flurry of British 'quota quickies' to satisfy quota demands. The Motion Picture Producers and Distributors of America (MPPDA; renamed the Motion Picture Association of America, MPAA, in 1945) gave what was to become the conventional American response to attempts by European countries to protect their industries, claiming that 'This government had adopted no restrictive regulations similar in any way to those enforced in certain foreign countries.' Nearly seventy years later, the same disingenuous free-trade rhetoric would be repeated in the 1993 Uruguay Round of the General Agreement on Tariffs and Trade (GATT).

American production involvement in Europe increased dramatically after World War II, the devistated continent now reliant on American aid and having little capacity or will to dictate strict import quotas. Equally, there were hundreds of American films, unreleased in Europe during the war, with which Hollywood could saturate European markets. At the same time, as Peter Lev has pointed out, 'European markets became a necessity, not a luxury, to American film companies in the 1950s, because the American audience for motion pictures was rapidly shrinking.' The Paramount decrees of 1948 which signalled the end of the vertical integration of Hollywood led to a drop in the number of films produced, and thus the increasing importance of the export market. In the face of the American strategy of market saturation, European countries returned either to quota systems or to a system of 'blocked funds' to try to counter American domination of domestic markets. The 1948 Anglo-American Film Agreement allowed US companies to withdraw only $17 million of their earnings, leaving over $40 million each year to accumulate in blocked accounts, the proviso being unlimited American access to the British market. The 1948 Franco-American Film Agreement allowed US firms to withdraw up to $3.6 million of their funds annually, leaving around $10 million blocked to be used for joint production with French companies and the construction of new studios, among other things. This latter agreement replaced the 1946 Blum-Byrnes trade agreement that had given America generous terms to export their films to France. Both 1948 agreements laid the ground for what became known as 'runaway productions', one of the three sorts of production that came to characterise the postwar relationship between Hollywood and Europe, the others being co-productions and what Peter Lev calls 'the Euro-American art film'.

With high unemployment in Hollywood in the 1950s and 1960s, and with lower production costs and more flexible labour regulations in Europe – especially Italy and Spain – the two immediate postwar decades saw a spate of European-American film production. 'Runaway productions' relied on a combination of European and American personnel and stars, were financed through blocked funds and tended towards the spectacular epic, films like *Alexander the Great* (1955), *Ben-Hur* (1959), *Lawrence of Arabia* (1962) or *55 Days at Peking* (1964); the ground-breaking Italian (so-called) 'Spaghetti' Westerns* of the mid-1960s should also be included here. Co-production agreements were increasingly part of the production structure of such films; although they had been tried in the 1920s, they became common practice only after World War II. Jean-Luc Godard's *Le Mépris/Contempt* (1963) is both a satire on the exigencies of co-production – Georgia Moll as the harassed interpreter caught between Jack Palance's overbearing American producer, Fritz Lang's urbane European director, Michel Piccoli's French screenwriter and Brigitte Bardot's alienated sex goddess – and the very incarnation of the Euro-American art film. Such a film, according to Lev, 'attempts a synthesis of the American entertainment film (large budget, good production values, internationally known stars) and the European art film (auteur director, artistic subject and/or style) with the aim of reaching a much larger audience than the art film normally commands'. While the 1960s can be seen as the high point of such ventures, a nominal list of some of the more celebrated examples of the Euro-American art film indicates the longevity of this production style: *Blowup* (1967), *Ultimo tango a Parigi/Last Tango in Paris* (1972), *Paris, Texas* (1984), *The Last Emperor* (1987).

The 1993 GATT talks illustrated the extent to which the relationship between Europe and Hollywood remains 'a two-way fascination and a one-way exploitation', to use Godard's phrase. American objections to European film subsidies and 'protectionist' measures resulted in a piece of concerted brinkmanship by the French government – supported by a prestigious group of film-makers and stars – over the issue of 'cultural exception', which threatened to scupper the entire GATT agreement, of which film and audiovisual issues constituted only a small part. 'Cultural exception' was the idea that films and audiovisual material – because of their 'cultural specificity' to a particular nation – should not be governed by the same terms applied to foodstuffs, minerals, cars, etc. At the eleventh hour this principle was effectively acknowledged in a piece of EU/US political legerdemain: in order to save the GATT treaty, it was agreed simply to exclude film and audiovisual material from its terms. That the French government was so active in facing down American *laissez-faire* petitioning was accounted for by the French film critic Michel Ciment in December 1993 as follows: 'If French cinema has survived it is because of two measures that an American interpretation of GATT could decide were illegal. The first is the quota imposed on films shown on televison (60 per cent of them must be European). The second is a 13 per cent tax on all tickets sold at the box-office, which is used to subsidise innovative films, art-house cinemas, independent distributors, film festivals, film schools and East European and African production.' In retrospect, this aspect of GATT looks less resolved than simply put on hold, and the pro-liferation of cable and satellite channels promises to pose questions of broadcasting territory and intellectual property rights as well as to challenge definitions of the 'national' that underwrite positions such as those adopted by the French over their film industry.

Aesthetically speaking, the relay between Europe and Hollywood has had complex and diverse consequences, from the fascination and support evinced in the 1920s by American studios for German direc-tors such as F. W. Murnau, Ernst Lubitsch and Paul Leni, to the sometimes uncomfortable exile that Hollywood offered to émigré European directors such as Lang, Jean Renoir, Douglas Sirk (Sierck) and Robert Siodmak in the 1930s and 1940s. A prime example of this international cross-pollination of film style can be seen in critical approaches to *film noir* as a hybridisation of American generic structures, German Expressionism and French Poetic Realism. The European New Waves and art cinemas of the 1950s and 1960s were often fascinated by Hollywood, a fascination epitomised by Godard's films, and in turn can be seen to have fed into the stylistics of American directors such as Martin Scorsese, Francis Ford Coppola and Brian De Palma of the 'New American Cinema' of the 1970s. This traffic of influence and mutual acknowledgment has been evident more recently in the American vogue for remaking successful European, and particularly French, films, for example Coline Serreau's *Trois hommes et un couffin/Three Men and a Cradle.* (1985) as *Three Men and a Baby* (1988), Luc Besson's *Nikita* (1990) as *The Assassin* (1993) and Daniel Vigne's *Le Retour de Martin Guerre* (1981) as *Sommersby* (1993). (Chris Darke)

Bib: Peter Lev, *The Euro-American Cinema* (1993).

EUROPEAN COMMUNITY [NOW EUROPEAN UNION] AND THE CINEMA

While European cinema production had previously fallen under gen-eral EC legislation and directives on trade and industry, it was not until the 1980s that the Brussels authorities developed a coherent pol-icy specifically concerning film and other European media. The issue had been brought to a head by a 1984 proposal from French president François Mitterand to establish a pan-European co-production fund for work in cinema and television. Mitterand's plan was rejected but it had started the ball rolling.

In 1986 the Commission's Directorate for Information, Communication and Culture put forward its *Mesures pour Encourager le Développement de l'Industrie de Production Audio-Visuelle* (or MEDIA for short). Once accepted by the Council, MEDIA began a pilot phase in 1987, to last until 1990, under the control of the EC Ministers for Cultural Affairs. As a symbol of the EC's commitment to its MEDIA programme, 1988 was designated European Cinema and Television Year. Events included the first ever European Film Awards*, although somewhat ironically the Berlin ceremony garnered very little media attention. During the same year, in an attempt to emphasise the economic implications of MEDIA, the suffix '92' was added to the programme's acronym. MEDIA 92 was to be a high-profile test case for the new EC internal market, encouraging collaboration between the twelve member states.

The full MEDIA programme was adopted by the Council of Ministers of the EC in December 1990 and was retitled MEDIA 95. From 1991 to 1995, MEDIA was awarded a budget of 200 million ECU (roughly £340 million). Most of this money was designated as 'seed' funding, a system of repayable advances with the programme's initiatives sharing in any profit they had helped to create. Thus it was hoped that the MEDIA budget would largely become self-perpetuating in years to come. In an attempt to broaden the scope of MEDIA (and its funding), European states from outside the EC have been encouraged to join the programme's activities. In 1992 MEDIA initiatives were opened to five members of the European Free Trade Association (EFTA) – Austria, Finland, Iceland, Norway and Sweden – as well as to Poland, Hungary and Czechoslovakia.

MEDIA is made up of an ever-increasing programme of initiatives which support the development, production and distribution of European audiovisual culture. Of these, nineteen are partly or wholly concerned with film. The remit of the respective initiatives can usually be gleaned from their catchword titles. CARTOON, for example, comprises a package of measures to support European animation production, including a database of contacts and incentives to encourage cooperation between studios. The most important MEDIA initiative with regard to development is the European Script Fund (SCRIPT). Recognising that securing finance for the development of projects is often the biggest hurdle faced by European film-makers, SCRIPT provides loans and advice to help get proposals up and running. The loans, averaging 50 per cent of a project's pre-production budget, become reimbursable if the project goes into production. Completed films which have benefited from assistance by SCRIPT include *Acción Mutante* (1992, Spain), *Daens* (1992, Belgium/France/Netherlands) and *Naked* (1993, UK). For projects that have made it to the production stage, Euro Media Garanties (EMG) provides film-makers with a measure of financial security. Supporting ventures that involve producers from at least three Council of Europe members, EMG will guarantee up to 70 per cent of the loan finance taken out on the project.

142

Perhaps the biggest success story of the MEDIA programme, the European Film Distribution Office (EFDO) has helped many films reach wider markets, both within the continent and around the world. EFDO's main remit is to support distribution between EU member states, but through 'EFDO Abroad', which presents films at festivals outside Europe, it now also promotes European cinema to countries worldwide. With the vast majority of European cinema consisting of low-budget projects which are only ever distributed in their country of origin, EFDO has been particularly beneficial to smaller productions. In fact 80 per cent of EFDO's available funds are set aside for films costing no more than 2.25 million ECU (£3.825 million). Covering up to 50 per cent of distributors' pre-costs, EFDO offers interest-free loans to films which have secured a distribution deal for no less than three EU countries. Moreover, the loan is only repayable if the release is successful. Conversely, if a supported film does especially well at the box-office, EFDO becomes entitled to a small share of the profits, or 'success dividend', which can then be reinvested. Among the well-known films to have received support from EFDO are *Babettes gaestebud/Babette's Feast* (1987, Denmark), *Spoorloos/The Vanishing* (1987, Netherlands/France) and *Volere volare* (1991, Italy).

Another film to have benefited from EFDO money, *Toto le héros/Toto the Hero* (1991, Belgium/France/Germany), serves as a testament to the package of MEDIA initiatives and the spirit of cooperation they have fostered within European cinema. A co-production of three member states, *Toto* was aided at every stage by European funding, beginning with support from SCRIPT and ending with the promotion of the video release by Espace Vidéo Européen (EVE). Yet one of the film's major sources of funding came from outside the MEDIA programme, via an initiative of the Council of Europe, EURIMAGES.

Set up in 1988, EURIMAGES is a co-production fund in the mould of that proposed by François Mitterand four years earlier. Providing financial support for films made by production partners from at least three member countries, the fund initially comprised twelve Council countries. A notable absentee from the final agreement, though, was the UK. Displaying the all too prevalent combination of ignorance about what is happening in Europe and a belief that the British still lead the way, the UK government soon established its own European Co-Production Fund (ECF). In the meantime EURIMAGES has gone from strength to strength and the UK finally joined in 1993.

European government initiatives aimed at the media industries are completed by the Audiovisual EUREKA programme (AVE). Again proposed by Europe's prime mover in this field, François Mitterand, AVE's remit is somewhat less specific than those of MEDIA or EURIMAGES. AVE exists primarily to encourage the development and application of advanced audiovisual technology. It also differs from the other major programmes in that it has a wider membership base of nearly thirty countries and responds to specific proposals from the industry rather than attempting to initiate projects itself.

At the time of writing (early 1995), the MEDIA programme is preparing to enter a new phase, MEDIA 2. Although details are still to be confirmed, MEDIA 2 looks quite different from its predecessor, reducing the nineteen initiatives to three strands: training, development and distribution. MEDIA 2 should also have a considerably larger budget for its next five-year programme, but the decision not to provide any specific measure in favour of exhibition has already proved controversial.

Each EU country now has a Mediadesk to provide information and answer queries about the MEDIA programme. (Simon Horrocks)

EUROPEAN FILM AWARDS (FELIX)

Established in 1988 as part of the European Community's Cinema and Television Year, the FELIX awards were intended as a European rival to the Oscars. Yet their initial impact can be measured from the challenge made by Sean Day-Lewis after the first ceremony in Berlin went almost unnoticed: 'Hands up anybody who can name one of the winners or, come to that, anybody who knows whether the epoch-making occasion happened at all.'

FELIX largely follows the format of its Hollywood counterpart, awarding its major prizes in the categories of Best Film, Best Actor/ Actress and so on. One innovation is the prise for Best Young Film, recognising the achievements of up-and-coming talents in European cinema. Suitably, the first recipient of this award was the *enfant terrible* of Spanish film, Pedro Almodóvar, for his *Mujeres al borde de un ataque de nervios/Women on the Verge of a Nervous Breakdown* (1988). As if to emphasise the 'European-ness' of the awards, the annual FELIX ceremony does not have a permanent home, visiting Berlin, Paris and Glasgow in its first three years. Reinforcing FELIX's identity, the prefix 'European' was added to the award categories from 1990, Best Film becoming European Film of the Year, etc. In 1991 responsibility for FELIX was assumed by the newly founded European Film Academy (EFA), bringing with it the respected name of the Academy's president, Ingmar Bergman. But perhaps the most significant change was made to the awards in 1993. While the European Film of the Year continues to be judged on artistic merit, potential winners now have to achieve a designated amount of box-office revenue before qualifying for nomination. FELIX thus recognises that commercial viability is as important as critical acclaim if European cinema is to resist Hollywood's continued domination of the market.

Although the European Film Awards have undoubtedly made significant progress since their inception, FELIX has a long way to go before it can hope to compete with the Oscars in the popular imagination. In the words of EFA chairman Wim Wenders, 'our handicap is that the awards should have started at least twenty years ago'. (Simon Horrocks)

144

The winners in the major FELIX categories so far are as follows:

Best Film (European Film of the Year from 1990)

1988 *Krótki Film o Zabijaniu/A Short Film About Killing* (Krzysztof Kieślowski; Poland)

1989 *Topio stin Omichli/Landscape in the Mist* (Thodoros Angelopoulos; Greece/France/Italy)

1990 *Porte aperte/Open Doors* (Gianni Amelio; Italy)

1991 *Riff-Raff* (Ken Loach; UK)

1992 *Il ladro di bambini/Stolen Children* (Gianni Amelio; Italy/France)

1993 *Urga. Territoriya lyubvi/Urga. Territory of Love* (Nikita Mikhalkov; Russia/France)

1994 *Lamerica* (Gianni Amelio; Italy)

1995 *Land and Freedom* (Ken Loach; UK/Spain/Germany)

Best Young Film (Young European Film of the Year from 1990)

1988 *Mujeres al borde de un ataque de nervios/Women on the Verge of a Nervous Breakdown* (Pedro Almodóvar; Spain)

1989 *300 Mil do Nieba/300 Miles to Heaven* (Maciej Dejczer; Poland/Denmark)

1990 *Henry V* (Kenneth Branagh; UK)

1991 *Toto le héros/Toto the Hero* (Jaco van Dormael; Belgium/France/Germany)

1992 *De Noorderlingen/The Northerners* (Alan van Warmerdam; Netherlands)

1993 *Orlando* (Sally Potter; UK/Russia/France/Italy/Netherlands)

1994 *Le Fils du requin* (Agnès Merlet; France) and *Woyzeck* (Janos Szasz; Hungary)

1995 *La Haine/Hate* (Mathieu Kassovitz; France)

Best Actor (European Actor of the Year from 1990)

1988 Max von Sydow for *Pelle Erobreren/Pelle the Conquerer* (Denmark)

1989 Philippe Noiret for *La Vie et rien d'autre/Life and Nothing But* (France) and *Nuovo Cinema Paradiso/Cinema Paradiso* (Italy)

1990 Kenneth Branagh for *Henry V* (UK)

1991 Michel Bouquet for *Toto le héros/Toto the Hero* (Belgium/France/Germany)

1992 Matti Pellonpää for *La Vie de bohème/Bohemian Life* (Finland/France/Sweden)

1993 Daniel Auteuil for *Un Cœur en hiver/A Heart in Winter* (France)

[1994: no award]

Best Actress (European Actress of the Year from 1990)

1988 Carmen Maura for *Mujeres al borde de un ataque de nervios/Women on the Verge of a Nervous Breakdown* (Spain)

1989 Ruth Sheen for *High Hopes* (UK)

1990 Carmen Maura for *¡Ay, Carmela!* (Spain)
1991 Clothilde Coreau for *Le Petit Criminel* (France)
1992 Juliette Binoche for *Les Amants du Pont-Neuf* (France)
1993 Maia Morgenstern for *Balanta/Le Chêne/The Oak* (Romania/
      France)
[1994: no award]

FESTIVALS

Film festivals gather films (as well as film-makers and stars) in one
venue for the purpose of promotion and information. Although such
events have taken place since the 1910s, the first festival in the modern
sense of the term was Venice*, opened in 1932, followed by Cannes in
1946 and Berlin in 1951. These three constitute the major league of
European film festivals, joined by Karlovy Vary and Locarno in 1946,
Edinburgh in 1947, London in 1957, and a host of others. Festivals'
raison d'être, apart from media and tourist appeal, is to be a market
place for new product and, incidentally (and often controversially), a
forum for critical evaluation. Many award prizes and a Cannes, Venice
or Berlin prize carries promotional value. Since the early 1980s, as the
theatrical market for film has shrunk, festivals in Europe have taken
on a vital role, as the *only* place of exhibition for an increasing number of films, at worst creating the ghetto of the 'festival circuit', but at
best a springboard for media exposure and occasional release: the
films of Emir Kusturica and Kira Muratova are two examples of the
latter. Concurrently a veritable explosion of smaller festivals has taken
place, especially in western Europe, where they are substantially supported by central and local state funds, catering for a wide variety of
specialisms (animation, horror, shorts, thrillers, women's films, gay
and lesbian films, children's films, silent cinema, realist cinema,
national cinemas, etc.). While the market value of the smaller events
is negligible, they perform a crucial cultural function, continuing and
to some extent replacing the work of film clubs as a forum for discovery and debate, and providing an opportunity to circulate other
European and non-American films. (Ginette Vincendeau)

Below is a *selective* list of film festivals. For further details, see:
Directory of International Film Festivals, published by the British
Council, and the *BFI Handbook* (both yearly).
   Albania hosts a biennial national film festival in Tirana. **Austria** has
three main annual film festivals. The Viennale – Internationale
Filmfestwochen Wien (Vienna international film festival, every
autumn) is subsidised by the Vienna City Council and a private spon-
sor, and includes symposia and publications. The other two festivals
are dedicated to Austrian cinema: the Österreichische Film Tage Wels
(Austrian Film Days, in Wels) since 1984, and the Diagonale – Festival
des Österreichischen Films (festival of Austrian cinema) held in

Pier Paolo Pasolini

The second incarnation of Maciste: Gordon Scott in Giacomo Gentilomo's *Maciste contro il vampiro (Goliath and the Vampires*, 1961).

Francesco Rosi's *Salvatore Giuliano* (1962).

Stefania Sandrelli
with Jean-Louis
Trintignant in
Bernardo Bertolucci's
The Conformist
(1970).

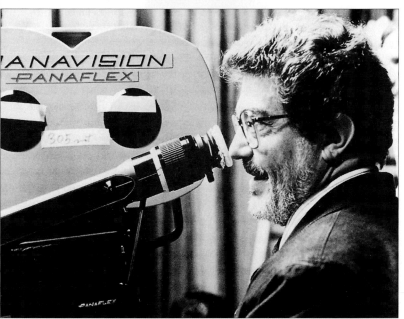

Ettore Scola

Vincent Spano
and Joaquim de
Almeida in the
Taviani brothers'
*Good Morning,
Babilonia* (1986).

Ugo Tognazzi

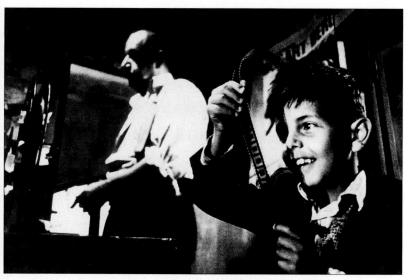

Philippe Noiret and Salvatore Cascio in *Cinema Paradiso* (1988).

Totò

Alida Valli and Farley Granger in Luchino Visconti's *Senso* (1954).

Monica Vitti in Michelangelo Antonioni's *L'avventura* (1960).

Tómas Milian and Lee Van Cleef in Sergio Sollima's
La resa dei conti (1967).

Nicoletta Braschi and Roberto Benigni in *Johnny Stecchino* (Robert Benigni, 1991).

Isa Miranda in *Malombra* (Mario Soldati, 1942).

Salzburg since 1993 and organised by the Austrian Film Commission. **Belgium**'s most famous, though short-lived, festival was Exprmntl (experimental films) at Knokke-le-Zoute which ran in 1949, 1958, 1963, 1967, 1971 and 1974, and remains legendary for both its films and its passionate climate of debates and 'happenings'. Out of the country's large number of festivals should be mentioned the Brussels international film festival (January), the Brussels international festival of fantasy and science-fiction film and thrillers (March), and, also in Brussels, Cinédécouvertes (cine-discoveries) in July and Filmer à tout prix ('To film no matter what') in October. In November, a festival of European film is held in Virton. Ghent holds the Internationaal Filmgebeuren (international film festival) in October and an art film festival in February. **Bulgaria**'s main festival is the international festival of comedy films in Gabrovo in May (odd years). There is also an animation festival in Varna in October (odd years). **Czechoslovakia**. First held in 1946 and established permanently in 1950, Karlovy Vary (now in the Czech Republic) has been the main festival. Until 1992 it alternated bi-ennially with Moscow and functionned as the Communist block alternative to Cannes and Venice*, showcasing Eastern European cinema, but also 'Third World' cinema. Bratislava (now Slovakia) holds several festivals, including the Forum (festival of first feature films, November–December). **Denmark**. The main festival is the Odense international film festival (August, odd years). There are also a film and video festival in Copenhagen (June, even years) and the Copenhagen gay and lesbian film festival (September, annually).

Finland. The Midnight Sun festival takes place every June (since 1986) in Sodankylä, a small Lapland community, focusing on new Finnish cinema and silent films. Espoo ciné, in southern Finland, started in 1990. Kettupäivät ('The Fox-days') in Helsinki in early November is a forum for new Finnish shorts, documentaries and videos. The international children's film festival (launched in 1982) takes place in Oulu in late November. The Tampere short film festival in early March (since 1970) is an important forum for new Finnish film-makers. MuuMedia in early March in Helsinki (since 1991) concentrates on video and the new media. **France**. Founded in 1938 to counter the fascist influences thought to contaminate Venice*, Cannes' opening was delayed by World War II. Since 1946, it has been the international film industry's most prominent meeting place. The festival takes place in May. The most important specialist events are: the Annecy festival (January), the Clermont-Ferrand short film festival, the Cognac festival of thrillers, the Créteil international women's film festival (March–April), the Cinéma du réel (documentary) festival in Paris (March) and the Deauville festival of American cinema in September (notoriously boycotted in the early 1980s by French Minister of Culture Jack Lang). The Institut Lumière in Lyons and the Cinémathèque Française organise regular retrospective festivals, the latter in particular with Cinémémoire (Paris, November), which shows newly restored prints. **Germany**. The most important German Festival is in Berlin, founded in 1951. The Internationale Kurzfilmtage Oberhausen (Oberhausen international short film festival), held annually since 1955 (in April), exhibits a wide variety of short films. The Internationales Film-Festival Mannheim (November), established in 1952, emphasises debut features and documentaries. The Internationale Hofer Filmtage (Hof International Film Days) has since 1967 been a meeting place for younger German film-makers, especially film school graduates. The Leipzig festival (November–December), launched in 1957, is a forum for politically committed documentary film-making. Although its political focus has shifted since the end of the GDR to Third World film, it still functions as a window for central and eastern Europe. Germany has two major women's film festivals, Feminale (Cologne, May, since 1984) and Femme totale (Dortmund, since 1987). The Stuttgart animation festival has been running since 1982. **Greece**. The major cinematic event in Greece is the Thessaloniki festival, founded in September 1960. **Hungary**. The main festival is the Hungarian Film Week, which provides a survey of Hungarian cinema, including documentary, experimental and student films. It is usually held in February, a week before Berlin. **Ireland**. Established in 1956, the Cork festival was the first in Ireland. It was joined in 1986 by the Dublin festival as well as festivals in Galway, Derry and Belfast.

Italy. For many years Venice* was Italy's sole major film festival. Since the early 1960s many smaller festivals have emerged. A pioneering role was played, from 1960, by the Festival del Cinema Libero at the Apennine resort of Porretta Terme, for films made outside or on the fringes of the system. This was followed in 1965 by the Mostra del Nuovo Cinema at Pesaro (June). Founded by critic Lino Miccichè, Pesaro has devoted itself to the discovery or rediscovery of *auteurs*, movements and national cinemas, promoted conferences, and produced a steady stream of important publications. Throughout the 1970s and early 1980s numerous local initiatives followed. Among the most important were the Salso Film and TV Festival at Salsomaggiore, devoted (until its demise in the 1990s) to research and experiment; Filmmaker in Milan, dedicated to independent production; the Festival Cinema Giovani in Turin, with retrospectives of the 'New Waves' of the 1960s; and the Bergamo Film Meeting, a festival-market for quality films awaiting distribution. Among specialist festivals the most noteworthy are Mystfest at Cattolica, near Rimini, for thrillers, and the Pordenone festival of early cinema (October). **Netherlands**. The three main festivals are the Netherlands Film Festival (formerly Dutch Film Days), in Utrecht (September), where an independent film festival (Cinemanifestatie) ran 1966–71; the documentary festival in Amsterdam (December); and the Rotterdam festival (January–February). **Norway**. The main Norwegian film festival is held in Haugesund annually (August–September). In addition, a festival takes place in Oslo in November, and a short films festival in Trondheim in June. **Poland** has four annual festivals. The festival of Polish feature

148

films in Gdansk/Gdynia (September) presents Poland's latest productions, and holds the annual meeting of the Association of Polish Filmmakers. The Cracow festival of short films (late May) celebrated its thirty years as the major Polish short film festival in 1993. The Warsaw International Film Festival has grown in recent years from a student film club event to a well organised festival of recent international releases (modelled on London). The Lubuskie Lato Filmowe, run by the Association of Film Societies (Dyskysyjne Kluby Filmowe) at Lagow in western Poland, presents the latest films produced in Poland and eastern and central Europe.

Portugal. Among Portugal's numerous festivals are the Espinho festival (November) for animation, the Encontros Internacionais de Cinema Documental (documentaries) in Odivelas, the Fantasporto (fantasy films) in Oporto in February, the Figueira da Foz festival (September) and the Troia festival (June–July). **Romania**. There is a biennial animation festival in Mamaia; the national film festival has taken place at Costinesti since 1976, but its future is in doubt. **(Former) Soviet Union**. The major film festival of the Soviet Union has been Moscow, in July (odd years, alternating with Karlovy Vary), traditionally the showcase for Soviet and eastern European socialist cinema; other festivals are held in St Petersburg (June), Sochi (May–June) and Tashkent (May–June). Among other festivals in the ex-Soviet states are the International Film Forum 'Arsenal' in Riga (Latvia) in September, for experimental film, the 'Golden Taurus' festival in Kaunas (Lithuania) in June and the 'Molodost' international film festival in Kiev (Ukraine) in October. **Spain**. The San Sebastián Film Festival (annually in September, since 1953) initially contributed glamour and an indirect legitimacy to Franco's regime, showcasing films which were then further cut or prohibited in Spain. After the transition to democracy, it is still Spain's premier film event; under Pérez Estremera, San Sebastián presents a competitive section built around the pick of Spanish autumn releases and the best new Latin American films, plus major international titles. Under Fernando Lara, festival director since 1983, the Valladolid International Film Festival (October) premieres major art films, complemented by tributes and retrospectives. Spain's other large festivals are Sitges (October) for fantasy and horror, and Valencia for Mediterranean cinema.

Sweden's main festivals are in Stockholm (November) and Uppsala (October, specialising in short films); there is also a festival in Gothenburg (February). **Switzerland**. Apart from Locarno, founded in 1946 as a showcase for the international film market, the main festivals in Switzerland are Nyon and Solothurn. Emerging from the 'Festival du film amateur' (Rolle 1963–64, Nyon 1965–68), Nyon is concerned with documentary. Its director was Moritz de Hadeln (also Locarno's director 1972–77) until 1980, when Erika de Hadeln took over, pursuing the festival's remit of showing politically and socially committed films. Solothurn, or the Solothurner Filmtage (Solothurn Film Days), held annually in the last week of January since 1966, is the most important venue for domestic productions, together with theme-specific films by foreign directors, exhibitions and round-tables on issues of national film policy. Solothurn has since the early 1990s opened up towards video, television and co-productions. Video art finds a place at the Internationale Film- und Videotage in Lucerne, the International Video Week in Geneva and the Video Festival at Locarno. **UK**. Apart from Edinburgh, established in 1947 as the first British film festival, the major event is the London Film Festival (November), held at the National Film Theatre and other London cinemas, created as a non-competitive 'festival of festivals' to present material shown at other festivals earlier in the year, as well as films released in their own country but not in Britain. The National Film Theatre also hosts the London lesbian and gay film festival (March) and the Jewish film festival (October). Smaller film festivals in the UK include Aberystwyth (November), Birmingham (October), Brighton (May), Cambridge (July), Leeds (October), the Norwich Women's Film Weekend (May), Nottingham ('Shots in the Dark', a thriller film festival, May–June) and Southampton (September). **(Former) Yugoslavia**. There is an international festival of animated films in Zagreb (Croatia) in June (even years). The Pula (Croatia) festival was first held in 1954, as the national film festival of Yugoslavia. In 1993 it was remodelled the national Croatian film festival. Fest was established in Belgrade in 1970 as a 'festival of festivals' and it became a major gathering point for international filmmakers. It collapsed under the economic and cultural embargo of Serbia in 1993 (Croatia).

GAY CINEMA IN EUROPE – see LESBIAN AND GAY CINEMA IN EUROPE

HERITAGE CINEMA IN EUROPE

The term describes period films made since the mid-1970s. Characteristic, successful examples include *Jean de Florette* (1986, France), *A Room with a View* (1985, UK), *Babettes gæstebud/Babette's Feast* (1987, Denmark) and *Belle Epoque* (1992, Spain). The term suggests an affinity with what has been called the heritage industry, notably retro fashion and the popularisation of museums and historical sites through the use of simulacra, lighting and sound effects and actors in period costume. Films may be characterised by use of a canonical source from the national literature, generally set within the past 150 years; conventional filmic narrative style, with the pace and tone of '(European) art cinema'* but without its symbolisms and personal directorial voices; a museum aesthetic, period costumes, decor and locations carefully recreated, presented in pristine condition, brightly or artfully lit; a performance style based on nuance and social observation.

It is arguable whether this is a distinct phenomenon. There are precedents (for example, the French costume dramas of the 1950s such as *Les Misérables*, 1958), but heritage films may be distinguished from many period films in a number of ways. While displaying high production values, they are generally small-scale and intimate, not spectacular; they do not (on the whole) deal with the great events of history, as conventionally understood, or even, like *Senso* (1954, Italy) or *Angi Vera* (1978, Hungary), treat such events through their impact on personal lives; much less do they address the construction of historical representation, like *Ludwig – Requiem für einen jungfräulichen König/ Ludwig – Requiem for a Virgin King* (1972, Germany) or *Amarcord* (1974, Italy). However, it is not a uniquely European genre, except perhaps in the sense of Eurocentric, since it has been important to the cinema of most white settler nations, notably Australia, Argentina and Canada.

The focus of the films is, typically, on attractively presented everyday bourgeois life. Critically they are an interesting case study. Often hugely popular in their country of origin, they tend to be sold as art cinema outside it. Though the market research is not available, it seems likely that they are especially popular with middle-class audiences, in a period when this class has become the majority or at least a significant minority in many European countries. They are thus embraced by the same class from which the critical establishment is drawn, yet the latter has generally viewed them negatively. Often characteristics such as nostalgia or attention to fixtures and fittings are criticised without considering the potential of the former to be a critique of the present or the sensuousness of the latter and its iconographic expressivity (typically requiring the skilled reading of a female spectator). Equally, the genre has provided a space for marginalised social groups, a sense of putting such people back into history, for instance women: *Rouge Baiser* (1985, France), *Rosa Luxemburg* (1986, Germany), *Howards End* (1991, UK); lesbians and gay men: *El diputado/Congressman* (1978, Spain), *Ernesto* (1979, Italy), *Avskedet/The Farewell* (1980, Finland); even ethnic minorities (*Cheb*, 1990, France) and the disabled (*My Left Foot*, 1989, Ireland). None of this argues for the merit of the genre, but suggests a critical issue of some complexity that warrants exploration. (Richard Dyer)

Bib: Andrew Higson, 'Re-presenting the National Past: Nostalgia and Pastiche in the Heritage Film', in Lester Friedman (ed.), *British Cinema and Thatcherism* (1993).

LESBIAN AND GAY CINEMA IN EUROPE

It is generally assumed that European cinemas have a good track record on homosexuality: more images, sooner, less prejudiced, more often produced by openly lesbian/gay people. This account needs qualification and explanation, and more research.

Lesbian/gay representation has been all but entirely absent from East European cinemas. In Western Europe, lesbian/gay stereotypes are widely used, not only in popular comedies and thrillers but in canonical *auteur* works: *Die Büchse der Pandora/Pandora's Box* (1929, Germany); *Roma città aperta/Rome Open City* (1945, Italy), *La Fiancée du pirate/Dirty Mary* (1969, France). They are not necessarily the same as in Hollywood, nor are stereotypes unambiguously negative, something radical gay/lesbian films have often taken up, as in *Un hombre llamado Flor de Otoño/A Man Called Autumn Flower* (1977, Spain), or *Madame X – eine absolute Herrscherin/Madame X – an Absolute Ruler* (1978, Germany). The greater number of lesbian/gay representations in Western European cinemas has much to do with identifying markets with which Hollywood did not compete: pornography and the educational film, not always firmly distinct genres. Soft-core heterosexual pornography has been a mainstay of many European industries and invariably includes lesbian sequences. Sex education films have treated male and female homosexuality and have often been enlightened as texts even when marketed as titillation, for instance *Anders als die Anderen/Different from the Others* (1919, Germany) or *Der Sittlichkeitsverbrecher/The Sex Criminal* (1962, Switzerland).

At the same time, European cinemas dealt with homosexuality in a serious manner much earlier than others. This did not only occur in films of blatant high seriousness: among the most cherishable early images of homosexuality are the male relationship in the highly strung melodrama *Geschlecht in Fesseln/Sex in Shackles* (1928, Germany) and the lesbian character in the French thriller *Quai des Orfèvres* (1947). The earliest known representation is in *Vingarne/The Wings* (1916, Sweden), with the earliest lesbian representation perhaps *Die Büchse der Pandora*. *Anders als die anderen* and *Mädchen in Uniform/ Girls in Uniform* (1931, Germany) represent the earliest explicitly progressive treatments, a tradition taken up in the postwar years by *Victim* (1960, UK): the presence of contemporaneous, relatively strong homosexual rights movements in these countries is significant in accounting for these breakthroughs.

Government policies in many countries have facilitated *auteur* cinema, in which many more or less openly lesbian/gay directors have worked (Chantal Akerman, Pedro Almodóvar, Jean Cocteau, Rainer Werner Fassbinder, Marleen Gorris, Derek Jarman, Ulrike Ottinger, Pier Paolo Pasolini*, Luchino Visconti*), as have (straight) women directors who treated homosexuality in a sympathetic, even at times envious, manner – among others, Mai Zetterling's *Älskande par/ Loving Couples* (1964, Sweden), Margarethe von Trotta's *Das zweite Erwachen des Krista Klages/The Second Awakening of Krista Klage* (1977, Germany) or Diane Kurys' *Coup de foudre/Entre Nous/At First Sight* (1983, France). In recent years, the European heritage* film has been remarkably hospitable to lesbian/gay themes, as for instance in *Novembermond/November Moon* (1984, Germany), *Maurice* (1987, UK), *Meteoro ke skia/Meteor and Shadow* (1962, Greece); one might consider Jacqueline Audry's *Olivia* (1950, France) an important early example. *Auteur* and heritage cinema do not treat homosexuality as an issue or problem, but are not always lacking in anguish, as for instance in *Tystnaden/The Silence* (1962, Sweden), or melancholy, as in *Gli occhiali d'oro/The Gold-rimmed Spectacles* (1988, Italy), and few European films have had the (often bland) affirmative impulse of post-gay liberation cinema in the USA. (Richard Dyer)

Bib: Richard Dyer, *Now You See It: Studies on Lesbian and Gay Film* (1990).

SEXUALITY, EROTICISM AND PORNOGRAPHY IN EUROPEAN CINEMA

Representations of sexuality and eroticism are as old as the cinema in Europe. While 'actualities' and little comic scenes entertained audiences in fairgrounds, short pornographic movies drew a few of them into brothels. A wide underground network of porn or 'stag' films flourished, usually unknown to mainstream audiences and film history alike, except when they surfaced in 'scandalous' manifestations, as with the Romanian-born French entrepreneur Bernard Natan [> PATHÉ] who directed, and starred in, a large number of them. In the 'legitimate' cinema, eroticism quickly became a feature too, in early French movies for instance and, notoriously, in the pre-World War I Danish erotic melodrama, credited with the 'invention' of the on-screen passionate kiss.

In 1935, the American authorities burned a print of the Czech film *Extase/Ecstasy* (1932, dir. Gustav Machatý), in which Hedy Lamarr appeared naked. This took place five years after the introduction of the notoriously censorious Hays Code in the US and, for a good thirty years afterwards, the cinema of Europe was regarded as comparatively free in its depiction of sexuality. Of course, such 'freedom' was, as it would be later, within the confines of dominant (and often misogynistic) representations of women as sexual icons. It was also subject to censorship laws in the European countries themselves. Germany, for example, banned *Extase*, but that was on the grounds of Lamarr being Jewish. And if, in Arletty, the French cinema of the 1930s and 1940s had an icon of 'independent' female sexuality, her brief 'nude' shower scene in *Le Jour se lève* (1939) was nevertheless excised.

The national cinemas of postwar Europe, particularly those of France and Italy, began to redefine the permissible limits of cinema's depiction of on-screen sexuality. The Italian neo-realist* cinema achieved an immense international visibility based on the perceived 'realism' of its depiction of specific social milieux. Such success might equally be said to have been achieved by its depiction of female sexuality. The 'earthiness' of Silvana Mangano* in *Riso amaro/Bitter Rice* (1949) and the revealing filming of Anna Magnani*, not to mention the barely concealed lesbian subplot in *Roma città aperta/Rome Open City* (Roberto Rossellini*, 1945), prepared international audiences for the appearances in the 1950s and 1960s of Italian stars such as Gina Lollobrigida*, Sophia Loren* and Claudia Cardinale*.

In France, in a string of films starting with *Caroline Chérie* (1950), Martine Carol continued the line of French female stars whose presence guaranteed that their vehicles would be, as Claude Beylie wrote, 'lightly spiced with a pleasant eroticism'. If Carol and others, such as Françoise Arnoul, gave international currency to certain ideas of French cinema and French femininity, the advent of Brigitte Bardot in *Et Dieu ... créa la femme/And God Created Woman* (1956) promoted different, modern versions both of this femininity and this cinema. The same might be said, forty years on, of Béatrice Dalle, whose explosive performance in *37°2 le Matin/Betty Blue* (1985) can be read as a reprise of the Bardot sex-kitten persona, treated with *Emmanuelle*-like explicitness.

In François Truffaut's *Les Quatre cents coups* (1959), Jean-Pierre Léaud steals a publicity still of an Ingmar Bergman film showing Harriet Andersson in a revealingly off-the-shoulder outfit. It is a moment in which one European art cinema*, the French New Wave, addresses the important figure of Bergman, the most celebrated European *auteur* of the period, via the concern common to both: the 'realistic', 'adult' and hence 'explicit' treatment of sexual themes. These three terms, often interchangeable, became associated with the European art cinemas of the 1960s. It was equally the case that the 'adult' treatment of sexuality by these cinemas was accompanied by the *frisson* of the well-publicised relationships between male *auteurs* and their leading actresses, Roberto Rossellini and Ingrid Bergman, Jean-Luc Godard and Anna Karina, Michelangelo Antonioni* and Monica Vitti*, Ingmar Bergman and Liv Ullmann. Interestingly, the postwar rise in European art cinema was also paralleled by the burgeoning genre of pornography.

If the difference between pornography and eroticism is that between display and suggestion, the late 1960s and the 1970s saw a short-lived convergence of the two. While the sex industry in Europe had formerly restricted itself in the 1950s to low-tech 'stag films' and 'loop movies' for peep shows, and with cinema encroaching progressively upon its territory either in pseudo-documentaries on naturism, so-called 'nudie cuties' and American B-movie exploitation, the late 1960s saw a major increase in the profile of films normally associated with the sex industry.

Two moments are worth isolating in the growing explicitness of sexually oriented material – the first production of hardcore pornography in colour magazines in Scandinavia in 1967, and the international *suc-*

cès de scandale of the Swedish film *Jag är nyfiken – gul/I am Curious – Yellow* (1967), which dispensed with any documentary alibis in its straightforwardly explicit depiction of (simulated) sexual action. These two events presaged the increasing commercial importance of explicit sexual content in European cinema of the 1970s. The first half of the decade saw the great commercial success of Bernardo Bertolucci's* *Ultimo Tango a Parigi/Last Tango in Paris* (1972), whose superbly performed confection of stellar cast, hack psychoanalysis and chic sodomy set a model that many *auteurs* would follow throughout the decade. Most notable among examples of this increasing hybridisation of art cinema and pornography were Dušan Makavejev's Brechtian disquisition on sexual theorist Wilhelm Reich, *W. R. Misterije organizma/ W. R. Mysteries of the Organism* (1971), Bertrand Blier's anarchic, misogynistic *Les Valseuses/Going Places* (1973); Alain Robbe-Grillet's vacuous exercise in softcore imagery and narrative origami, *Le Jeu avec le feu/Giochi di fuoco* (1975, Fr./It.); Pier Paolo Pasolini's* punishing Sadian parable of Italian fascism, *Salò o le 120 giornate di Sodoma/Salò* (1975); Nagisa Oshima's brilliant, French co-produced excursion into hardcore, *Ai no corrida* (1976); and Jean-Luc Godard's highly mediated take on sexuality and domesticity, *Numéro deux* (1975).

The 'sexual revolution' of the 1960s created a climate in which the explicit depiction of sex was more acceptable to a mainstream audience. For a while, softcore and hardcore pornography flourished on European screens, especially in France where censorship began to be phased out from 1967. The most spectacular example of mainstream softcore success was *Emmanuelle* (1974), the top-grossing film of its year, making an international star of its lead actress, Sylvia Kristel. A year later, French hardcore took to similarly mainstream screens with *Exhibition* (1975). The response of the French government was not so much one of outright censorship as a fiscal and institutional one that created, in the law of 31 October 1975, the 'X' certificate to designate pornographic films, the creation of a specialised distribution circuit and the imposition of taxes on domestic pornography and a heavier tax on imported porn. While this approach kept the domestic pornography industry marginalised but financially healthy for a short period, it equally serviced the conventional film industry through the siphoning off of porn-tax income into the 'avances sur recette' funding of art cinema. However, the bubble soon burst and by the 1980s the porn cinema accounted for only 5 per cent of the national audience.

The brief foray into mainstream public consciousness that the 1970s bought to the genre of pornography, particularly in France, also saw, towards the end of that decade, the beginnings of the video boom. The European porn industries latched onto video as a means of bypassing cinematic censorship but also as a way of producing low-budget porn. While the genre of 'amateur porn' began inauspiciously in Germany in the 1970s with the so-called *Hausfrauenporn* (housewife porn), by the 1990s video had become hugely lucrative and the standard means of distribution, so that in France an organisation such as 'Nanou Contact' can organise casual sexual encounters, tape them and market them as product. Equally, the European porn industry has its own stars, many of them celebrities beyond their particular fan-base: Brigitte Lahaie and Tabatha Cash in France, Teresa Orlovski in Germany and La Cicciolina (Ilona Staller) in Italy.

If censorious worries with on-screen sexual explicitness have recently been replaced with a concern over levels of violence, it is clear that, as screens themselves have multiplied, the concern is now as much over access to such images as over their contents. The French pay-channel Canal Plus, for example, programmes soft and hardcore pornography regularly. The extension and multiplication of the audio-visual media throughout Europe with cable and satellite will doubtless revivefy the old debates. (Chris Darke)

Bib: Nick Anning and David Hebditch, *Porn Gold: Inside the Pornography Business* (1988).

APPENDIX I

European Production and Audience Statistics*

* Sources from *Encyclopedia of European Cinema*

FILM PRODUCTION FIGURES

Dates

	1945	1946	1947	1948	1949	1950	1951	1952	1953	1954	1955	1956	1957	1958	1959	1960	1961
Albania	–	–	–	–	–	–	–	–	–	–	–	–	1	–	1	1	1
Austria	1	3	13	25	25	15+2	23+5	16+3	18+10	16+6	22+6	28+9	24+2	19+4	17+2	18+2	21+2
Belgium	9	3	1	2	1	0	1	1/0	0	0	0/5	8	3	4+1	3+2	2/0	6+0
Bulgaria	2	3	4	–	1	1	3	3	1	2	4	6+1	6+4	7+2	12	11	7
Czechoslovakia	3	12	22	20	–	20	8	17	18	15	17	21+1	24+3	29	33+2	35+1	44+1
Denmark	10	13	8	8	8	14	15	16	13	14	13	17	17	14	16	17	24
Finland	21	12	14	16	16	12	18	26	23	29	29	17	20	18	17	15	20
France	72	94	72	91	99+8	99+18	94+18	88+21	64+47	52+46	76+34	90+39	81+61	75+51	68+65	79+79	69+98
Germany (East)	–	–	–	–	–	10	–	–	–	–	13	18	21	25	28	29	27
Germany (West)	–	1	9	23	61+1	73+9	57+3	78+4	89+15	94+15	120+8	115+8	96+11	98+17	85+21	85+10	69+11
Greece	5	4	5	8	13	13	15	22	21	14	24	30	31	51	52	58	68
Hungary	3	–	–	6+0	–	4	8	5	8	7	11+0	9	16	13	18	15	19
Iceland	–	–	–	–	–	–	–	–	–	–	–	–	–	–	–	–	–
Ireland	0	–	–	–	–	0	0	2	–	–	1	–	4	3	3	2	2
Italy	–	62	60	54	76	92+0	104+0	119+13	125+21	144+46	74+52	68+23	66+71	76+65	83+81	94+66	117+88
Luxemburg	–	–	–	–	–	0	0	0	1	0	3	0	0	0	2	0	0
Netherlands	2	0	1	2	2	1	0	1	1	–	3	2	2	4	2	5	1
Norway	4	6	2	5	5	4	11	10	7	10	11	9	10	12	8	8	8
Poland	0	1	2	4	4	4	4	1	9	6	9	13	10	23	15	19+2	24
Portugal	4	9	10	4	7	2	4	8	4	–	5	4	1	4	5	2	2
Romania	1	–	–	–	1	1	2	2	2	3	0	3	4	4	5	8	10
ex-Soviet Union	19	23	23	17	18	13	9	24	45	51	81+3	104	108	121	137	119	133
Spain	33	38	49	45	36	47+2	37+5	33+7	37+7	56+13	49+7	53+22	50+22	51+24	50+17	55+18	72+19
Sweden	44	42	45	32	38	36	32	33	32	37	37	34	32	29	21	24	18
Switzerland	1	0	1	1	1	0	1	2	–	–	3	3	4	3	5	4	7
UK	51	66	73	120	125	99	102	132	142	148	115	130	164	135	140	157	151
ex-Yugoslavia	0	–	2	4	3	4	6	5	9	4+3	12+2	11+1	14+2	14+2	13+2	15+1	32+0

	1962	1963	1964	1965	1966	1967	1968	1969	1970	1971	1972	1973	1974	1975	1976	1977	1978
Albania	1	1	1	1	–	–	–	–		3		–	6	10	14	–	10
Austria	16+4	13+2	11+8	11+5	7+11	7+5	2+5	1+2	3+4	2+3	4+5	3+3	4+4	2+4	3+2	4+4	1+2
Belgium	5+0	0/1	1+1	1/1	1/1	3/1	5/1	10/0	3/1	3/4	11/3	9/4	4/2	–	8/0	3/2	3/3
Bulgaria	9	11	13	11+1	12+2	12+2	13+2	13+2	14+2	17+1	22	19+1	19	22+3	26+2	19+2	30
Czechoslovakia	35+4	39	41	42+3	40	49	44+1	42+8	52+2	57+2	45+4	65+3	63+3	54+8	65+3	61+2	48
Denmark	19	21	17	18	19	20	20	20	20	28	18	20+0	22+0	16+2	20+0	16+0	17+0
Finland	19	11	9	9	6	3	12	11	9	8	8	7	2	7	9	7	10
France	43+82	36+105	45+103	34+108	45+85	47+73	49+68	70+84	66+72	67+60	71+98	97+103	137+97	160+62	170+44	190+32	116+44
Germany (East)	27	20	15	15	–	–	–	–	–	–	10+7	14+2	14+1	15+1	17+1	16	–
Germany (West)	43+18	44+22	35+42	25+47	27+33	56+40	61+46	82+39	86+27	68+31	57+28	80+18	58+22	47+26	42+18	38+14	50+7
Greece	82	92	93	101	117	99	108	98	87	90	64	44	42	38	17	17	15
Hungary	16	18+1	19+1	23	21	21+1	36+1	22+1	21+2	15+4	21	21	19+1	19	19	24+1	28
Iceland	–	–	–	–	–	–	–	–	–	–	–	–	–	–	–	–	–
Ireland	3	2	3	1	3	1	1	0	5	2	6	4	2	0	2	0	1
Italy	139+106	135+95	135+155	94+109	89+143	130+117	130+116	146+103	132+99	128+88	169+111	171+81	176+55	177+53	203+34	142+23	119+24
Luxemburg	0	0	0	0	0	0	0	0	1	0	0	0	0	0	0	0	–
Netherlands	6	5	3	1	5	–	–	–	4	4+1	6+1	8+3	8	16	8+2	7+2	1
Norway	6	6	7	9	6+1	4	7	5+1	11	7+1	8	9+2	12	13+1	14	9	7
Poland	23	27	23	20+0	25	–	–	–	24+0	27	19	19	27	20+1	–	27	31
Portugal	4+1	7+1	5+3	6	5	5+2	4	4	4	7	6	3	–	6	6	9	21
Romania	12	14	14	14+1	11+4	16	6+2	12+2	9+2	15	19	22	22	24	10	23	24
ex-Soviet Union	121	133	–	167	159	175	161+2	194+2	215+3	208+6	230+4	166	162+7	176+8	150+6	146+2	–
Spain	64+24	59+55	67+63	53+98	67+97	55+70	49+68	55+70	42+63	48+43	52+51	73+45	71+41	89+21	90+18	83+19	77+30
Sweden	17	21	19	25	29	23	36	28	23	17	19	15	21	25	18	26	15
Switzerland	4	2	4	10	5	2	3	5	5	6	6+2	17+3	13+4	28+2	19+1	16+4	–
UK	171	150	126	97	99	140	107	112	122	67	131	98	89	91	92	73	77
ex-Yugoslavia	22+0	14+4	17+1	18+2	17+3	33+3	32+1	27+4	23+0	21+3	20+2	20+3	14+1	17+2	14+0	20+0	20+1

Figures are for feature film production by country. 47+2 indicates films + co-productions. 5/1 indicates division of French language/Dutch and Flemish language films produced. Zero (0) indicates no films produced. A dash (–) indicates no figure available.

FILM PRODUCTION FIGURES (continued)

Dates

	1979	1980	1981	1982	1983	1984	1985	1986	1987	1988	1989	1990	1991	1992	1993
Albania	12	–	–	–	7	14	12	–	–	–	11	5	0	1	–
Austria	5+1	5+2	3+2	12+1	8+3	16+1	9+3	11+2	8+2	8+1	10+1	10+5	11	10+0	–
Belgium	8/2	4+2	1/2	4/1	4/3	3/2	6+1	4+1	7+5	4+11	10+0	9+11	3+3	3+9	4+4
Bulgaria	29	31	42	–	32	–	40	23	35	15	20	19	22	3	5+3
Czechoslovakia	47	52	48	–	66	–	50	63	55	58	70	62	17	15	20
Denmark	9+0	13+0	12+0	7+0	11+0	10+1	7+2	10+0	9+2	14+2	16+2	12+1	9+2	10+5	11+3
Finland	9	7+3	12	17	16	17	13	23+1	12	10	7+3	14	11	20	20
France	126+48	144+45	186+45	134+31	101+30	120+41	106+45	97+37	96+37	93+44	66+70	81+65	73+83	72+83	67+85
Germany (East)	–	17	–	16	16	–	16	16	5	–	–	–	–	–	–
Germany (West)	53+12	37+12	60+16	57+13	69+8	62+13	46+18	45+15	47+18	49+8	53+15	38+10	53+19	53+10	50+17
Greece	27	25	46	48	37	40	30	27	26	13	14	10	15+0	6+4	15+3
Hungary	21+5	26	25	–	25	11+6	21	26	26	14+6	37	23	15+4	17+5	9+7
Iceland	–	2	3	3	4	5	4	2+0	1+0	2+0	2+0	2+0	4	1+2	0+2
Ireland	1	5	2	1	3	2	2+0	3+1	1+3	2+3	2+1	3	1	3+1	3+3
Italy	122+24	128+32	79+24	99+15	101+9	86+17	81+8	94+15	106+10	103+21	102+15	98+21	111+18	114+13	86+20
Luxemburg	0	0	3	0	0	1	1	1	1	1	3	1	1+1	1+2	0+4
Netherlands	–	7	11	10	10	12	10+1	13+0	15+3	8+2	13	13	14	13+0	16+0
Norway	13	10	10	10	8	6	10	13	7+2	10	11	9	10	8	9
Poland	32	33+6	17+2	23+3	31+5	35	37	34	35	34	22	27	–	8+13	11+10
Portugal	6	9	6	8	4	8	8	6	9+2	16	4+3	2+7	6+3	2+6	10+6
Romania	28	32	31	32	32	–	26	30	26	23	23	4+5	15+4	12+6	10+5
ex-Soviet Union		156	–	–	–	–	158	142	158	153	160	300	400	65	137
Spain	56+33	82+36	92+45	118+22	81+18	63+12	65+12	49+11	62+7	54+9	43+5	37+10	46+18	38+14	41+15
Sweden	20	23+3	22+3	14+4	17+6	16+2	12	17+3	26+1	13+8	15+6	20+5	10+17	9+11	13+14
Switzerland	–	13	11	–	–	20	15	3+19	6+15	6+12	8+8	8+11	5+12	3+6	0+16
UK	77	61	66	46	56	51	53	29+6	42+6	38+2	22+5	39+8	24+22	29+13	31+29
ex-Yugoslavia	27+1	24+2	23+3	32+2	30+3	30+3	30+2	21+4	23+4	28+7	26+7	21+4	–	3	–

Figures are for feature film production by country. 47+2 indicates films + co-production. 5/1 indicates division of French language/Dutch and Flemish language films produced. Zero (0) indicates no films produced. A dash (–) indicates no figures available.

AUDIENCE FIGURES (Millions)

Dates

	1945	1946	1947	1948	1949	1950	1951	1952	1953	1954	1955	1956	1957	1958	1959	1960	1961
Albania	–	–	–	–	–	–	–	–	4.6	–	5.9	–	5.9	6.6	8.0	–	7.6
Austria	–	–	–	–	–	92.5	93.9	94.1	107.9	110.0	114.0	116.1	119.9	122.0	114.9	106.5	100.5
Belgium	–	–	–	–	–	116.4	114.1	110.4	112.2	111.4	106.0	109.7	106.7	99.9	88.7	80.0	71.7
Bulgaria	–	–	–	–	–	–	37.0	39.0	42.0	55.2	60.0	69.0	77.9	89.4	101.2	112.1	118.0
Czechoslovakia	47.0	–	–	–	–	–	128.0	135.0	144.0	152.0	162.6	185.5	186.2	183.3	178.0	176.5	166.0
Denmark	36.3	53.8	54.4	–	–	52.2	56.6	57.3	59.0	58.7	55.0	52.1	51.3	50.0	46.7	44.0	42.0
Finland	–	30.0	29.6	29.1	26.2	25.7	26.8	26.8	29.4	30.3	33.5	31.2	31.3	28.8	25.5	24.6	23.8
France	402.0	419.0	424.0	–	–	370.7	372.8	359.6	370.6	382.8	394.9	398.9	411.7	371.0	353.7	354.7	328.4
Germany (East)	–	–	–	–	–	184.0	–	–	–	–	310.0	–	–	273.1	258.6	237.9	–
Germany (West)	–	–	–	–	–	487.4	554.8	614.5	680.2	735.6	766.1	817.5	801.0	749.7	670.8	604.8	516.9
Greece	–	–	–	10.0	–	37.5	38.8	41.3	42.6	45.3	49.5	56.9	62.2	66.8	74.8	84.2	86.3
Hungary	–	–	–	–	35.6	47.1	63.0	69.0	73.0	98.0	115.8	113.6	133.4	131.0	135.0	140.1	135.4
Iceland	–	–	–	–	–	–	–	–	–	–	–	–	–	–	–	–	–
Ireland	–	–	–	–	–	46.1	47.8	49.1	50.7	54.1	50.9	52.1	49.8	45.6	43.8	41.2	38.0
Italy	–	411.0	525.0	580.0	600.0	661.5	705.7	748.1	779.9	800.7	819.4	790.2	758.4	730.4	747.9	744.8	741.0
Luxemburg	–	–	–	–	–	–	–	–	–	–	4.0	5.0	5.0	5.0	5.0	4.5	5.0
Netherlands	–	–	–	–	–	63.9	63.5	63.1	63.7	65.1	66.0	69.9	65.6	64.2	55.5	55.4	51.0
Norway	–	30.1	–	–	–	30.0	32.0	34.0	33.0	34.0	33.0	35.0	35.0	35.0	35.0	35.0	33.9
Poland	–	–	–	–	–	–	121.0	136.0	152.0	166.0	208.3	198.0	231.4	205.3	195.5	196.0	186.0
Portugal	–	17.7	20.9	20.7	19.9	20.6	20.9	23.0	22.1	24.1	25.9	27.0	27.9	26.5	26.6	26.6	26.1
Romania	–	–	–	–	–	52.4	66.0	67.0	83.0	84.0	85.4	113.0	119.0	113.5	134.1	150.3	164.3
ex-Soviet Union	–	–	–	–	–	–	–	–	–	–	2506.0	–	3063.0	3392.0	3519.0	3610.0	3849.0
Spain	–	–	–	–	–	–	315.0	310.0	314.0	320.0	310.0	324.0	360.0	362.0	365.0	370.0	370.0
Sweden	–	–	–	–	–	–	60.0	67.0	70.0	65.0	60.0	67.0	65.0	70.0	60.0	55.0	54.0
Switzerland	–	–	–	–	–	–	–	33.0	–	–	34.0	37.0	40.0	42.0	44.0	40.0	40.0
UK	1585.0	1635.0	1462.0	1514.0	1430.0	1395.8	1365.0	1312.1	1284.5	1275.8	1181.8	1100.8	915.2	754.7	581.0	515.0	449.1
ex-Yugoslavia	–	–	–	–	–	–	64.0	60.0	68.0	85.0	97.0	101.4	108.0	114.3	125.0	130.1	129.0

AUDIENCE FIGURES (Millions) (continued)

Dates

	1962	1963	1964	1965	1966	1967	1968	1969	1970	1971	1972	1973	1974	1975	1976	1977	1978
Albania	–	–	–	7.8	–	–	–	8.4	–	8.4	–	8.4	–	–	–	–	–
Austria	90.8	84.9	76.0	72.1	65.8	57.7	50.6	39.5	32.9	28.5	26.7	23.9	23.4	20.8	17.5	17.9	17.4
Belgium	63.9	52.7	46.6	40.9	39.5	36.7	33.9	31.5	30.5	29.8	29.4	26.3	26.5	24.9	23.2	22.3	21.7
Bulgaria	122.8	124.0	125.0	126.4	124.1	119.9	114.0	110.2	109.6	111.1	112.3	114.0	112.3	114.3	114.7	113.4	111.3
Czechoslovakia	152.0	140.7	134.2	128.4	127.0	118.8	118.7	120.6	114.8	110.7	98.4	89.3	87.7	85.9	85.3	86.4	84.7
Denmark	39.3	34.5	33.2	33.9	33.5	29.7	26.8	25.6	24.3	22.1	20.7	18.9	19.2	18.9	18.6	16.7	17.4
Finland	17.8	13.2	10.6	14.0	15.1	14.5	10.1	10.5	11.7	13.0	10.1	10.9	9.6	9.6	8.9	9.0	9.8
France	311.7	292.1	275.8	257.2	234.7	211.4	203.2	182.1	184.4	177.0	184.4	176.0	179.4	180.7	177.3	170.3	178.5
Germany (East)	191.2	–	140.6	119.0	–	99.2	100.6	93.3	91.4	83.4	81.5	84.5	79.5	76.9	79.7	84.1	–
Germany (West)	442.9	366.0	320.4	294.0	257.1	215.6	180.4	180.6	160.1	152.1	149.8	144.3	136.2	128.1	115.1	124.2	135.5
Greece	96.1	100.5	109.5	121.1	131.8	137.1	137.4	135.3	128.6	118.0	92.6	62.2	57.1	47.9	39.9	39.0	39.2
Hungary	122.0	115.7	111.1	106.0	104.6	96.8	84.5	82.2	79.6	79.7	74.7	74.4	77.9	74.4	73.6	76.0	71.7
Iceland	–	–	–	–	2.3	–	–	–	1.7	1.8	2.0	2.0	2.3	2.6	2.5	–	–
Ireland	35.0	–	30.0	30.0	–	–	–	–	20.0	–	–	–	18.0	15.0	–	–	–
Italy	728.6	697.5	683.0	663.1	632.0	568.9	559.9	550.9	525.0	535.7	553.7	544.8	544.4	513.7	454.5	373.8	318.6
Luxemburg	4.0	4.0	3.5	3.0	–	2.1	1.9	1.5	1.3	1.1	1.1	1.0	1.0	1.1	0.8	0.7	–
Netherlands	47.9	43.1	38.7	36.4	34.3	31.6	27.4	24.8	24.1	25.7	25.0	26.5	28.1	28.3	26.5	26.2	28.4
Norway	32.8	26.5	24.5	23.0	21.8	21.0	19.2	19.2	18.6	18.9	18.3	17.5	17.9	18.5	16.8	16.8	16.8
Poland	194.0	164.8	177.0	168.0	164.7	163.1	–	141.3	137.8	130.4	136.2	140.6	142.8	143.4	144.2	131.6	116.0
Portugal	25.6	24.8	24.5	25.7	26.1	27.7	26.6	26.4	28.0	27.2	28.1	28.9	35.7	41.6	42.8	39.1	34.0
Romania	181.0	191.0	181.7	204.7	216.1	209.2	203.7	200.4	198.8	189.2	179.7	177.4	182.3	185.7	191.2	183.5	187.9
ex-Soviet Union	3900.0	3900.0	–	4280.0	4200.0	4502.8	4715.0	4655.9	4651.8	4656.3	4569.0	4583.3	4566.9	4497.3	4211.0	4080.0	–
Spain	–	320.0	–	435.2	403.1	393.1	376.6	364.6	330.9	295.3	295.2	278.3	262.9	255.8	249.0	211.0	220.0
Sweden	50.0	39.5	40.0	38.2	37.3	35.4	32.6	30.4	28.2	26.0	26.7	22.9	22.1	23.7	23.7	22.5	23.5
Switzerland	40.0	39.0	37.0	45.0	34.0	32.0	35.0	33.0	32.0	30.0	28.0	27.0	25.5	23.7	20.4	21.2	20.0
UK	395.0	357.2	342.8	326.6	288.8	264.8	237.3	214.9	193.0	176.0	156.6	134.2	138.5	116.3	103.9	103.5	126.1
ex-Yugoslavia	121.8	117.0	123.0	121.2	114.6	104.9	100.2	90.3	86.3	81.5	84.2	86.3	83.3	81.7	79.7	75.8	75.4

	1979	1980	1981	1982	1983	1984	1985	1986	1987	1988	1989	1990	1991	1992	1993
Albania	–	–	–	–	–	–	–	–	–	–	3.8	–	–	–	–
Austria	17.5	17.5	18.2	16.6	17.9	16.1	17.0	12.6	11.5	10.0	11.8	10.2	10.5	9.3	12.0
Belgium	19.8	21.6	20.1	20.5	21.3	19.0	17.9	17.7	15.7	15.2	15.0	16.2	16.9	16.6	18.3
Bulgaria	109.4	100.0	91.4	92.5	93.5	–	95.5	93.2	84.2	81.0	79.0	65.0	25.7	30.0	11.0
Czechoslovakia	82.5	82.3	81.0	78.6	–	–	76.7	76.6	73.8	73.8	70.6	65.0	40.6	43.0	31.0
Denmark	17.2	15.9	16.2	14.3	13.7	12.0	11.3	11.3	11.4	10.0	10.3	9.6	9.2	8.6	10.2
Finland	10.1	9.9	9.4	9.1	9.1	7.6	6.7	6.3	6.5	6.7	7.2	6.2	6.0	5.4	5.8
France	178.1	174.8	189.2	201.9	198.8	190.8	172.2	163.4	136.7	124.7	120.9	121.8	117.0	115.9	133.3
Germany (East)	–	79.5	–	72.4	–	73.4	70.0	70.2	69.2	69.3	64.0	30.0	13.0	11.2	–
Germany (West)	142.0	143.8	141.3	124.5	125.2	112.1	104.2	105.2	108.1	108.9	101.6	102.5	106.9	94.7	57.7
Greece	34.1	43.0	40.5	35.3	35.0	22.0	23.0	22.0	22.5	17.0	17.5	16.5	6.2	6.7	7.0
Hungary	69.0	60.7	67.1	70.0	68.9	71.0	70.2	68.0	55.9	50.7	45.8	36.2	22.3	15.6	15.2
Iceland	–	2.6	–	2.2	–	–	1.4	1.2	1.3	–	1.2	1.2	1.2	1.2	1.2
Ireland	–	9.5	–	11.4	12.7	14.0	11.6	11.0	5.2	6.0	7.0	7.4	8.1	8.2	9.3
Italy	276.3	241.9	215.2	195.4	162.0	131.6	123.1	124.8	112.5	93.0	95.2	90.5	88.6	83.6	92.2
Luxemburg	–	0.8	–	0.7	0.7	0.7	0.7	0.7	0.7	0.5	0.5	0.5	0.6	0.6	0.7
Netherlands	25.8	27.9	24.7	20.5	20.2	17.4	15.3	14.9	15.5	14.8	15.6	14.6	14.9	13.7	15.9
Norway	17.8	17.5	16.4	15.1	14.8	12.8	12.9	11.1	12.4	11.5	12.6	11.4	10.8	9.6	10.9
Poland	96.2	96.9	91.1	89.4	99.7	127.6	107.0	100.0	94.0	95.3	86.4	38.0	18.0	12.0	13.7
Portugal	32.6	30.8	28.8	26.0	22.9	21.0	19.0	18.4	16.9	13.0	13.8	11.0	11.8	12.0	12.7
Romania	185.7	193.6	198.3	143.7	209.4	217.0	191.5	204.7	208.3	–	170.0	130.0	76.0	41.0	30.0
ex-Soviet Union	–	4260.0	–	4220.0	–	–	4100.0	–	3775.0	3920.2	3640.0	3500.0	2000.0	1000.0	–
Spain	200.0	176.0	173.7	156.0	141.0	118.6	101.1	87.3	85.7	69.6	78.1	78.5	79.1	83.3	87.7
Sweden	25.1	24.9	23.2	21.3	19.0	17.1	17.9	16.4	17.4	17.5	19.2	15.3	15.1	15.7	16.0
Switzerland	21.3	20.9	20.4	20.1	19.7	17.9	16.4	16.3	16.2	14.9	15.2	14.3	15.4	15.0	15.9
UK	111.9	101.0	83.0	64.0	65.7	58.4	70.2	72.6	74.8	84.0	96.0	98.2	101.6	103.6	114.4
ex-Yugoslavia	–	80.0	76.5	80.0	85.0	87.0	81.0	80.8	78.1	70.8	65.0	58.0	25.7	20.9	–

APPENDIX II

Select Bibliography for European and Italian Cinema

BIBLIOGRAPHY

Europe

Roy Armes, *The Ambiguous Image: Narrative Style in Modern European Cinema* (London: Secker and Warburg, 1976).

Grzegorz Balski, *Directory of Eastern European Film-makers and Films, 1945–1991* (Trowbridge, Wilts: Flicks Books, 1992).

Peter Cowie, *International Film Guide* (now *Variety International Film Guide*) (London: Andre Deutsch, annual from 1964).

Peter Cowie, *Scandinavian Cinema: a survey of film and film-makers in Denmark, Finland, Iceland, Norway and Sweden* (London: Tantivy Press, 1992).

Richard Dyer and Ginette Vincendeau (eds.), *Popular European Cinema* (London and New York: Routledge, 1992).

The European Film in the World Market (Vienna: The Austrian Film Commission, 1988).

David W. Ellwood and Rob Kroes, *Hollywood in Europe, Expressions of a Cultural Hegemony* (Amsterdam: Amsterdam University Press, 1994).

Daniel J. Goulding (ed.), *Five Filmmakers: Tarkovsky, Forman, Polanski, Szabó, Makavejev* (Bloomington: Indiana University Press, 1994).

Daniel J. Goulding (ed.), *Post New Wave Cinema in the Soviet Union and Eastern Europe* (Bloomington: Indiana University Press, 1989).

Thomas H. Guback, *The International Film Industry: Western Europe and America since 1945* (Bloomington: Indiana University Press, 1969).

Thomas H. Guback, 'Cultural Identity and Film in the European Economic Community', in *Cinema Journal*, vol. 14, no. 1, 1974.

Nicholas Hewitt (ed.), *The Culture of Reconstruction. European Literature, Thought and Film, 1945–1950* (Basingstoke and London: Macmillan, 1989).

Andrew S. Horton and Joan Magretta (eds.), *Modern European Film-makers and the Art of Adaptation* (New York: Frederick Ungar, 1981).

Mira and Antonín J. Liehm, *The Most Important Art: East European Film After 1945* (Berkeley and London: University of California Press, 1977).

David W. Paul (ed.), *Politics, Art, and Commitment in the East European Cinema* (New York: St. Martin's Press, 1983).

Duncan Petrie (ed.), *Screening Europe: Image and Identity in Contemporary European Cinema* (London: BFI, 1992).

James Quinn, *The Film and Television as an Aspect of European Culture* (Leyden: A. W. Sijthoff, 1968).

Pierre Sorlin, *European Cinemas, European Societies 1939– 1990* (London and New York: Routledge, 1991).

Italy

Adriano Aprà and Patrizia Pistagnesi (eds.), *The Fabulous Thirties* (Milan: Electa, 1979).

Roy Armes, *Patterns of Realism* (New York: A. S. Barnes, and London: Tantivy Press, 1971).

Aldo Bernardini (ed.), *Archivio del cinema italiano. Vol. 1: Il cinema muto, 1905–1931* (Rome: Edizioni Anica, 1991).

Aldo Bernardini (ed.), *Archivio del cinema italiano. Vol. 2: Il Cinema sonoro, 1930–1969* (Rome: Edizioni Anica, 1992).

Aldo Bernadini and Jean A. Gili (eds.), *Le cinéma italien de La Prise de Rome (1905) à Rome ville ouverte (1945)* (Paris: Centre Georges Pompidou, 1986).

Aldo Bernardini and Vittorio Martinelli, *Il cinema italiano degli anni Venti* (Rome: Cineteca Nazionale del Centro Sperimentale di Cinematografia, 1979).

Peter Bondanella, *Italian Cinema: From Neorealism to the present* (New York: Continuum, 1990).

Gian Piero Brunetta, *Cent'anni di cinema italiano* (Rome/Bari: Editori Laterza, 1991).

Gian Piero Brunetta, *Storia del cinema italiano. Vol. i: 1895–1945* (Rome: Editori Riuniti, 1980).

Gian Piero Brunetta, *Storia del cinema italiano. Vol. ii: Dal 1945 agli anni ottanta* (Rome: Editori Riuniti, 1982).

Giuliana Bruno, *Streetwalking on a Ruined Map: Cultural theory and the city films of Elvira Notari* (Princeton NJ: Princeton University Press, 1993).

Monica Dall'Asta, *Un cinéma musclé: le surhomme dans le cinéma muet italien (1913–1926)* (Crisnée: Editions Yellow Now, 1992).

Angela Dalle Vacche, *The Body in the Mirror: Shapes of history in Italian Cinema* (Princeton NJ: Princeton University Press, 1992).

Franca Faldini and Goffredo Fofi, *L'avventurosa storia del cinema italiano: raccontato dai suoi protagonisti, 1935–1959* (Milan: Feltrinelli, 1979).

Franca Faldini and Goffredo Fofi, *L'avventurosa storia del cinema italiano: raccontato dai suoi protagonisti, 1960–1969* (Milan: Feltrinelli, 1981).

Franca Faldini and Goffredo Fofi, *Il cinema italiano d'oggi, 1970–1984: raccontato dai suoi protagonisti* (Milan: Arnoldo Mondadori, 1984).

David Forgacs (ed.), *Rethinking Italian Fascism: Capitalism, Populism and Culture* (London: Lawrence and Wishart, 1986).

Vernon Jarratt, *The Italian Cinema* (London: Falcon Press, 1951).

Pierre Leprohon, *The Italian Cinema* (London: Secker and Warburg, and New York: Praeger, 1972).

Mira Liehm, *Passion and Defiance: Film in Italy from 1942 to the Present* (Berkeley, Ca.: University of California Press, 1984).

Millicent Marcus, *Italian Film in the Light of Neorealism* (Princeton, NJ: Princeton University Press, 1986).

Lorenzo Quaglietti, *Storia economico-politica del Cinema italiano, 1945–1980* (Rome: Editori Riuniti, 1980).

Sam Rohdie, *Antonioni* (London: BFI, 1990).

Sam Rohdie, *The Passion of Pier Paolo Pasolini* (London: BFI, 1995).

Francesco Savio, *Ma l'amore no: realismo, formalismo, propaganda e telefoni bianchi nel cinema italiano di regime (1930–1943)* (Milan: Sonzogno, 1975).